free jazz

also by Ekkehard Jost

Europas Jazz 1960-1980
Jazzmusiker. Materialien zur Soziologie der afro-amerikanischen Musik
Sozialgeschichte des Jazz in den USA
Sozialpsychologische Faktoren der Popmusik-Rezeption
"La musique speculative" von Nicolas Bergier
Akustische und psychometrische Untersuchungen an Klarinettenklängen

ekkehard jost

free jazz

DA CAPO PRESS • NEW YORK

Library of Congress Cataloging-in-Publication Data

Jost, Ekkehard.

Free jazz / Ekkehard Jost. —1st Da Capo Press pbk. ed.

      p. cm. — (The Roots of jazz)
  Originally published: Graz: Universal Edition, 1974. (Beiträge
zur Jazzforschung; 4).
        Includes bibliographical references, discography, and index.
        ISBN 0-306-80556-1
        1. Jazz — History and criticism. 2. Jazz musicians. I. Title.
II. Series.

ML3506.J67 1994

781.65'5—dc20   93-34779
                                                    CIP
                                                    MN

First Da Capo Press paperback edition 1994

This Da Capo Press paperback edition of *Free Jazz* is an unabridged republication of the edition published in Graz, Austria in 1974. It is reprinted by arrangement with Universal Edition, Vienna.

Copyright © 1975 by Universal Edition A. G. Wien

Published by Da Capo Press, Inc.
A Subsidiary of Plenum Publishing Corporation
233 Spring Street, New York, N.Y. 10013

Contents

PREFACE

The advantage in writing about music that is current, living and immediately within reach is offset by an equally great disadvantage, namely that the music concerned is subject to transformation while it is being written about. The validity of what was said yesterday is in danger of being superseded by what is played today. A book, unfortunately, cannot continue to evolve like a musical style; it is not a "work in progress," but something with a beginning and an end. This gives the observations it imparts a tinge of the provisional and hypothetical — especially when the book sets out to be more than just a compilation of historically documented data. This book, let it be said, is not to be taken as a "history of free jazz," but first and foremost as a critical exploration of its most essential musical directions. A lack of temporal distance to our subject may make it difficult to decide what is essential and what is of only peripheral importance. Nevertheless, a decision must be made. ("Time will tell," that popular and overworked phrase, usually means that the author hesitates to express his own opinion, or that he has no opinion at all.) The choice of the style portraits in this book will probably lead to criticism from people who consider other musicians and groups more important in the evolution of free jazz. No doubt other musicians and trends within the stylistic conglomerate of free jazz might have been included. If I have concentrated on a relatively few salient points, it was due not only to space limitations, but also to the conviction that a detailed discussion of what is typical in the music of just a few artists would be more rewarding than a global resumé of changing characteristics in the work of many.

In writing this book I was greatly helped by many friends. My thanks are due first to the late director of the jazz division of the Norddeutscher Rundfunk in Hamburg, Hans Gertberg. He and his successor Michael Naura gave me access to the division's huge collection of recordings and thus created one of the primary conditions for the realization of this book.

I would also like to thank my friends Dr. Artur Simon of the Ethnological Museum in Berlin, Dr. Peter Faltin of the National Institute of Musical Research in Berlin, and Dr. Dieter Glawischnig of the Institute of Jazz Research in Graz, whose critical comments on my manuscript were of great value. Further, I am indebted to Ludolf Kuchenbuch, not only for long discussions of theoretical matters, but also for practical musical experience gained from playing with him.

Finally, I owe the most thanks of all to my wife Helgi. Without her, this book would very likely still be lying in a desk drawer as an untidy manuscript.

Berlin, 1972   Ekkehard Jost

INTRODUCTION

"A saxophonist was asked to take part in a 'free' jazz session. When he turned up with his horn he was told to feel free to express himself, and to 'do his own thing'. — Anyway, he must have been feeling a bit nautical, because he played 'I do like to be beside the seaside' throughout the entire session. Apparently, his associates were extremely angry about this and told him not to bother to come again" (Jan Carr, 1971).

The beauty of any good anecdote is that in describing a specific occurrence it also describes a symptom. The experience of our anonymous saxophonist, who found that the song he played as an ostinato during a free jazz session was obviously at cross purposes with his colleagues' objectives, points up one of the many misunderstandings attached to the term "free jazz" and the music for which it stands.

At no period in the seventy-year history of jazz has a mixture of ideological and musical factors left such a lasting imprint on a stylistic direction, as it did on the music heard at the end of the Fifties as the *New Thing*, and later — the name came from the title of a record made by Ornette Coleman in 1960 — as *Free Jazz*[1].

The idea of total freedom which "free jazz" implied from the outset for its "fringe adepts" (that is, its non-practitioners) arose from a false estimation of the musical facts. So did the panicky reports of musical anarchism and the ruin of jazz, put out by a sector of jazz criticism which, clinging to tradition, lay paralysed by its own musical criteria. While these two parties indulged in a feud involving a good deal of verbal abuse, a third party — proceeding from positive, but as a rule wholesale judgements on free jazz — focussed on its socio-cultural and political background. A not unimportant source of motivation for this latter group of jazz commentators, who saw themselves as spokesmen of a "black cultural revolution" in the USA and as "nouvelle critique" in France, was the change in the way musicians regarded themselves. Renunciation of the mere role of entertainer, activities of a political nature, and the proclamation of an openly anti-European (or anti-American) slant by some of the most prominent exponents of free jazz, paved the way for a sociological (in some instances merely "sociologizing") approach to the analysis of the music. However imperative — and in many cases productive[2] — investigations into the social function of free jazz and its significance as a

---

1) The name *cosa nova* propounded by Leonard Feather got just as far — namely nowhere — as Stanley Dance's *nouvelle gauche*, an invective term which doubtless has more to say about its inventor than about the music.

2) *Cf. inter alia* Carles / Comolli 1971, Kofsky 1970.

cultural and political phenomenon may have been, the exclusivity of the approach did involve a risk: the autonomous musical aspects of the evolution of free jazz — *i. e.,* those aspects which escape a purely sociological analysis — often were ignored.

The prevailing abstention from detailed analyses of musical formative principles was due to two causes: first, the majority of the representatives of the so-called "nouvelle critique," whose qualifications were scientific rather than musical, felt no call to musical analysis; secondly, and more important, musicologists who had made names for themselves with penetrating investigations of earlier stylistic areas of jazz either were outspokenly negative toward free jazz, or — since their primary interests belonged to older styles — took hardly any notice of it.

Just as it is not enough to take the development of a musical style solely as a vehicle from which to derive sociological theories, it is equally unprofitable to reduce analysis to musically tangible facts only. Free jazz shows precisely how tight the links between social *and* musical factors are, and how the one cannot be completely grasped without the other. Several of the initiators of free jazz, for instance, had to contend for a long time with systematic obstruction on the part of the record industry and owners of jazz clubs (who continue to control the economic basis of jazz). This circumstance is by no means void of significance for the music of the men concerned. Being without steady work means not only personal and financial difficulties; it also means that groups may not stay together long enough to grow into real ensembles, that is, to evolve and stabilize a concept of group improvisation — an absolute necessity in a kind of music which is independent of pre-set patterns.

The chief motivation behind this book lies in the realization that the variety of musical formative principles existing in the stylistic conglomerate of free jazz has so far been obscured rather than brought to light by the sociological approach predominant in contemporary jazz literature. Obviously, questions of an extra-musical nature will have to be dealt with also, but these will be determined by the extent to which biographical data of free-jazz musicians and the social setting of the music itself can contribute to our understanding of it.

As in all other stylistic areas of jazz, conventions and "rules of the game" established themselves in free jazz — even though the latter's own creation was sparked by a break with most of the norms considered irrevocable before. The conventions of harmonically and metrically confined jazz styles, up to hard bop, could be reduced to a relatively narrow and stable system of agreements; therefore, analysis of a given style could concentrate on detecting and interpreting the congruities present in individual ways of operating within that system of agreements. With the advent of free jazz, however, a large number of divergent personal styles developed. Their only point of agreement lay in a negation of traditional norms; otherwise, they exhibited such heterogeneous formative principles that any reduction to a common denominator was bound to be an over-simplification[3]. The initiators of free jazz drew widely different consequences from the renunciation of harmonic-metrical patterns, of the regulative force of the beat, and of the structural principles of the "jazz piece." As a result, the conventions that arose in free jazz with regard to instrumental technique, ensemble playing, formal organization, etc., were never as universally binding as those in traditional areas of jazz. Variability of formative principles is inherent in free jazz; moreover, specific principles are tied up with specific musicians and groups. In coming to grips with this music, then, it is necessary to adopt a method fundamentally different from the method which still worked for bebop, cool jazz or hard bop. Rudolf Stephan, speaking with reference to avantgarde music in Europe (1969), drew attention to the absorption of the "musically universal" by the "musically particular." This is true of free jazz too; therefore, analysis demands a procedure that allows the particularities in the music of its most important exponents to be brought out, after which we can go on to discover general tendencies and trends. My approach in this book is to give "style portraits" of those musicians and groups who functioned as pioneers and initiators of free jazz, and those whose music may be considered to represent its different phases of evolution, and the musical characteristics that distinguish them.

Subjects for style portraits — and the order in which they appear — were chosen on the basis of experience gained from listening to several thousand recorded pieces and a large number of concerts. An element of subjectivity is of course unavoidable, but neither chance nor personal likes and dislikes had anything to do with the matter. The sample of these portraits is the result of an attempt to present, as clearly and comprehensively as possible, a labyrinthine evolution in the course of which innovation and imitation over-lapped, and continuity was frequently broken by mutual influences exerted by the leading musicians on each other.

Proof of the validity and the sequence of the style portraits in this book can be left to the text itself. A few preliminary remarks, however, may not be out of place. They concern (1) the role of the "pioneers" of free jazz, i. e. of those who paved the way for it, (2) the classification of free jazz as "black music," and (3) the development of free jazz in Europe.

(1) In jazz it is not always appropriate to ascribe the initiative for shaping new principles of creation, or abandoning old ones, to an individual or a small circle of innovators, who — in the front lines of a musical development — set the new standards which, not long after, a large army of "fellow-travellers" accepts for its own work. Only in the rarest instances does the one-to-one correlation of musical progress and individual genius, long since endemic in the personality-cult branch of jazz history writing

---

3) For example, the attempt by the Duke of Mecklenburg — in cooperation with Joe Viera — to present a summary of stylistic criteria of the New York school of free jazz ("Stilkriterien der New Yorker Schule des Free Jazz," 1969) shows how a global approach runs the risk, in view of the multiplicity of phenomena, of losing all touch with reality.

(Pekar 1966), do justice to the network of interdependencies that leads to the creation of a new stylistic trend. Nevertheless, there are certainly musicians who represent a stylistic upheaval to a special degree, in which case the chronology of "discoveries" of stylistic features is less important than the role those musicians play in making a definitive musical language out of a welter of innovations. Whether Charlie Parker, Dizzy Gillespie or Thelonious Monk was the first to introduce the tritone as the new "consonance" of bebop is of secondary interest; that all of them were central figures in the development of that music is indisputable.

Just as in bebop in the early Forties, a number of musicians appeared on the jazz scene at the end of the Fifties who were more responsible than others for breaking new musical ground. There can be some agreement that the threshold from hard bop to free jazz was crossed earliest and with the most determination by the groups of Ornette Coleman and Cecil Taylor. But we must also be aware that the multiple currents flowing in free jazz cannot be traced back just to the work of two outstanding musical personalities. The influences felt in the divergent personal styles of the Sixties encompass musicians like Sidney Bechet, Ben Webster, Thelonious Monk and Lennie Tristano as well as Stravinsky, Schoenberg and Cage. It would be highly unlikely that anyone would seriously call Sidney Bechet or John Cage "pioneers of free jazz." There are, however, a few musicians beside Coleman and Taylor whose influence is reflected not only in the personal expressive characteristics of many free jazz exponents, but who contributed as *pioneers,* in moulding fundamental formative principles that had more than just individual validity.

The roles and the chronological positions of Charles Mingus and John Coltrane, the pioneers whose music is discussed in the first two chapters of this book, are different. As early as the Fifties, Mingus worked out a concept of collective improvisation that later proved to be essential to the evolution of free jazz, but he never thought of himself as belonging to free jazz. At the start of the Sixties (by which time the old barriers had long since been demolished by Coleman and Taylor), Coltrane fulfilled the role of a pioneer for part of the so-called "second generation" of free jazz, and from 1965 on — at the latest — he was regarded as the "head of the school." John Coltrane's dual function — first a pioneer, then as the central figure of post-1965 free jazz — made it necessary for the sake of clarity to interrupt the discussion of his musical development at the point where he moved from the periphery of free jazz to its centre.

(2) LeRoi Jones, writer, jazz critic, and one of the most heated advocates of the Black Power movement during the Sixties, calls what we have become accustomed to term free jazz "New Black Music." This is not at all so inapt as a camp of Euro-American jazz criticism would have us believe, a camp that rejects Jones's phrase — on account of its claim to exclusivity — as an expression of chauvinism and racism. For although it cannot be argued that white jazz musicians, far from merely swimming along with the tide of free jazz, have in some cases made decisive contributions to its development[4], it

---

4) One need only recall the outstanding role of white bassists in the Ornette Coleman and Albert Aylers groups.

is plain that the early forms of free jazz and the innovations that marked its path came for the most part from black musicians. Furthermore, its most significant emotional components are not those of a diffuse "world music," but clearly derive from a music that is Afro-American in the broadest sense. After seventy years of jazz, the observation that white musicians play music that is "black" in essence should surprise us as little as the statement that 18th-century German composers wrote "Italian" operas.

The dominating role of Afro-American musicians in free jazz is reflected in the sample of style analyses compiled in this book. Without exception, black musicians stand in the foreground of every chapter; this is only a consequence of their dominating role and of the necessity of sticking to essentials, and has nothing whatsoever to do with a one-sidedness of musical preferences on the author's part or with a Panassié kind of purism.

(3) A conspicuous feature of jazz in Europe over the past decades was a tendency to take over — with a lesser or greater time lag — what American musicians had tried out earlier and consolidated into a style. Although formative principles, not traceable to American models, did occasionally develop in Europe, imitation generally predominated over innovation. Saxophonists who played "like Lee Konitz" at the beginning of the Fifties, "like Sonny Rollins" a little later, and finally "like John Coltrane," were not exceptions — and the same went for every other instrument. The gradual spread of free jazz changed the epigone role of most European musicians only slightly at first, but by the latter half of the Sixties there was a partial disengagement from American influences. Now there exist in Europe — and in Japan too — a number of soloists and groups pursuing a musical conception that is relatively independent of Afro-American free jazz. So free jazz has brought European musicians not only freedom from traditional standards of jazz improvisation, but also freedom from the tutelage of American jazz. It should be mentioned in passing that this declaration of European independence has often been accompanied by an overcompensation effect, that can be interpreted only in psychological terms: the musical anti-Americanism proclaimed by some people on the European free jazz scene, the assertion that whatever comes from "over there" is relatively old-fashioned, has much in common with the phenomenon of "spiritual parricide."

Nevertheless — or rather for that very reason — a detailed analysis of specifically European formative principles, such as those developed by the groups of Peter Brötzmann · Han Bennink, Wolfgang Dauner, Paul Rutherford · Barry Guy, Michel Portal, Alexander von Schlippenbach, etc., would be vitally necessary. There are two reasons why such an analysis is not found in this book — which thus excludes what is undoubtedly an important movement in free jazz.

In the first place, the history of free jazz in Europe is relatively short, and the lines of evolution are still for the most part so unsurveyable that a selection of significant phenomena would have at the most a hypothetical character. Further, extensive documentation of this development on records only began in recent years (mostly on the musicians' own initiative). The early stage of European free jazz, therefore, eludes analysis almost as much as does the early history of jazz itself.

In the second place — and this is in our case the essential factor — the evolution of European free jazz would require an analysis in keeping with its musical variety; otherwise, it would be merely fragmentary. To make such an analysis in this book would have meant doubling its dimensions.

"The precedence of the sound over the notation, whose relevance in jazz lies solely in assisting the 'memoria'[5], must be heeded in all methodological considerations" (Rauhe 1970, p. 27).

Neither verbal explanations nor examples given in a notational system — whatever kind it may be — can replace the music to which they refer; this is true not only of jazz, but of all music. But "in traditional occidental art music (discounting the exceptions) the composer's 'imaginatio' first emerges in the 'res facta' of the notation and only then is realized in sound by the 'interpretatio,' while 'imaginatio' and 'interpretatio' coincide as a rule in jazz, at least in improvisation. Thus a graphic record in the form of notation is replaced by a phonographic record on disc or tape . . . Transcription of it serves only to help the 'memoria' in analysing structure or style" *(op. cit.).*

In this respect the sound recording fulfils a similar function in the investigation of jazz (or any improvised music) as the score does in analysing traditional art music. But there are a few problems about records which must not be forgotten when one begins to interpret what one has perceived by analysis. Gunther Schuller (1968, X) correctly points out that in contrast to the score of a Beethoven or Schoenberg work, the recording of a jazz improvisation is the "definitive" version of something that was never meant to be definitive.

How relevant is an analysis of recorded improvisations made on a certain date and under certain circumstances (the group involved, the improviser's physical and mental disposition, the conditions imposed by the producer, etc.)? This will depend on the extent to which those improvisations can be taken, beyond the immediate musical facts, as indicative of the specific musicians' or groups' creative principles. In determining that, two conditions must be met:

First, formative *principles* are in fact present, *i. e.* the progress of an improvisation is not just left to pure chance, but is — at least in part — the result of the musical experience of the player or players and the conception based upon it. Analysing a piece that consists simply of accidental sound coincidences would have as little value as trying to calculate the probability of winning or losing in a game of dice where everybody has an equal chance.

---

5) This and the next quotation are taken from Hermann Rauhe's "Der Jazz als Object interdisziplinärer Forschung" (1970), a fundamental work for the methodology of jazz research. In using the Latin terms Rauhe refers to Siegfried Borris (1962).

Second, analysing and interpreting the features of a given improvisation demands that the analyst take into account everything he has learned from *other* improvisations by the same musician. The significance of general pronouncements on the stylistic features of an improviser, from whom one has just a single solo at hand, is minimal, while the likelihood of drawing false conclusions is very great.

Over the years of his development, the improvisations of a given musician form a chain of *non-definitive* phenomena, a "work in progress" (Schuller, *op. cit.*). The only way to arrive at definitive statements about those non-definitive phenomena is to analyse the most exemplary on record.

Records unquestionably provide the most important working foundation for jazz research, but they also involve some problems that must be touched on here.

We should not forget that the selection of information resources we have, so far as they are on records, is guided considerably by the circumstance that behind a record issue there has already been a process of selection. This by no means always or exclusively follows musical criteria. The businessmen, on whose cooperation jazz musicians normally have to depend, are not usually prompted by aesthetic motives; they want a product that will respond to the market. "Jazz is singularly unique in that the people who control it are thoroughly ignorant of it, know nothing about it" (Shepp, in Morgenstern 1966, p. 20).

Socio-psychological factors growing out of the dynamics of group relations within the *jazz community* also have a bearing. For example, whether a musician belongs to a certain clique and whether he is on good terms with recognized "stars," probably will have a great deal to do with his being invited to take part in a recording session or to make an LP with his own group.

In addition to extra-musical factors like these, which account for the presence or absence of material important for an investigation and thus control our stock of information resources, another problem is posed by the material itself. No matter with what technical brilliance records are produced, they always constitute a reduction of what was originally an audio-visual event to a purely acoustical one. In free jazz as practised by several groups discussed in the later chapters of this book, visual components have such a direct bearing on the music that the acoustical result on a record (for example, a Sun Ra concert) can reproduce only a part of what the musicians and their audience experienced when the take was made.

Nevertheless, records remain the only practicable basis for the scientific exploration of jazz, for two principal reasons:

(1) Only a recorded improvisation can be played as often as desired and thus be readily accessible to analysis. Musical impressions gained at concerts or other live performances

can contribute only in a supplementary way to perceptions gained by analysis; they may be able to direct analysis toward a certain point, but they can never replace it. Fleeting, unrepeatable impressions, and distortions caused by the levelling effect of memory, create a haziness regarding musical details that makes any statement about them suspect.

(2) The fact that improvised music can be reproduced by recordings guarantees that statements can be tested empirically and that subjective judgements can be evaluated critically. But the reader, too, must be in a position to check the results of analysis, and this means that the object of analysis must be easily accessible to him. That is the reason this book is based mainly on commercial recordings available to the reader, and not on the many private or radio tapes of concerts which circulate among "collectors."[6]

In discussing a kind of music, two of whose most pronounced traits are that it arises from *improvisation* and that it is moulded to a great extent by the *emotions* of the people who play it, one encounters a few more obstacles.

Putting technical musical details into words creates a problem that cannot always be solved, even when the strictest discipline is observed as to terminology, for the terminology of music is anything but universally binding. The most valuable expedient for the illustration of technical musical phenomena, difficult or impossible to verbalize, is the notation of excerpts. This is not the place to go into the questions frequently discussed in musical ethnology concerning the translation of musical sounds into written notation [7]. However, the reader is asked to bear two points in mind with regard to the transcriptions in this book:

(1) The musical examples I have reproduced are based on "protocol" transcriptions, intended to demonstrate different aspects of the music. This means that the nature of the transcription is always determined by the point it is supposed to illustrate. For example, it would make little sense to puzzle out, with the aid of a sophisticated electro-acoustical device, the time values of a melodic line played in a free tempo, and to notate them precisely on a graph divided into hundredths of a second, if the purpose of the example is merely to illustrate a particular kind of pitch organization. It would be equally fruitless to give the gliding fundamental frequencies of a sequence of run-together sounds obviously intended by the player as a "sound slur" and not as a melodic line, or to identify the individual components of a sound which must be comprehended not as a chord but as a cluster.

(2) As we know, the notation of a jazz improvisation — no matter how scrupulously exact — can comprehend only partial aspects; fundamental characteristics of tone and tone production, as well as minute rhythmic and dynamic shifts, which may be essential

---

6) In one instance an exception was made: the recorded concert discussed in the chapter on Don Cherry was included because there is not yet one document on discs for a very important phase of Cherry's musical development.

7) *Cf. inter alia* List 1963, Hopkins 1966, Stockmann 1966, Rauhe 1970.

to the stylistic identity of a musician, defy objectification by written notation. And if one tries for the highest possible degree of precision, by introducing a battery of auxiliary markings, the communicative function of a transcription is often crowded out in the process. Apart from the fact that a transcription gives an incomplete clue to an improvisation, we must not forget that the improvisation itself is usually only a part of the larger musical context, except when a musician improvises utterly "solo" (which happens relatively rarely). In every type of jazz there are as a rule more or less strong interactions between the improvising soloist and the rhythm section "accompanying" him. In free jazz this is even more the case, since, in the course of its development, the accompanying function of the rhythm group has been increasingly eliminated in favour of interaction between *all* the musicians in a group. The import of such reciprocal effects must be taken into account when one is confronted with the transcription of an improvisation divorced from its musical surroundings. The question as to whether certain accentuations, rests, emphases, etc., result solely from the improviser's flow of ideas, or whether they are stimulated by impulses from the "background" against which he plays, can rarely be answered by a transcription of the whole musical situation, for it is usually impossible to dismantle the complex structure of free jazz. In view of the interactive processes operative in the course of an improvisation, the sonic example is a necessary complement to the notated or notatable extract taken from it.

Weightier, and of fundamentally another nature, than the problems having to do with the presentation of technical musical phenomena are those that arise in connection with emotional content. Emotions in jazz do not usually play merely an accessory role to an otherwise intellectually guided formative process; on the contrary, they frequently are pre-eminent in the scale of musical necessities, for the musician as well as the listener. In view of this fact, it would be quite unproductive (and not in keeping with the nature of our subject) to describe only what can be reproduced by musical notation and other graphic devices. The observation that the melodic line of a solo is simple or complicated can be immediately verified by consulting the musical text (remembering that both attributes are purely relative). But to say that the same solo is "aggressive" has an element of subjectivity whose validity — like that of a value judgement — can either be accepted or challenged. Attempts have been made to reduce musical expression, by psychometric tests and statistical methods, to a few globally applicable dimensions[8]. Profitable as they may have been, they have understandably produced no universal formula to objectify what is to a high degree a subjective phenomenon.

The author of this book has, nevertheless, not hesitated to set foot on the unsteady ground of emotions (influenced as these are by personal listening habits and expectations) or to include expressive elements — utterly inseparable from music like free jazz — in technical musical analyses. This he has done, trusting in the critical ear of the reader.

"Neither the description and analysis of musical events nor the notation of excerpts from recordings can present the full experience. The reader must also listen" (Schuller 1968, X).

---

8) *Cf.* Keil 1966, Kleinen 1968, Reinecke 1970, Jost 1970.

16

Chapter 1

JOHN COLTRANE AND MODAL PLAYING

At the end of the Fifties, Ornette Coleman made the programmatic statement, "Let's play the music and not the background" (from Williams 1970, p. 207). By "background" he meant the general framework of jazz improvisation which had established itself soon after the birth of jazz as a more or less incontestable norm. With an aura of inviolability, it had survived all the stylistic upheavals that followed — swing, bebop, cool jazz and the rest. This framework consisted of a code of agreements which made up — to paraphrase Stephan's words — the "musically universal" in jazz, and remained constant throughout the years of jazz evolution, while the "musically particular" changed. Earlier stylistic upheavals in jazz were triggered primarily by the extension of technical resources, or else by increasing complexity in the structure of the background. Around 1960, however, the background itself started to disintegrate. The evolution of jazz, which until then had followed a straight line, took a sudden turn[1].

To get a clear idea of what happened, and of how it happened, let us quickly review what the "musically universal" in jazz means, or rather what it meant until 1960.

One of the first things that strikes one in traditional jazz is its formal simplicity. The theme, taken as a basis for improvisation, determines — by the chord progressions underlying it, and by its disposition into a metrical scheme — the formal and harmonic progress of a whole piece. The theme will, of course, frequently reflect the musical particularities of a stylistic area, but on the whole it serves primarily to provide a harmonic and metrical framework for the improvisations that follow. It became evident in bebop during the Forties, that thematic material could more or less be replaced at will by other material, when musicians began writing new themes whose melody and rhythm agreed with their own style, on the chord progressions of "standards." In this way, *How High the Moon* could become *Ornithology,* without the improviser having to depart one bit from the old familiar chord patterns of the original tune.

In jazz, the improvisatory treatment of given material was always considered more important than the material itself. Accordingly, musicians hardly ever consciously felt the formal rigidity to be a problem. On the contrary, as long as the laws of functional harmony were in force, as long as they enabled the "musically particular" to unfold, the

---

1) The general introductory remarks in this chapter are based on an article by the author in "Die Musik der sechziger Jahre" (*cf.* Jost 1972).

acceptance of strictly applied and relatively easy-to-handle formal patterns was the real prerequisite for ensemble improvisation. The upheaval we are going to discuss took place at a time when the functional harmonic models were worn out as a basis for improvisation; when the constant reinterpretation of chord patterns, although increasingly complex, appeared with inexorable regularity during a piece and led more frequently to clichés, from which even the most inspired improvisers could not escape.

Finally, the "musically universal" of traditional jazz includes a continuous, accentuated fundamental rhythm — the beat — which, as we know, fulfils the function of metre but is not identical to it. The process of breaking up the beat had gone on continuously since the march-inspired music of the New Orleans veterans. But apart from a few exceptional cases on the periphery of jazz, it had never been abandoned — for good reason too, since one of the most important rhythmic elements of jazz, namely swing, owed much to the conflict between beat and off-beat. Without going into great detail in what is necessarily a quick survey of traditional jazz conventions, we may sum up as follows: the interpretation of a given piece by two musicians or groups playing in different stylistic areas of traditional jazz, will differ in the choice of rhythmic, harmonic, melodic and tone-colour resources, but will not differ in principles used.

The emancipation from traditional jazz laws first significantly infiltrated that area of jazz where the restrictions had become most noticeable, *i. e.* in functional harmony.

On April 2, 1958, a sextet led by trumpeter Miles Davis recorded a piece whose harmony — to the horror of the jazz critics in those days — apparently consisted of only two degrees. The piece was constructed on the *almost* conventional formal pattern A - A - B - B - A; one harmonic degree was assigned to the A sections, the other to the B sections (Example 1). What was first regarded as a total weakness in harmony, was in reality aiming at a new concept of improvisatory creation. *Milestones,* the piece in question, was a first step on the road to *modal playing.*

A SECTIONS (G Dorian)   B SECTIONS (A Aeolian)

EXAMPLE 1   MILESTONES

Like the musical language of medieval Europe, modal playing in jazz uses scales[2] whose structure does not necessarily correspond to our familiar major and minor scales. The

---

2) In these remarks, scale and mode are synonymous, in contrast to the "material scales" known to ethnomusicology which always only denote the tonal material, without implying its order or arrangements.

characteristic features of each mode are determined by the intervals between its successive tones, or more precisely, by the location of whole tones and semitones within the mode. For example, the Ionian mode (which happens to match our major scale) is arranged 1-1-1/2-1-1-1-1/2, while the Dorian mode has the sequence 1-1/2-1-1-1-1/2-1 (1 indicating a whole tone, 1/2 a semitone). By using, say, two modes, the improviser will have two differently arranged sets of tonal material. And if a mode is harmonized in its own modal terms, a closed system is created, within which everything is possible and permissible that does not overstep the boundaries of the mode. In *Milestones* (Example 1) the improviser is given two scale types: the A sections of the piece are in the Dorian mode on G (g-a-b flat-c-d-e-f), with the 11th forming the bass (C); the B sections follow the Aeolian mode on A (a-b-c-d-e-f-g).

What prompted the introduction of modal playing at the end of the Fifties cannot be said for sure. It is unlikely that modal playing arose from any direct reference to the tradition of early European church modes, or the modes of antiquity. It is equally unlikely that Indian ragas served as models; in the late Fifties there were as yet no signs of a trend toward exotic musical genres that a few years later would sprout into fashion. At the time, only very few musicians were involved — consciously and with programmatic intent — with oriental music. Modal playing, however, had no programmatic air; it came about spontaneously at a point in jazz history when the rigidity of the harmonic framework had brought about the perpetual reinterpretation of traditional patterns, no matter how sophisticated they may have become in the meantime.

Modal playing led to consequences of fundamental importance to the development of free jazz. With vertical chordal movement reduced to a minimum, there was room for freedom in a horizontal direction, for the abolition of functional harmony made a schematic division into eight, twelve or sixteen-bar patterns unnecessary. As a series of compositions from the late Fifties shows, it was of course still possible to play modally within traditional formal patterns. In principle, however, the presence of modality as an alternative to a functional harmonic framework (the so-called changes) demanded a form not limited by patterns of bars. If such patterns were still retained (as in *Milestones*), it was by force of habit, rather than inescapable necessity.

As the central point in the earliest evolutionary phase of modal playing, at the end of the Fifties, stands the collaboration of *John Coltrane* and *Miles Davis*.

Coltrane was born on September 23, 1926, in Hamlet, North Carolina. After years of "paying his dues," some of which were spent in rhythm-and-blues bands, he was hired by Miles Davis for his quintet in 1955. Like most of his fellow tenor saxophonists, Coltrane had taken Lester Young and Coleman Hawkins as his models, and had grown into the modern jazz of the Forties under the influence of Dizzy Gillespie and Charlie Parker. As early as 1947, he played a few jobs with Sonny Rollins in Miles Davis's group, but after a short time he left Davis to work with the tenor saxophonist Jimmy Heath, and later in the bands of Dizzy Gillespie, Earl Bostic and Johnny Hodges.

When he joined the Miles Davis Quintet in 1955, attracting the attention of critics and public for the first time, Coltrane was one of the many "hard" tenor saxophonists who, as antipodes of the cool players of the same epoch, split jazz fans into two opposing camps — one enthusiastic, the other negative. His manner of playing at the time was exploratory; he was working out material whose laws were to determine large stretches of his later development. Coltrane began to take the smallest possible note values as basic metrical units, logically finding his way to a strongly slurred articulation, which contrasted greatly to the emphatically staccato phrasing of Sonny Rollins, and which a little later led to the kind of melodic structure dubbed with the unfortunate term "sheets of sound."

The first recordings with the Miles Davis Quintet in 1956 - 57 show a hesitant Coltrane. His ideas seem to be there, but there are shortcomings in their realization. Martin Williams (1967) rightly comments on Coltrane's tendency to finish his phrase endings with blurred tone successions, or to swallow them altogether.

In mid-1957, Coltrane left the Davis Quintet to play with Thelonious Monk for a few months. Collaboration with that "musical architect of the highest order," as Coltrane called Monk in a *Down Beat* article (1960), was of benefit to his musical growth in two important ways: first, Monk showed Coltrane how to play two or three tones simultaneously on the tenor; secondly, he assisted him in his harmonic explorations. The method of stacking supplementary intervals on fundamental chords had already been developed in bebop; Coltrane now went a step further, by piling related chords on the fundamental chords, thus creating harmonic structures of the utmost complexity. This kind of stylistic innovation did not come about spontaneously in improvisatory playing, but contemplatively in theoretical study, or by experimenting at the piano. Coltrane said of this phase of his development: "I've been devoting quite a bit of my time to harmonic studies on my own, in libraries and places like that. I've found you've got to look back at the old things and see them in a new light" (Coltrane 1960).

When Coltrane rejoined Miles Davis's group (now expanded to a sextet) in 1958, he found Davis in the middle of a period of stylistic change. Like Coltrane, Davis had previously worked with multi-chordal structures. He was, as Coltrane said, "interested in chords for their own sake." But now, in 1958, he seemed to be going in the opposite direction: above a minimum of chord changes he was improvising in free-flowing lines, and was much more interested in melodic, horizontal continuity than in the harmonic structure. About his tendency to give chief emphasis to melody while reducing chordal movement, Davis remarked at the time: "When you go that way, you can go on forever. You don't have to worry about changes and you can do more with the line. It becomes a challenge to see how melodically inventive you are. When you are based on chords, you know at the end of thirty-two bars that the chords have run out and there's but to repeat what you've just done — with variations. I think that there is a return in jazz to emphasis on melodic rather than harmonic variation. There will be fewer chords but infinite possibilities as to what to do with them. Of course, several classical composers have been writing this way for years. Too much modern jazz has become thick with chords" (from Hentoff 1961, p. 208).

For Coltrane, this concept acted like a trigger. Although he tried at first to suit his vertical-harmonic achievements to the new modal style, he soon recognized the wider potential Miles Davis's music offered him. "I could play three chords on one. But on the other hand, if I wanted to, I could play melodically. Miles's music gave me plenty of freedom" (Coltrane 1960).

In March and April 1959, about a year after *Milestones,* the second LP representative of the early phase of modal playing was recorded, *Kind of Blue,* by a sextet made up of Davis on trumpet, Coltrane on tenor, Julian Adderly on alto, Winton Kelly alternating with Bill Evans on piano, Paul Chambers on bass, and Jimmy Cobb on drums. The exemplary modal pieces are *So What* and *Flamenco Sketches.* But even *All Blues* and *Freddie Freeloader* — although on the 12-bar blues pattern — bear the stamp of modal playing too; there are no harmonic accessories like substitute chords, secondary dominants, etc., but only the unadorned blues pattern of three four-bar sequences.

More obviously than in *Freddie Freeloader* (a theme whose interval structure and melodic motion are strongly reminiscent of the old Goodman standard *Soft Winds*), the turn toward modal playing can be heard in *So What.* This Miles Davis composition takes the conventional A - A - B - A form of the so-called song pattern. But compared to the old familiar "songs," there are two impressive modifications:

(1) Within the eight-bar periods there is no functional harmonic movement at all; the improvisation material is based in the A sections on the Dorian mode on D, and in the B sections likewise on the Dorian mode, but on E flat.

(2) Any trace of a functional relationship between the periods is avoided: the B section is a chromatic shift of the basic scale from D to E flat, not a leap of a fourth or fifth.

So What became the modal composition par excellence; not long after *Kind of Blue* was issued, legions of amateur groups proceeded to cut their teeth on it. But the most consistently modally worked piece on the disc is *Flamenco Sketches.* This composition — and here that word must be understood in its broadest sense — has no actual theme, that is, it does not proceed from a specially composed melody. This practice is, of course, not new; in all jazz epochs, and especially in bebop, improvisations were played on a given harmonic framework, without necessarily bringing in a theme that fit it. This was particularly so in the case of the 12-bar blues, where the first chorus was frequently an improvisation (*e. g.* Parker's *Mood, K. C. Blues,* etc.). That kind of improvising, however, always maintained a constant pattern throughout the whole piece. The improvisations in *Flamenco Sketches,* on the other hand, are not based on a pattern divided into a fixed number of bars. The piece cannot be said to derive either from the blues form, or the different types of song forms. It consists of five sections of different lengths, each based on another mode (Example 2). This means — and this is the important point — that the individual improvisations are not given a different length by the soloists playing different numbers of choruses (as in traditional jazz), but by their expanding or contracting the periods on the various modes within one chorus. A diagram of the sequence of solos in *Flamenco Sketches* is given in Example 3; each vertical line indicates one bar.

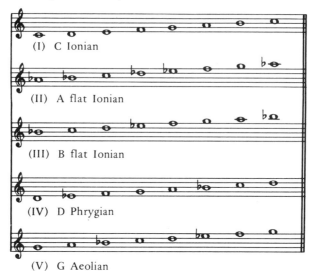

(I) C Ionian

(II) A flat Ionian

(III) B flat Ionian

(IV) D Phrygian

(V) G Aeolian

EXAMPLE 2   FLAMENCO SKETCHES

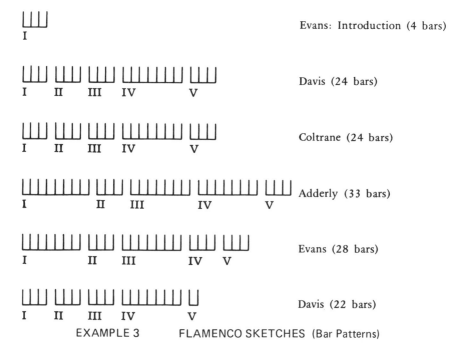

I   Evans: Introduction (4 bars)

I   II   III   IV   V   Davis (24 bars)

I   II   III   IV   V   Coltrane (24 bars)

I   II   III   IV   V   Adderly (33 bars)

I   II   III   IV   V   Evans (28 bars)

I   II   III   IV   V   Davis (22 bars)

EXAMPLE 3   FLAMENCO SKETCHES (Bar Patterns)

Improvising on a number of modes whose sequence is established but whose duration is variable brought with it consequences for ensemble playing which were of fundamental importance for the further development of free jazz. The moment the convention of a standardized bar pattern is dropped, the members of a group are forced to listen to each other with intensified concentration. In the case of *Flamenco Sketches,* all the players had to be able to tell when a change was made from one mode to the next. Since the improviser could not be expected to announce his intentions by facial expressions or gestures, musical signals with the requisite "invitatory" character were established. In some situations, signals like these are introduced and perceived subconsciously, that is, they do not have an agreed signal function; rather, that function is musically immanent.

In *Flamenco Sketches,* the transition from one mode to another is signalled in quite different ways: during Miles Davis's solos, the change is usually indicated by the bassist Paul Chambers, who prepares the ground of the next mode by suspensions; "Cannonball" Adderly leads to the new mode by melodic, modulatory twists; John Coltrane points the shift to a new mode primarily by kinetic cumulation, interrupting the relatively calm melodic progress of his improvisation with interpolated 16th or 32nd figures (*cf.* Example 4). By avoiding modulatory flourishes, which automatically suggest a functional harmonic connection between the modal blocks, he most consistently utilizes the modal concept.

The immediate consequences of modal playing must not be overestimated. *Flamenco Sketches,* and the breach it caused in the standardized concept of bar patterns, was an exception, and remained an exception for some time. While pieces like *So What* found their way into the repertoire of countless jazz groups (Miles Davis recorded the composition with almost all of his later groups), they still inspired hardly any musicians of that time to leave the well-trod track of hard and fast formal patterns.

A month after recording *Kind of Blue,* the Miles Davis Sextet broke up. Davis went back to working with Gil Evans, a collaboration responsible for famous dialogues between trumpet and big band, like *Sketches of Spain, The Meaning of the Blues* and *Lament;* in his small groups, however, he at first did not go beyond the concept developed in *Kind of Blue.* After a bossa nova digression, Julian Adderly returned with his brother Nat to the lucrative fields of soul jazz, winning with *This Here* a public whose range far exceeded that of jazz enthusiasts. It was left to John Coltrane to expand the principle of modal playing.

In May 1959, Coltrane recorded *Giant Steps,* his first important LP as leader of his own quartet. *Giant Steps* reverts to the multi-chordal structures Coltrane was working on earlier. The title tune of the record again runs through all the possibilities of harmonic-melodic creation, at breakneck tempo and with half-bar chord changes; the harmonic framework, however, goes far beyond the simple patterns of hard bop. The foundation here is not the customary "once around the circle of fifths"; the shifts are to mediants,

EXAMPLE 4   FLAMENCO SKETCHES

chords a third away[3]. The melodic line is given no decorative details, as was the case in the melodic overlaying of standards in bebop, but serves primarily to accentuate the chord progressions.

---

3) In this sense the title *Giant Steps* doubtless has programmatic significance. Where Martin Williams (1967) heard an E flat pedal tone in this piece, and a B flat in the (non-existent) bridge, is impossible to imagine.

At a first hearing, Coltrane's improvisatory treatment sounds very impressive, but a more detailed analysis is disillusioning. The exaggerated tempo suggests a stream of melodic ideas, but what in fact occurs is an uninterrupted sequence of arpeggiated chords — in the final analysis, a masterfully presented, well-planned etude. Some melodic patterns in the first chorus, like those underlined in Example 5, also appear note for note in the following choruses.

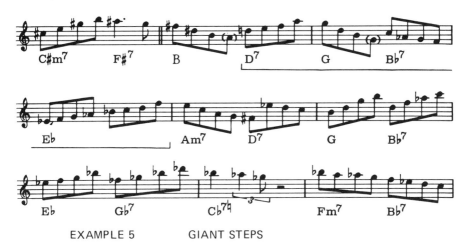

EXAMPLE 5   GIANT STEPS

This example of Coltrane's work played a negative role — but perhaps an important one precisely for that reason — on the road to free jazz. In the *Down Beat* interview of September 1960 (already quoted above) Coltrane said concerning the improvisation technique based on broken chords: "I haven't completely abandoned this approach, but it wasn't broad enough. I'm trying to play these progressions in a more flexible manner now."

About a year after *Giant Steps,* the restrictions of vertical-oriented improvising led Coltrane to return to modal playing and thus to concentrate again on horizontal melodic development. In October 1960 he recorded *My Favorite Things,* with musicians who were to become pillars of the Coltrane Quartet for years: pianist McCoy Tyner and drummer Elvin Jones. They proved to be of considerable importance for Coltrane's stylistic progress; in the years that followed they comprised — at every stage of his innovations — a rhythm section that matched the various phases of his own development.

The title tune of the record, *My Favorite Things,* is a rather insignificant waltz from a musical by Richard Rodgers. Coltrane gives it a certain oriental charm by playing it not on his main instrument, the tenor saxophone, but on soprano, the nasal timbre evoking exotic associations. As it stands, *My Favorite Things* is not a theme that obviously demands modal treatment; there is not, to be sure, much chordal motion in its first eight bars, but the next period contains a modulation from E minor to G major, and finally a whole tone shift to F. Completely ignoring these changes as a springboard for improvisation, Coltrane works with another element of the theme, namely the E minor scale in the last four bars (Example 6), plus a scale in E major introduced as an interlude after the second presentation of the theme. These two scales form the material of the

EXAMPLE 6   MY FAVORITE THINGS

improvisations and also give the piece its formal structure. The soloists, McCoy Tyner and John Coltrane, each improvise first on the minor scale and then on the major, with regular returns of the theme as fixed points, in what seems to be a boundless, open form. The duration or number of bars of each improvisation varies, depending to a great extent on the improviser's flow of ideas. Still, an inner division of traditional eight-bar units does become obvious; it is recognizable above all in repetitions of rhythmic patterns such as

or in the comping figures of the piano. This kind of inner division has a tension-building function similar to the riffs in jazz of the swing era or the comping patterns of the "funky" piano in hard bop (as played for example by Horace Silver). The danger of monotony immanent in improvising on scales instead of chord progressions, is warded off here by a further element of tension.

Coltrane's manner of improvisation in *My Favorite Things,* compared to his solos with the Davis Sextet, is much freer in two respects. First, in the modal pieces by Davis, Coltrane's phrasing usually matched the periodic division; here he plays across the patterns set up by the rhythm section, mostly ignoring the four or eight-bar units they create. Secondly, he expands the material of the E minor and E major scales by putting in tones foreign to the scale at exposed points. With Davis, he used them at the most as passing tones or cambiatas, as we can see from the transcription of *Flamenco Sketches.* Here, they take on a definite value of their own; this hardly presages a coming dissolution of tonality, but it does extend the scope, and stretches the laws, of modal improvising. Example 7 shows a passage of Coltrane's improvisation on the minor scale; at two particularly exposed spots, g sharp (*i. e.,* a major third) jeopardizes the minor scale.

EXAMPLE 7   MY FAVORITE THINGS

The Coltrane recordings that followed *Favorite Things* constantly move back and forth between stylistic innovation and already proven procedures. The records made with trumpeter Don Cherry, the same year as *My Favorite Things,* are not as progressive as the title of the album, *The Jazz Avantgarde,* would lead one to think. Cherry, at the time a member of the Ornette Coleman Quartet and therefore one of the best known exponents of the "new thing," plays more conventionally on this session than he does with Coleman's group. And in such company, Coltrane acts in a curiously hesitant way, if not downright erratically; hectic, short phrases alternate with arpeggios à la *Giant Steps.* Of the flowing lines that distinguish *My Favorite Things* and that were to reappear in *Olé* a few months later, there is hardly anything to be heard.

The significance of the recording session with Don Cherry, then, was more symbolic than immediately musical — an attempted rapprochement between various currents of jazz. But a meeting with far-reaching consequences for Coltrane's path towards free jazz occurred the next year. At the end of 1961, Eric Dolphy — alto saxophonist, flautist and bass clarinettist rolled into one — began to play with the Coltrane Quartet as second wind soloist. This was the start of a partnership between two musicians whose musical backgrounds were not identical, but whose thinking moved in the same direction, namely the expansion of musical scope and the achievement of new ways and means of expression. About his collaboration with Eric Dolphy, Coltrane said in a *Down Beat* interview: "Eric and I have been talking music for quite a few years, since about 1954. We've been close for quite a while. We watched music. We always talked about it, discussed what was being done down through the years, because we love music. What we're doing now was started a few years ago. — A few months ago Eric was in New York, where the group was working, and he felt like playing, wanted to come down and sit in... I'd felt at ease with just a quartet till then, but he came in, and it was like having another member of the family. He'd found another way to express the same thing we had found one way to do. — After he sat in, we decided to see what it would grow into. We began to play some of the things we had only talked about before. Since he's been in the band, he's had a broadening effect on us. There are a lot of things we try now that we never tried before" (from DeMichael 1962).

When Dolphy joined the Coltrane Quartet in 1961 he had a musical background marked by an immense variety of associations. Born in Los Angeles in 1926, he began his career in groups led by — among others — Gerald Wilson and Buddy Colette, and first attained international fame by playing with Chico Hamilton in 1958/59. He came into contact with the jazz avantgarde of the day while working in the groups of Charles Mingus and George Russell.

At the start of the Sixties, Eric Dolphy, like Coltrane, was musically on the borderline between the gradually growing offshoots of hard bop and the more radical innovations of free jazz, as it was evolving in the Coleman and Taylor groups. But while Coltrane steadily gained independence from traditional norms, step by step and year by year, Dolphy moved back and forth between the stylistic poles. On the one hand, we have the radical renunciation of traditional harmony and rhythm in Ornette Coleman's double quartet record *Free Jazz,* in which Dolphy participated as co-leader in 1960; on the other hand, we have his recordings with Oliver Nelson or Booker Little, oriented on hard bop, made a year later. His dialogue with Charles Mingus in *What Love* (1960) is free of all formal ties; the pitch functions of the bass and bass clarinet are irrelevant as such, and both instruments produce vocalized sounds resembling speech, hollers or shouts. Contrasted with this are flute ballads of classical beauty, such as *Don't Blame Me* (1961) or *You Don't Know What Love Is,* which Dolphy recorded shortly before his death in 1964.

Like few jazz musicians of the Sixties, Dolphy was at home in all the stylistic areas of the time, without ever giving up anything of his personal style. That style embraced the maximum technical potential of his three instruments, with "traditional" techniques expanded by a quite specific kind of articulation, intonation and phrasing. For Dolphy, as for Ornette Coleman, tempered intonation (which in any case is accepted only in a limited way in jazz) was of secondary interest. His flute playing awakes associations with bird-song not only in the listener; Dolphy himself openly said that bird-song was the source of it — to the considerable astonishment of the critics (*cf.* DeMichael 1962). On the bass clarinet, Dolphy developed sounds not related to a precisely definable pitch, giving them an independent identity; the subsequent evolution of free jazz took them for granted. These and his dragged, or smeared, tones on the alto saxophone are not merely effects grafted onto an otherwise conventional way of playing. The "tricks," as Dolphy's critics called them at the start of the Sixties, are in reality fully integrated stylistic elements, although their expressive quality, akin to that of the human voice, must have been a source of suspicion to listeners trained on conventional sounds[4].

Dolphy's collaboration with Coltrane lasted just a few months and produced only a few records which, moreover, do not reflect more than a small part of the impression the group made in live performances in the USA and Europe. One of the principal documents we have was recorded live at a club date in November 1961; it has the programmatic title *India* (on *Impressions*). Although *India* — as one may gather from the name — is a modal piece, it is clearly a symbolic bow to Indian music (keenly appreciated by Coltrane), rather than an attempted musical fusion on the order of the German recordings *Jazz Meets India,* or Joe Harriot's *Indo Jazz Suite.* Coltrane's *India* picks up the concept of *Favorite Things* and *Olé,* and carries it further. Again the theme is only of secondary importance for the progress of the piece. It sets the emotional mood, without providing a rhythmic, harmonic or formal foundation. Two simple, signal-like motives are opposed to one another; the second, consisting of the notes g-e-c-d, is later taken over by the pianist as an accompaniment pattern during the solos of Coltrane and Dolphy. Preceding the theme, Coltrane plays an improvised passage on soprano, intro-

---

4) Much the same thing happened to Lester Young, thirty years earlier, when he broke with then current standards of tenor saxophone tone production, doctored pitches by "false fingerings" and estranged himself from the arpeggio players of the time by his use of a linear conception of melody.

ducing the mode on which succeeding solos are based, or rather (in this case), on which the soloists orient themselves (Example 8). The mode in question is G Mixolydian,

EXAMPLE 8   INDIA

comparable to G major with a minor seventh. In *India*, the mode is treated much more freely than in Coltrane's earlier modal pieces. This is perhaps due to the influence of Dolphy, who tends to stray from a strict observance of the mode; even the entrance to his chorus has a distinctly bitonal character. By using flattened intervals at the focal points of phrases, he gives his melodies a minor coloration which now and then collides violently with the mode of the piece, and thus with the pianist's chord progressions (*cf.* Example 9).

EXAMPLE 9   INDIA

Coltrane's melody shows a great deal more proximity to the Mixolydian mode than Dolphy's, but a clear shift away from the original material is also noticeable in the course of Coltrane's improvisation. In *Favorite Things,* he still accepted the mode as more or less binding, occasionally aiming away from it, so to speak, at tones foreign to the scale (Example 7); here, however, he plays *around* the mode more than *in* it.

Two modifications in Coltrane's style of playing may have been inspired by his collaboration with Dolphy, and were possibly among the things he "never tried before," as Coltrane said in the conversation quoted above (DeMichael 1962). The first is working with single tones whose sound coloration is frequently reminiscent of Dolphy's sound on bass clarinet. Coltrane had already experimented with tone colour before, for example when he played multiple sounds in his composition *Harmonique*. In earlier pieces, such sound manipulations had more the character of stylistic additives, but here they are

29

fully integrated into the solo and neither act like ornamentation nor sound unnatural[5]; they function as culminating points of the melody.

The second new feature of Coltrane's playing, which likewise hints at Dolphy's influence, is the use of large intervals, sixths and sevenths. The use of volatile melodic elements had for some time been one of Dolphy's most pronounced improvisational traits and had provoked frequent attacks (mostly unjustified, in my opinion) for what critics claimed was a tendency to produce clichés. Coltrane works a good deal more sparingly with these rather hectic wide intervals than does Dolphy. For the most part, these intervals serve as melodic — and also rhythmic — contrasts to the rounded melodic curves built of 8th-note or 16th-note chains, and moving as a rule in seconds or thirds. In the passages with large leaps, Coltrane moves furthest away from the modal frame of reference, as a comparison of Examples 8 and 10 will clearly demonstrate.

EXAMPLE 10   INDIA

An essential factor in the musical structure of *India* is the treatment of the rhythm, which takes on a special weight — among other ways — by the presence of two bassists (Reggie Workman and Jimmy Garrison) in the rhythm section. The drummer Elvin Jones provides the beat, but also camouflages it in a very subtle way, by dividing it between his percussion instruments, a quasi "open-work technique." At the same time, he makes an orientation toward "one," the down beat, an Alpha and Omega of traditional jazz, practically impossible by superimposing asymmetrical rhythmic flourishes. The bassists add to the process of rhythmic disorientation by bringing in two-bar rhythmic patterns whose accent distribution often jeopardizes the fundamental rhythm (Example 11).

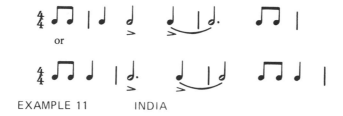

EXAMPLE 11   INDIA

These patterns are of note because they are not used in a schematic way; they vary throughout the piece, therefore constantly giving new impulses to the rhythmic flow, and admittedly contributing to the listener's insecurity. In the same way, the

---

5) The German verb "verfremden" as applied to sounds, can be given as "to denature," "to render unnatural" or unaccustomed (translator's note).

pianist McCoy Tyner uses the pattern derived from the second thematic motive (g-e-c-d) quite independently of periodic divisions; only very faint here are reminiscences of the stereotyped four or eight-bar comping figures in *Favorite Things.*

India is just one of the pieces that grew out of the John Coltrane - Eric Dolphy partnership, and it is probably not even the best one. Nevertheless, it very forcefully marks a phase of modal improvisation, distinguished by a consistent exploration of all the potentialities inherent in it; at the same time, however, its limitations are exposed. Except for the theme, all formal schematism in *India* is given up in favour of procedurally developing structural contexts, their organizational development dependent both on the spontaneous creative power of the individual musicians, and on their willingness and ability to integrate their creative potential into a larger whole. The inner order of the piece — in its horizontal development — is necessarily asymmetrical, governed as it is by the soloists' phrasing, the changing patterns of the bassists and pianist, and the extremely variable rhythmic foundation laid down by the drummer. Vertical cohesion is achieved in principle by the modal framework, but that principle does not absolutely hold. No longer does the modal material bind the whole piece together; instead, it functions as a starting and landing point for melodic excursions, which are just one short step removed from polytonality.

In the early Sixties, Coltrane was obviously fully aware of the magnitude of that "short step," and for a long time was not willing to take it. *India* remained, for the time being, without direct consequences. It should be regarded as a temporary, probing venture, rather than as the germ-cell of a new concept. Here, it may be well to digress for a moment to the reactions of jazz critics at the time, for only in that way can we really get an idea of the climate in which these innovations — which are relatively harmless when viewed historically — took place. While Coltrane and Dolphy were conducting their experiments aimed at expanding modal playing, the catchword "anti-jazz" raised its head in critical circles. On November 23, 1961, the co-editor of *Down Beat,* John Tynan, wrote: "At Hollywood's Renaissance Club recently, I listened to a horrifying demonstration of what appears to be a growing anti-jazz trend exemplified by these foremost proponents (Coltrane and Dolphy) of what is termed avant garde music. — I heard a good rhythm section . . . go to waste behind the nihilistic exercises of the two horns . . . Coltrane and Dolphy seem intent on deliberately destroying (swing) . . . They seem bent on pursuing an anarchistic course in their music that can but be termed anti-jazz" (from DeMichael 1962).

"Nihilism, anarchism, anti"; as we see, reactionary criticism's invective vocabulary is the same everywhere. One of the main charges levelled at the John Coltrane group was the excessive length of their pieces. This is interesting to note, since long pieces were not really new in the history of jazz. In informal jam sessions of the swing and bebop eras, and at "Jazz at the Philharmonic" concerts, one-hour pieces had never drawn such furious reactions. The stumbling block, then, was not the duration *per se*, but that in modal improvisation the listener lost familiar aids to orientation. The abandonment of functional harmony made traditional formal patterns obsolete, and a readily comprehensible time-division went with them. As we know from experimental psychology, non-divided time (whether apparent or real), is always subjectively felt to be longer than divided time. Coltrane was not attacked for blowing *too many* choruses, but for blowing *one* too-lengthy chorus, on what was apparently just *one* chord.

At bottom, criticism of the duration of pieces was nothing other than the reaction of bewildered observers, standing before the razed barriers of traditional patterns. But the accusation of "nihilistic exercises" was based also on other — if not necessarily sounder — arguments. When critics said that "swing," one of the most substantial elements of jazz, had been "destroyed," they were implying that swing as a rhythmic quality was something unmistakably definable, holding it up as a constant in all varieties of "real" jazz, and forgetting to make allowance for the fact that swing was a phenomenon with many forms and expressions. The swing of the Count Basie Orchestra is not "better" than that of a bebop group or a soloist like Stan Getz; it is qualitatively different, and the point is not who swings *more*, but how the swing of various musicians and styles differs.

The post-*India* modal pieces by the Coltrane Quartet are all comparatively conventional. In pieces like *Up Against the Wall, Alabama* or *Promise,* the dominance of the mode is scarcely infringed on. The bassist of the group, usually Jimmy Garrison, plays close to the beat, and even the standardized formal patterns — already claimed to be obsolescent — are usually observed.

In many respects, this procedure of sticking to proven quantities is symptomatic of John Coltrane's whole musical progress. Every step forward is followed by what looks like a pause for relaxation. On closer scrutiny, however, it proves to be a phase of consolidation, a pulling together of the experiences gained from the previous stage of experimentation.

The climax and conclusion of this period is Coltrane's first Suite, *A Love Supreme,* recorded in December 1964. The psychological and spiritual aspects of this "great prayer of hymnic force" (Berendt 1968, p. 96) have been stressed again and again by jazz publicists. It is doubtful whether the same piece, under a different title and without Coltrane's religious confession on the record jacket, would have attracted the kind of attention it ultimately did. Even so, the influence it had, as the manifestation of a new, spiritual attitude, on many young musicians in the New York free jazz circle, cannot be overlooked. With *A Love Supreme,* Coltrane's role as a pioneer of technical musical innovations — which he had pursued from the beginning of the Sixties — was transformed into the role of pioneer of a new self-realization on the part of free jazz musicians.

Musically, *A Love Supreme* is the consummate product of an assimilation process in which Coltrane sums up five years of musical experiences and perceptions. As such, it achieves a synthesis of the most varied formative principles. Each of the four movements of the Suite presents the improvisers with a differently structured frame of reference: a relatively freely treated modality in *Acknowledgement*; cadential eight-bar periods in *Resolution*; a twelve-bar blues pattern with a modal flavour in *Pursuance*; and finally, strict modality in *Psalm,* a piece of intensive simplicity.

With respect to form, *A Love Supreme* shows a new feature in Coltrane's work: motivic ties between sections. At the beginning of the first movement *(Acknowledgements),* for example, Coltrane opposes to the principal theme (Example 12) — played by the bass and later presented vocally — a contrasting melodic line (Example 13), from which, during the first movement, he takes a phrase and systematically varies it. The same phrase, in a new rhythm and over new harmonic progressions, forms the theme of the third movement *(Pursuance).*

A typical procedure of Coltrane's later development occurs at the end of the first movement: taking the central motive of the main theme, he sequences it through all keys (Example 14), superimposing it on the modal foundation in the bass and piano — an emphatic cumulation created by relatively simple means, and one of the essential expressive features of the recordings he made in the ensuing years.

EXAMPLE 12   A LOVE SUPREME

EXAMPLE 13   A LOVE SUPREME

EXAMPLE 14   A LOVE SUPREME

The boundaries Coltrane accepted with the frames of reference underlying *A Love Supreme* are clearly drawn, but they are seen to be relatively flexible when one traces Coltrane's path from his work with the Miles Davis Sextet, to *Favorite Things* and *India,* and on to this Suite.

Coltrane's gradual departure from the musical norms of hard bop, the decisive move being the turn to modal playing under the influence of Miles Davis, led him by the mid-Sixties to a position which Martin Williams (1967) called the "man in the middle." Around 1965, however, Coltrane was in reality further removed from the stiff, routine forms of post bop, and closer to the formative principles of free jazz being developed by Ornette Coleman and Cecil Taylor. The step from *A Love Supreme,* still "music of the middle," to *Ascension* (*cf.* Chapter 5) which Coltrane recorded a half-year later, meant more for his musical growth than any step before. With it he left a position difficult to define in terms of established stylistic categories. The "man in the middle" became one of the central figures in a group of young New York musicians, the "second generation" of free jazz, who -- building on the musical achievements of Coleman and Taylor — now found in Coltrane one of their chief musical and human models.

Chapter 2

CHARLES MINGUS

At the beginning of the Sixties, the search for new techniques and means of expression was carried on with a vigour that was viewed with mistrust by some critics and fans — not to mention musicians of the older generation. Others were plainly alarmed, and minced no words in their comments. In the midst of the turmoil stood, firm as a rock, bassist and composer *Charles Mingus,* with a conception whose most important features had already been worked out in the mid-Fifties, and which at the same time anticipated some of the basic elements from which varieties of free jazz later crystallized. Coltrane's development, as we have seen, was a gradual stylistic progression which, as time went on, took him further and further away from his starting point. When one talks about his "style," therefore, one must also mention dates. Mingus, on the other hand, took elements from widespread areas of music, and fused them into a whole whose characteristics are valid in a way that is relatively independent of dating.

Mingus got his earliest and most formative musical impressions from the gospel songs of the Negro church congregations in Watts, a slum suburb of Los Angeles where he spent most of his youth. The call-and-response patterns of the hymns sung in the Holiness churches, and particularly their strong emotional content, are still one of the foundations of Mingus's music today, and give it at times an intensity that makes the neo-gospel effects of so-called soul jazz seem like nothing more than fashion accessories.

The second, and not less decisive, experience for Mingus was the Duke Ellington Orchestra, which he first heard over the radio at the age of eight. The fascination was heightened when Mingus attended an Ellington concert: "When I first heard Duke Ellington in person, I almost jumped out of the balcony. One piece excited me so much that I screamed" (from Hentoff 1961, p. 164).

Ellington and gospel music, and later blues, are the most influential sources of Mingus's musical inspiration, but they are not the only ones. At a very early stage, Mingus had a strong affinity for European impressionist composers like Debussy and Ravel. But above all, he had practical experience in almost all areas of jazz. By working as sideman of such dissimilar musicians as Kid Ory, Louis Armstrong, Lionel Hampton, Red Norvo, Art Tatum and Charlie Parker, Mingus got intimately acquainted with a broad spectrum of styles. In fact, it is doubtful whether any other musician has ever had quite the same amount of direct access to so many different kinds of jazz.

The diversity of these influences has brought about a style which takes into account such disparate things as the ensemble sound of the Ellington Orchestra and the collective improvisation of New Orleans bands, the call-and-response patterns of gospel music and bebop phrases, impressionistic sound structures and the rhythms of Spanish-Mexican folklore.

For all his eclecticism, Mingus has created an unmistakably personal idiom, not merely a stylistic mish-mash; the whole is always more than the sum of its parts. Credit for this achievement must go first and foremost to the strength of his personality; his "dissonant intensity" (if one may call it that) may have brought him a lot of trouble and misunderstanding outside the music field, but it has given his music a unique individuality. And it is the eclectic side of Mingus that has had a decisive influence on young musicians of the next generation, who — consciously or unconsciously — repeat in their own way Mingus's borrowing from past epochs of jazz, from folklore and the art music of the West.

As a bassist, Mingus is one of the great virtuosos. This impression may have paled with the passing of time and the rise of a new generation of bass players for whom — to gather from their technical derring-do — nothing seems impossible. Even so, one must recall the effect that the brilliance of Mingus's playing had on listeners during the Fifties: "He invariably gives the impression of accomplishing what the instrument was never intended for" (Balliett 1963, p. 169). What set Mingus apart from the bassists of the Fifties, however, was not so much his consummate command of technique, but chiefly the way in which he placed that technique at the service of his overall musical conception.

At the time, the signal virtue of a bassist was to play four beats cleanly, even at the fastest tempo. Solos (rare enough) were as a rule not much more than ensemble bass playing minus the ensemble, or — at the other extreme — virtuoso technical demonstrations that frequently had nothing to do with the musical context. Mingus proceeded to partly dispense with the time-keeper function of the instrument in favour of rhythmically independent lines running contrapuntally to the melody, lines that were both a foundation and a counter-part to the others. The excerpt from Mingus's composition *What Love,* in Example 15, shows this kind of emancipated bass playing.

Along with giving the bass an autonomous position in the ensemble, Mingus introduced a number of technical innovations. These, however, are not used predominantly for their own sake as soloistic ear-catchers; on the contrary, they always function as integrated components of the overall musical structure. He developed, for example, urgent pizzicato tremolos as a means of heightening tension; these give the impression of sustained swelling and fading tones. By articulation and phrasing, he makes the bass "speak" when he carries on the already mentioned dialogue with Dolphy in *What Love.* And in his reminiscences of the turbulent atmosphere in a Mexican border town *(Tijuana Moods),* he played flamenco-inspired guitar patterns long before bassist Jimmy Garrison caused a furore with his "flamanco bass" solos in the Coltrane Quartet (*cf.* Example 16).

EXAMPLE 15   WHAT LOVE

EXAMPLE 16   YSABEL'S TABLE DANCE

Only to a slight extent did Mingus's immediate contemporaries take over his technical innovations or join the move to free the bass from its servant role. There was not much room for Mingus's kind of bass playing in the rhythmic conception of hard bop. The outstanding bassists of the late Fifties — Paul Chambers, Sam Jones, Doug Watkins, for example — leaned more toward Ray Brown than toward Mingus. Only later did New Jazz bassists like Charles Haden, Scott la Faro, Steve Swallow and others, adopt Mingus's achievements, expanding them to match the rhythmic demands of free jazz.

37

Mingus's role as a pioneer of free jazz is by no means limited to his work as a bassist. He was of much greater importance for the music of the Sixties as a composer, and above all as the leader of his "jazz workshops," as he significantly called his groups. His predilection for Ellington is expressed not only in the sound texture of his compositions and in his brilliant interpretations of some Ellington pieces, but more so in the way he realizes his musical conception with his groups. Like Ellington, Mingus brings his musicians directly into the compositorial process; he does not compose *for them*, but *with them*. He does not hand them a definitive score, but sketches for them — usually at the piano — the musical and emotional framework of a piece. This is more, however, than a head arrangement, such as is used in a jam session or at informal recording sessions, where only externals, the order of solos, riffs, endings, etc. are given. When suggesting a certain manner of interpretation to his workshop musicians, when demonstrating the scales or chord progressions on which a piece is to be based, Mingus at the same time gives his players the freedom to make their own contribution, not only in solos — which will be individual in any case — but (more importantly) in collective ensemble playing. In this way, a feedback process is set up in which the musicians' reactions and the bandleader's ideas are almost equally important. Much of what happens musically is not planned in advance, but arises from spontaneous interactions within the group. Mingus says: "As long as they start where I start and end where I end, the musicians can change the composition if they feel like it. They add themselves, they add how they feel, while we're playing" (from Hentoff, Atl. 1377).

An important factor in this process is the cooperation between Mingus and his drummer Dannie Richmond. Together since 1957, they are one of the longest-lived teams in the history of jazz, and Richmond has developed over the years a quasi somnambulist empathy with his leader's intentions. With Richmond's support, Mingus guides the playing of his groups, steers the dynamic progression, introduces sudden changes of tempo, forces a continuous accelerando, or alters metre and rhythm. Obviously, this demands much more from the musicians in a Mingus group than just playing arrangements and solo choruses. Jimmy Knepper, a trombonist who worked for some years with Mingus, says: "It takes a little while to get in the spirit of some of his tunes . . . But once you learn [them], once you *feel* how they should be played, they come easily. He expects quick results, but understands the musician's problems. And he doesn't impose his own ideas on you but wants individual interpretations" (from Wilson 1966, p. 71). As Dannie Richmond puts it: "Mingus and I feel each other out as we go . . . The best way I can explain is that we find a beat that's in the air, and just take it out of the air when we want it" (from Hentoff, AM 6082). This may sound a bit mystic, but it hits the mark. It is doubtless this "feeling," this intuitive response, that has given Mingus's music part of its tension and fascination — and at a time when free group improvisation and changing tempos were by no means so self-evident as they are today.

One of Mingus's primary virtues as a bandleader is that he always found for his "jazz workshops", musicians who could fulfil his demands, who could follow both his angry musical outbursts and his lyrical ballad interpretations, who knew the spirit of New

Orleans collective improvisation, as well as the sound of the Ellington Orchestra. Some of these musician's came to Mingus's workshop as apprentices and left it as masters who had found their musical identity and had acquired the ability to attain a higher order of discipline in a seemingly undisciplined setting. "I figure if I can work with this cat [Mingus], I can work with anybody," says alto saxophonist Charles McPherson (from Hentoff, AM 6082), and a number of other musicians like Roland Kirk, John Handy III, Ted Curson and Clifford Jordan confirm that statement in a musical way.

The strong interactions between Mingus and the musicians in his groups had a notable effect, in that the outward features of Mingus's music changed, depending on who was playing. Without the essence, the specifically Mingus flavour being lost, various stylistic components of the music were pointed up at various stages. Collaboration with experiment-minded musicians like Teddy Charles, John la Porta and Teo Macero produced results — conditioned by the musical background of those players -- that showed European influences. On the other hand, the blues origins of Mingus's music came to the fore when musicians like Roland Kirk or Booker Ervin played with the group. The size of the ensemble also had much to do with the means of expression: in a 22-piece band, like the one Mingus used to record the LP *Pre-Bird,* collective improvisation is naturally not practicable to the extent it is in a quintet or quartet.

The two achievements of Mingus's music that are probably the most significant for his role as a pioneer of free jazz, are his treatment of form and tempo, and his approach to collective improvisation. Mingus's compositions, and what grows out of them in cooperation with his musicians, only rarely fit the formal structures common in the late Fifties and early Sixties. This comes about not so much by departing from prevailing bar patterns — Mingus uses 16 and 32-bar forms and 12-bar blues again and again — but by breaking away from the conventional formula of "theme — improvisation — theme."

Unlike Coltrane, who in following the principle of modal improvisation cut across schematic boundaries to arrive at a certain indeterminate form, Mingus accepts the old formal patterns, but alters them by filling them with new content. His pieces are always more than the tunes of hard bop, even though they are sometimes identical in form, and can hardly be distinguished as to the number of bars and the chord progressions. Mingus's pieces very often have the character of suites, their abundance of contrasting moods frequently recalling the masterpieces by the "father of jazz composition," Jelly Roll Morton, whom Mingus greatly admires. Sometimes Mingus will superimpose the melodies of two popular songs to create dissonant polyphonic structures that successfully mask the banality of the originals. In other cases, he alters the standard tunes so thoroughly that even a listener trained in the melodic and harmonic reshaping of bebop[1] will have trouble distinguishing just what the model is. The thematic origins of the Mingus title

---

1) In 1967 Frank Tirro introduced the apt term "silent theme tradition" for this practice.

All the Things You Could Be by Now if Sigmund Freud's Wife Was Your Mother are easier to deduce from the verbal joke than from the music itself.

The means Mingus uses to expand the formal axioms of jazz, to get contrast, to build and reduce tension, are many and varied. His most obvious method of formal expansion is to juxtapose several contrasting themes which, of themselves, give differentiation to the musical structure and thus establish various emotional levels. The possibilities of multi-thematic work are especially evident in programmatic compositions like *Reincarnation of a Lovebird* (dedicated to Charlie Parker), in *New York Sketchbook* and in *Passions of a Woman Loved,* the latter conceived as a jazz ballet. But also monothematic pieces and even 12-bar blues, in which nothing but the key and a few rhythmic patterns are agreed upon, reflect Mingus's formal ideas. By handling the instrumentation of his ensemble in a highly variable way, he creates pieces in which no two choruses are alike. Particularly in large formations, like the one that recorded *Black Saint and Sinner Lady,* passages with the most diverse instrumentation follow one another, producing — by alteration of tone colour and dynamics — formal units which signify much more than just a change from one soloist to the next. But Mingus and his group achieve a variable sound even in a quartet; seeming intuitively to follow the laws of combination, they pass through a series of spontaneously changing groupings. In *Folk-Forms No. 1,* for example, duets — trumpet and alto (unaccompanied!), trumpet and bass, or alto and drums — are inserted between the ensemble passages, thus creating timbric and dynamic gradations that are always different.

Another means of formal differentiation in Mingus's music is his treatment of tempo, metre and rhythm. There is hardly one Mingus piece in which the tempo set at the beginning is kept throughout. The change is frequently limited to a double-time that breaks into a calm pace (calm for Mingus, that is); this is executed not only by the drummer — as was customary at the time — but by the bassist too, which makes it seem that much more urgent. Just as often, however, Mingus will drive the tempo forward with an accelerando until — preceded by a roll from Dannie Richmond — he suddenly pulls it back. Continuous accelerations of up to four times the original tempo (= 56 to = 288 in *Black Saint and Sinner Lady*) are not at all rare.

Mingus frequently combines tempo changes with an alteration of the basic rhythm, and sometimes of the metre too. In his metrical variation, he is usually content with transitions from 4/4 to 3/4 (e. g. *Los Mariachis* in *Tijuana Moods*), or with the superimposition of three and four-beat metres *(Fables of Faubus).* The rhythmic make-up of his pieces, however, is much more inventive, attaining at times a variety that matches the variety of instrumental coloration. In the blues piece *Prayer for Passive Resistance,* for example, there are contrasting choruses with a steady beat, a triplet basis, stop-time and shuffle rhythms. In *Tijuana Moods,* Latin-American patterns (   ) alternate with jazz rhythms; and in *Black Saint and Sinner Lady* rhythmically free, late-Romantic-flavoured piano cadenzas are followed by an Ellington-inspired ballad on a steady beat, while later an alto saxophone-guitar duet (again rhythmically free) leads to the rhythm of a Spanish march (♪♫♫ ♪♪♫).

It was mainly through the principle of collective improvisation, however, that Mingus brought his players directly into a process of spontaneous co-creation. Collective improvisation was the very life and breath of older jazz; the smooth orchestral sound of the swing bands glossed it over, and emphasis on individual solo playing by "stars" pushed it completely out of sight, until it became a museum piece in the revival bands of jazz veterans and their young emulators. Attempts to revive collective improvisation in the Fifties, initiated mainly by white musicians like Gerry Milligan and the Al Cohn - Zoot Sims tenor duo, usually stopped at inserting an improvised dialogue of two horns before the last theme of a piece. Moreover, they were of a much too casual character to have had any far-reaching effect. Some experiments on the part of cool musicians headed by pianist Lenny Tristano went further: Tristano's *Intuition* (1949) is based exclusively on group improvisation, but it is oriented not so much on jazz practices as it is on contrapuntal techniques of European Baroque music. Furthermore, it was so far beyond the musical pale of Forties' and Fifties' jazz that it remained an exception, even within the narrower periphery of cool jazz.

The collective improvisations of Mingus's workshop groups have a great deal of the raw vitality of early jazz and very little of the sterile smoothness of cool jazz. As in New Orleans jazz, they often form the emotional climax of a piece. Passages already pointed toward an emotional culmination by a continuous intensification of tempo and dynamics are even more strongly emphasized by the polyphonic textures of a collective improvisation. The group improvisations of Mingus's large ensembles in particular have a sonic density and a driving force that were long absent from jazz and that do not appear again until the group improvisations of free jazz. The step from the collective improvisation of three horns over Mexican rhythms in *Ysabell's Table Dance* recorded in 1957, to Don Cherry's *Eternal Rhythm* eleven years later, is much smaller than the intervening period of time would make it appear.

The transition from arranged sections to improvised ensemble passages is often fluid in Mingus's pieces. Occasionally, rhythmic patterns are fixed which turn up again and again as ostinatos in the collective choruses; shifted, placed one against the other, they give the music a dogged, screwdriver quality. In other pieces a written-out theme may be played against improvised accompanying parts which, in their independent rhythmic and melodic construction, are more than just background or a "sound-carpet" for the soloist. Alongside such "semi-collective" improvisation — its New Orleans parallel is the contrast between the trumpet playing the theme, and the clarinet and trombone playing around it — Mingus attains (less frequently, to be sure) a kind of *total* collective improvisation that involves not only the horns but the whole group. The 1960 quartet recording of *Folk Forms No. 1* (*cf.* Example 17) contains long stretches in which the traditional roles of the rhythm section and soloists are set aside in a way unknown even

EXAMPLE 17   FOLK FORMS NUMBER ONE

in the early music of Ornette Coleman, the most talked about exponent of free jazz at the time. In the group improvisations of *Folk Forms,* one rarely hears a steady beat, and hardly any continuous harmonic basis. Nobody accompanies, nobody solos. The general mood of this music is hectic, nervous, but not chaotic. Although each part is on a par with all the others, it adapts itself to the rest, forming a whole whose conciseness stems not so much from any convention as from an intuitive understanding between the musicians. The players in the Mingus group "feel each other out," as Dannie Richmond said. The parts they play are autonomous but *not independent;* as in a conversation, there are pauses, and the exclamations of one player are corroborated by another. (Notice for example how the accent just before "four," set up by Mingus in bars 1 and 3, is taken over by Eric Dolphy in bar 5 and Ted Curson in bar 9.) Another source of order on the brink of chaos lies in the framework within which Mingus experiments: *Folk Forms* is based on a 12-bar blues. It is characteristic of Mingus that in striving for a synthesis of the past and future, he builds his innovations on one of the strongest traditional foundations of jazz.

Chapter 3

ORNETTE COLEMAN[1]

It is hard to dispassionately analyze the music of Ornette Coleman, without first recalling the turbulent extra-musical circumstances that accompanied its appearance at the end of the Fifties.

Now, controversy about the value of a novel stylistic direction was nothing new for the disputatious devotees of jazz. But never was the arrival of any one musician, utterly unknown a few short months before, greeted with such a spontaneous outcry in jazz journals and in private and public discussions.

In 1959, more or less overnight, Ornette Coleman became a figure of contention that split the jazz community straight across. He was hailed as "the new Charlie Parker," as the man who symbolized a departure for new musical shores; and he was ridiculed as a charlatan and a primitive.

To a greater degree than usual, jazz musicians themselves were drawn into the fray. Until this time, it had mostly been left to jazz criticism to announce the "decline of jazz" in polemic debates, or — usually late — to "discover" new talents. But where Ornette Coleman was concerned, a majority of the musicians joined the dissonant chorus of opposing opinions, providing the critics with additional ammunition for their guerrilla war[2].

The reticence of jazz musicians toward their "colleagues'" music is proverbial, as is their tendency to "put on" the instant a critic arrives on the scene.

Their unusual volubility in Coleman's case had a number of causes. One was that the innovations Coleman brought to the jazz of the Fifties seemed so revolutionary that a large percentage of "traditional" jazz musicians practically feared for their livelihood. Nat Hentoff describes his observations in the New York jazz club, "Five Spot," where Ornette Coleman had his first long engagement in 1959: "For months, grimly skeptical jazzmen lined up at the Five Spot's bar. They made fun of Coleman but were naggingly

---

1) This chapter is based on an article published in *Jazzforschung 2* (*cf.* Jost 1970a).

2) In his "Encyclopedia of Jazz in the Sixties" (1966) Leonard Feather published a collection of interviews about Ornette Coleman (blindfold tests) with musicians of all stylistic camps; the views are so divergent that one wonders if everybody was talking about the same musician.

worried that he might, after all, have something to say — and in a new way" (Hentoff 1961, p. 226)[3]. A critical point for his fellow musicians was Ornette Coleman's instrumental technique, or rather what they thought to be his lack of it; compared to other sax players, trained in the standard set by Charlie Parker, Coleman was anything but a virtuoso. True, the fashion of cutting contests, the conscious attempt to outblow other musicians in technical prowess, was no longer prevalent, as it had been during the swing era. Still, acceptance into the inner circle of New York musicians' cliques frequently depended on proficiency — and that meant, among other things, technical perfection. (The example of Julian Adderly, who as a newcomer from "down south" found immediate recognition with virtuoso choruses on the "test piece," *I'll Remember April,* is only one of many.)

The allegedly slipshod technique with which Coleman presented his innovations was one failing in the eyes of New York musicians; his negligible musical background was another. He could neither point to years of paying his dues in one of the better-known big bands, nor was he a recognized quantity in any other jazz centre. When Coltrane and Dolphy appeared a little later, they were tolerated — at least in their own ranks — because of their background. But the presence of Coleman was taken as a slap in the face. He had turned up on the New York jazz scene seemingly out of nowhere. His music had already been labelled "The Shape of Jazz to Come" by a record producer whose business sense was rather more pronounced than his tact. And his quartet was holding down one of the most sought-after New York club jobs. The ill-humour of a large part of the jazz community was unpleasant, but it was somehow understandable.

As it happens, Coleman's breakthrough was the result of a stroke of luck after years of watching, waiting, and frustrations that would probably have made most other musicians throw in the sponge.

Coleman was born on March 19, 1930, in Fort Worth, Texas. At 14 he began to play the alto, mainly self-taught; after 1949 he worked sporadically (and without much success) in various rhythm-and-blues bands in the southwest. His almost ten-year musical and human Odyssey, up to the end of the Fifties, has been described in detail on a number of record sleeves and in countless articles[4]. Very little is known about his playing during this time, but judging from the humiliation he suffered in commercial rock-oriented bands and in jam sessions with better-known musicians in Los Angeles, his saxophone style must have been as unconventional at the beginning as it was later, when he attracted the attention of a broad public.

Ornette Coleman's career began with a recording for Contemporary in February 1958, which came about more or less by accident. During his lean years in Los Angeles, he had

---

3) Hentoff gives a good survey of the various opinions on Coleman's music.

4) *Cf.* especially A. B. Spellman's "Four Lives in the Bebop Business" (1967), in which one of the four chapters is devoted to Ornette Coleman.

devoted himself increasingly to studies in music theory, especially composition. On the advice of some musician friends, he went to see record producer Lester Koenig to offer some of his compositions for use in recording sessions. The outcome of their talk, during which Coleman played his tunes for Koenig on his plastic also, sounds like one of those Hollywood stories with an inescapable happy end. Not only did Koenig accept Coleman's compositions, he also asked him to record for Contemporary, with a group of his own.

Two LPs were made during the next months: *Something Else! The Music of Ornette Coleman,* and *Tomorrow is the Question,* in which alongside Coleman, trumpeter Don Cherry, his friend and old comrade-in-arms, played a decisive role. Cherry, who was later to become one of the principal figures in free jazz, went east with Coleman in 1959. There they both took part in the summer courses at the Jazz School in Lennox, thanks to the good offices of composer, teacher and jazz writer Gunther Schuller, and the leader of the Modern Jazz Quartet, John Lewis. At the same time, they were put under contract by Atlantic, for whom they recorded six LPs during the next two years. In the autumn of 1959, Coleman and Cherry, together with bassist Charlie Haden and drummer Billy Higgins, began the already mentioned, now legendary engagement at the "Five Spot" in New York. At the end of 1962, following a triumphal concert in New York's Town Hall, Ornette Coleman retired from the jazz scene for two full years, concentrating on composing and two new instruments, trumpet and violin. When he came back into the public eye in January, 1965, with a trio including the bassist David Izenzon and drummer Charles Moffet (both of whom had played in his Town Hall concert), Coleman's unconventional treatment of his new instruments caused a shock similar to that of his debut at the "Five Spot" five years earlier.

Since that time the waves of indignation have calmed. Coleman's achievements have become essential and self-evident ingredients of the musical language spoken by a new generation of musicians. The revolutionary aura at the beginning has given way to general recognition that he is one of the great masters of free jazz.

Ornette Coleman's musical innovations, and the shock effect they had on jazz listeners at the time, proceeded partly from the negation of a quasi-axiomatic prerequisite of late Fifties' jazz: the use of a pre-determined harmonic framework as a formative element and as a basis for improvisation. This negative definition alone does not, of course, capture the character of Coleman's music, but it is important to establish that the *lack* of the features we have mentioned — the "law and commandments" so far as the listening habits of the jazz public were concerned — was the cause of the general perplexity about his music. What Coleman had to offer in place of the rules which he threw overboard was less apparent, and only became evident with intensive listening.

As early as the 1958/59 recordings for Contemporary, the most pronounced features of Coleman's saxophone playing were set. His bent for improvisations that were largely unrestrained harmonically is evident, even in pieces whose outward make-up is anything but revolutionary. These recordings suffer from a rhythm section that is mostly inadequate to his way of improvising. The rhythm sections, with musicians like bassists Red Mitchell and Percy Heath, and drummer Shelly Manne, would certainly have been ideal for a more traditional newcomer, but for Coleman they proved unsuitable.

As was the custom, the bassists play lines based on functional harmony; these are often ignored by Coleman and Cherry. The presence of a pianist on Coleman's first record, *Something Else,* leads to still more incoherence. Coleman was forced to improvise by and large on the given changes, if he did not want to risk head-on collisions with the pianist's chord patterns. This resulted in choruses that are a weird mixture of bebop-oriented clichés and explosive, hectic phrases, which in this context often sound bizarre. Especially in *Yayne,* a piece based on the changes of *Out of Nowhere,* the discrepancy between what Coleman wants and what his surroundings permit is often painfully evident.

On Coleman's next LP, *Tomorrow is the Question,* there is already a better balance between the rhythm section (no piano) and his improvisations, and more compatibility with his ideas. Again the bassists constantly play functional harmonic patterns, but the register and sound of the bass make them less binding for the soloists. The outcome is that Coleman's and Cherry's solos are harmonically freer; there are fewer bebop phrases, and the overall expression of the music is more even.

By adding bassist Charles Haden and drummer Billy Higgins to the quartet in 1959, Coleman and Cherry solved the personnel problem for good. Haden, as Leonard Feather has remarked, is more a participating than an accompanying bassist. He follows the horn lines independent of functional harmonic thinking and, playing preferably in low registers, provides a basis that allows the improvisers to evolve free lines while serving at the same time as a point of reference and a framework. *The Shape of Jazz to Come* and *The Change of the Century,* made with Haden and Higgins for Atlantic on the West Coast in 1959, contain some of the most tightly-knit music the quartet ever recorded.

Some of the most significant traits of Ornette Coleman's early style of improvising can be gathered from Example 18, which shows the first three choruses of a 12-bar blues, *Tears Inside.* The harmonic development is reduced to the most rudimentary changes, and in this respect the piece is more like early forms of folk blues than bebop blues, with their many substitute chords. The progressions do not go beyond the "archaic" changes: I (4 bars) – IV (2 bars) – I (2 bars) – V (2 bars) – I (2 bars).

The division into three four-bar periods — the groundwork of the blues form — is observed by Coleman to a far greater extent than was usual in post-bebop jazz improvisation. Whereas bebop musicians and their successors tried to bridge the period endings by long phrases, to give a certain continuity to a rigid formal design, Coleman not only accepts the given formula, but accentuates it by placing rests at period endings (see the arrows in Example 18). It is important to point out that in this respect *Tears Inside* is *not* unique. Of the eighteen compositions recorded for Contemporary, only two, *Mind and Time* and

Compassion, do not follow a standard bar-pattern. Ten have the A-A-B-A-form and six are 12-bar blues. In all these fixed-form pieces, period endings are observed — and in the improvisations, too.

The conformity with conventional frameworks is only an external feature of Coleman's music, however, and has little to do with its essence. The same goes for the procedure, common in bebop, of having a soloist improvise on the bridge of a theme and otherwise being content to follow the "theme-improvisation-theme" formula. It becomes clear from the first three choruses of *Tears Inside* that while Coleman may accept the formal structure of the blues, he rejects its harmonic implications and the resultant hierarchy of the three 4-bar periods. His point of reference is not changes but a kind of fundamental sound, for whose focal tone the term "tonal centre" was coined in the jazz literature of the Sixties.

As understood by present-day music theorists, tonality does not necessarily involve functional harmonic progressions; rather, it implies first and foremost a relationship to *one* tone. For that reason, Coleman's music at this stage — and, generally speaking, later too — can be regarded as entirely *tonal.*

The tonal centre of *Tears Inside* is D flat, if one is guided by the melodic line of Coleman's improvisation. On the other hand, the piece is in the *key* of D flat major, if one follows the bass lines of Percy Heath who — unlike his successor Charles Haden — abides by all the consequences a key implies, and plays changes. This discrepancy between solo and accompaniment is (as we have mentioned) a characteristic of most early Coleman records; it will be of no further interest to us here.

For Coleman, the tonal centre D flat in *Tears Inside* is valid for the whole piece, not just for the blues segments normally in the tonic (*i. e.* bars 1-4, 7-8 and 11-12). It acts like an imaginary pedal point: Coleman's melodies proceed from it, are oriented toward it, and it is even present subliminally when seemingly cancelled by dissonant intervals.

A comparison of the *tonal centre* with the principle of modal improvising — as worked out by John Coltrane and Miles Davis at about the same time — suggests itself. It shows that while both led to a dissolution of functional harmonic progressions, neither infringed upon the formal designs *at the start.* But whereas modality, in choosing a scale, chooses a set material which obeys an inner order, the tonal centre does not imply a fixed material, and thus permits a much broader scope. There is a danger of stagnation in both methods, and the degree to which this is compensated depends on the expressive potential of the player.

Ornette Coleman overcomes the tonal centre's monotonous tendency by two stylistic elements that are closely connected with one another: (1) a new kind of *motivic improvisation* leading to (2) temporary shifts to *secondary tonal centres.*

EXAMPLE 18   TEARS INSIDE

49

The recognized father of motivic improvisation in modern jazz is Sonny Rollins[5]. But while Rollins derives his motivic material as a rule from the themes he uses, thus making recognition easier for his listeners (the so-called "aha effect"), Coleman invents, as he goes along, motives independent of the theme and continues to develop them. In this way — independently of the chord progressions, let it be noted — an inner cohesion is created that is comparable to the stream of consciousness in Joyce or the "automatic writing" of the surrealists: one idea grows from another, is reformulated, and leads to yet another new idea. For this procedure, which is of the utmost importance for the understanding of Coleman's playing, we would like to introduce the term *motivic chain-association*[6].

In Example 18, motivic chain-associations are marked a 1, a 2, b 1, b 2, etc. They take many shapes: in phrases a 1 - a 2 the linkage is created in the phrase ending by the falling interval and repeated tones. The beginning of b 2 is a variant of the beginning of b 1, at a different pitch level and embellished by a 32nd-note run. The latter part of b 2 is, except for the last interval (d flat - d), a literal repetition of b 1. At the same time, it establishes a link with the end of c 1: the rhythmic and melodic pattern ♩ ♫ (d flat - d on both occasions), which in turn provides the model for c 2. Phrases d 1 - d 3 show how Coleman works on a motive, the fifth b flat - e flat, by giving it a different "prefix" each time.

Occasionally Coleman does not limit his motivic associations to phrases that follow one another directly, but takes up ideas that are, so to speak, several links back in the chain, and creates larger contexts in this way. In Example 18, for instance, at the start of the fourth chorus he reverts to the rising figure and sustained note of the opening of the third chorus. Examples of Coleman's motivic chain-associations could be presented indefinitely. An important means of establishing musical organization, especially in his later music which is completely divorced from formal patterns, they replace, in a certain sense, the traditional framework with a new one.

One direct outgrowth of Coleman's motivic chain-association is a habit of leaving motives "open," of stopping just short of the goal for which he is heading and placing a dash — instead of an exclamation mark. For example, he brackets the tonal centre d flat at the end of the first chorus with the interval of a third (c flat - e flat); the d flat itself is postponed until the end of the bar where, at the octave, it serves as upbeat to the next chorus. The phrase endings from d flat to neighbouring tones (*e. g.,* chorus 2, bars 2 and 9), similarly point to the tendency to leave ideas incomplete, open-ended for linkage with

---

5) Gunther Schuller has made a detailed analytical study of this aspect of Rollins's improvisation technique (*cf.* Schuller 1962).

6) This term is borrowed from experimental psychology, where a "chain of associations" denotes a series of "free" word-associations. These are not guided by any rational criterion such as "categories" or "sound similarity," but depend strictly on the stream of consciousness of the person doing the associating.

new motives derived from them. Thus, in the second chorus (bar 2) the unfinished idea expressed by the half-step d flat - d leads to a new idea. With d as its starting point, it logically leaves the tonal contre d flat. The phrase marked c1 has a distinctly G minor flavour[7].

Short moves like this away from the tonal centre clearly show that while Coleman takes a general tonal frame of reference, usually valid for a whole piece, it is not imperative throughout in that it permits shifts to *secondary centres*. For the most part, the shifts do *not* arise from functional harmonic changes but from motivic chain-association, and are thus independent of any time-order. They create elements of surprise by running counter to what the listener expects, and have a function similar in a way to the "modal disorientation" of Coltrane's style of playing in *India*.

It must be noted, however, that motivic chain-association is not the only way in which Ornette Coleman's improvisations are guided to secondary tonal centres. In the late Fifties, Coleman's repertoire, as we have said, still included compositions whose formal structure suggests a kind of modulation, even when there is no definite harmonic framework. One such piece is *Chronology* (recorded in May 1959). In principle, its structure follows the 32-bar song form A - A - B - A. But there is a very important difference: together, the four sections of the form do make up a metrical framework, but the individual sections imply no harmonic differentiation whatever; instead, they are related to various tonal centres. Example 19 is an excerpt from Ornette Coleman's solo in this piece (his second chorus). As we see, there is no harmonic development at all within the four 8-bar periods, but section B (bars 17-24) stands distinctly apart from the A sections (bars 1-16 and 25-32) in its tonal relationships. Coleman, then, accepts the song pattern quasi as an "empty form," but he does not completely ignore its functional harmonic implications. He observes the "bridge" function of the B section by shifting to a secondary tonal centre.

Closely related to Ornette Coleman's attitude toward tonality is his treatment of pitch. One of the things he was accused of at the very beginning was "wrong intonation." Now, "wrong" is a purely relative term in this connection, that is, what may be considered wrong in reference to European tempered tuning may be perfectly "right" in another musical context. Equal temperament is, *a priori*, nothing other than an agreement accepted by Occidental musical culture for the sake of practical considerations. By a process of acculturation too complex to be gone into here, it was later adopted by jazz. As we know, the equal tempered scale — synthetic at bottom — never became a hard and fast norm in jazz to the exclusion of everything else. There have always been things "foreign" to it. For example, blue notes are — strictly speaking — "atonal," but were refunctioned into minor thirds and sevenths by the use of the piano, and by pseudo-jazz genres à la

---

7) This is not the chromatic suspension to the subdominant (G flat) that was so popular in bebop, since the subdominant that would have to occur in bar 5 does not materialize.

EXAMPLE 19   CHRONOLOGY

Gershwin. Another example are the individual shadings of intonation: bent or slurred tones must not be regarded as accidental; on the contrary, they are part of the individual language of musicians and are an intentional means of expression.

In this context, a few fundamental observations on the phenomenon of "pitch" are necessary. To begin with, the objective comparative quantities set up by a tuning, of whatever kind, are frequencies, vibrations per second, not pitches. The pitch of a musical sound, on the other hand, is a subjective quality; although closely correlated to its fundamental frequency, it additionally depends on several other physical parameters, among them the overtone spectrum of the sound.

These observations are of special importance for Coleman's "wrong" intonation. A series of measurements[8] has shown that the frequencies of Coleman's sounds do in fact often deviate from the tempered system. As it happens, however, most of these deviations are well within the range we usually tolerate in an opera singer or violin virtuoso[9]. And it is frequently the case that even tones whose aural impression leads one to suspect greater deviations are likewise within this tolerance range. These "subjective" deviations result not from a change of frequency, but from an alteration of the sound itself.

Looking at it from this angle, one realizes what Ornette Coleman means when he speaks of the "human quality" of his intonation, of "human pitch" or "vocalization of the sound." A sound is vocalized not by intoning it higher or lower, but by playing it *differently.* "When I play an f in a song called 'Peace,' I think it should not sound exactly like the same note in a piece called 'Sadness'" (from Berendt 1968, p. 100). Coleman is not saying — as Berendt infers — that the f's should not be equal in vibrations; he is saying only that they should *sound* different. The saxophonist can achieve this in several ways: by increasing his breath pressure, which shifts the overtone complexes of the sound; by an unconventional use of the octave key and so-called "false fingering"; or by a "loose" embouchure at the secured end of the reed.

These very subtle sound manipulations are used by Ornette Coleman in two sorts of context and for different purposes: first, as he says himself, to give his music that human vocal sound, which is such a marked contrast to the sterilized tone quality of West Coast jazz, in whose geographical vicinity his music first became known (examples are found at every stage of Coleman's playing, especially in slow pieces like *Lorraine, Lonely Woman, Sadness,* etc.); second, alterations of the timbre of single tones serve as a means of syntactic organization; in many of his pieces he emphasizes long tones in this way at the beginning or end of phrases.

---

8) The measurements were made by the author at the State Institute of Musical Research, Berlin, with the aid of electro-acoustical processes.

9) Berendt's statement that in Coleman's playing "almost every one of his tones . . . is pushed up or down," would seem to be an exaggeration.

In spite of these considerations, we must not overlook the fact that in his early recordings, Ornette Coleman did frequently play off-pitch in the real sense. Very fast runs sometimes go out of control, and there are clashes which cannot always be interpreted as "expressive means." Presumably, the unprecise articulation and shaky intonation in such runs were the consequence of the lack of opportunities to play on steady jobs. The recordings made in 1961, following his six-months' engagement at the "Five Spot," can be taken as evidence that his earlier unsteadiness was probably unintentional. On records like *Ornette!* and *Ornette on Tenor*, Coleman's runs — even in the fastest tempos — are neither blurred in their articulation nor off-pitch in their intonation.

Ornette Coleman's rhythm — compared to that of, say, Charlie Parker — is simple in principle. Much more than other jazz musicians of his era, he plays evenly accentuated lines of quarter and eighth notes, or simple patterns like ♩♫♫♫ or ♩ ♫♫♩, familiar from swing[10]. Superimposed uneven rhythms (quintoles, septimoles, etc.), as developed by Coltrane in his "sheets of sound," are relatively rare in Coleman; also rare is the ♩♪♩♪ beat division that is one of the commonest patterns in jazz.

Occasionally, the simplicity of Coleman's rhythm gives his music a touch of folksong naiveté, plus a certain roundness that makes up for the less accustomed features of his approach to tonality and sound. Two examples from the Coleman double quartet recording *Free Jazz* — to be discussed in detail later — can serve as illustrations (Examples 20a and 20b). Against a rather hectic, strongly rhythmical background, Coleman plays phrases whose song-like character is unmistakable.

EXAMPLE 20a   FREE JAZZ

EXAMPLE 20b   FREE JAZZ

Obviously, rhythm of this sort, with its even pulse and simple patterns, could easily become "corny." Coleman's timing, his disposition of the phrases in relation to the basic

10) On this point *cf.* Don Heckman (1965).

rhythm, saves it from that fate. After playing a series of eighth notes *on the beat,* Coleman often introduces new patterns, just as simple, but plays them *off-beat,* creating a strong feeling of tension. In *Tears Inside,* Coleman uses a model that, taken out of context, is utterly simple: ♩ ♩ ♫ 𝄾 . What makes it a source of tension is that it is superimposed on the rhythmic bases *against the beat* (Example 21).

A similar way of heightening tension is Coleman's practice of subdividing lines of eighth notes into alternating groups of three, four, or five notes, by shifts of accent arising from the melody. Example 22, from *Forerunner* (on *Change of the Century*), shows this procedure: what we see is not different superimposed rhythms — *i. e.,* three against two or five against four — but an even eighth-note motion, accentuated in a way that runs counter to the metre. We can also see from Example 22, that a bar division is very often irrelevant in Coleman's music. True, *Forerunner,* like almost all the recordings of this epoch, is based on a regular beat (here clearly tending toward 4/4), but Coleman's phrasing makes it difficult to determine "one" in his melodic line. The effect is complexity achieved by simple means, a phenomenon that could not be more typical of the general nature of Coleman's music.

EXAMPLE 21   TEARS INSIDE

EXAMPLE 22   FORERUNNER

Long before Ornette Coleman's improvisation gained wider recognition, his compositions were accepted by the jazz public as well as by musicians and critics. The themes he and Cherry played in a unison whose roughness is reminiscent of early Parker-Davis records, have, in their often unconventional lines and metrically angular structure, a freshness lacking in most of the hard bop tunes with all their gospel effects and bebop clichés. Tenor saxophonist and poet Archie Shepp significantly described these Coleman compositions as follows: "His tunes have about them the aura of a square dance telescoped through the barrel of a machinegun" (Shepp 1966, p. 40).

In the early Sixties, many jazz listeners were fond of arguing that there was no relation between the themes of Coleman's pieces (which themselves were universally admired), and the improvisations by Coleman and Cherry. "He's putting everybody on. They start with a nice lead-off figure, but then they go off into outer space. They disregard the chords and they play odd numbers of bars. I can't follow them" (from Hentoff 1961, p. 228). This complaint by trumpeter Roy Eldridge is typical of many opinions about Coleman's music. Listening habits then demanded that relations between theme and improvised choruses be established exclusively by chord progressions, identical in both. And that sort of relation quite obviously did not exist in most of Coleman's music.

In fact, however, there is a unity of theme and improvisation in Coleman's music that goes much deeper than just reinterpreting a predetermined set of chord patterns following a fixed number of bars. The nature of that unity is more emotional than formal[11]. In traditional jazz, the theme very often functions merely as the purveyor of chord progressions or scales; in Coleman's music it above all determines the expressive content of his improvisations[12].

In passing, we mention that even the title of a composition may be brought into a congruity of theme and improvisations, as for example in the lament for the deceased pianist Lorraine Geller *(Lorraine)*, the hectic and gay *Rejoicing*, or the "dancing" *Una muy Bonita*.

More than one hundred Coleman compositions have been recorded to date. Each has its own specific musical make-up. Even so, several types have crystallized during a period of ten years. We will consider the two most significant here.

At the end of the Fifties, many of Coleman's themes are still based on patterns from bebop and its derivatives. They retain the traditional bar units and their interval structure often reminds one of compositions by Charlie Parker *(Chippie, The Disguise, Alpha)*, or of tunes played in the orbit of the Art Farmer-Gigi Gryce Quintet *(The Blessing)*. But already in Coleman's second recording session for Contemporary, a composition was included that shows many of the characteristics that later became part and parcel of free

---

11) The countless double-time improvisations on ballads such as *Lover Man* make one realize that emotional unity of theme and improvisation in jazz is not so evident as one might suppose.

12) With the help of the semantic differential technique, I tested 10 Coleman pieces (using 10 observers each) for subjective congruence of emotional expression in theme and improvisations. The correlations as a rule were significantly positive.

jazz. *Mind and Time* is actually nothing more than a melodic-rhythmic line that determines the emotional nature of the improvisations, and beyond that, only the tempo and tonal centre. It has no implicit harmonic progressions, nor does it fit into one of the common metric schemes. As far as that goes, a division of this melody into bars (which at the same time implies an accentuation of certain beats) is irrelevant; since the tune is 11½ "bars" long, notes falling on "one" the first time round would fall on "three" in the repeat[13] (*cf.* Example 23).

EXAMPLE 23   MIND AND TIME

Leaving aside their asymmetrical form and harmonic indetermination, themes like *Mind and Time* are, in a certain sense, the successors to bebop themes. By means of a melodic-rhythmic line, a relatively non-obligatory framework is established; the only further influence it has on the following improvisations derives from its range, motion and perhaps, dynamics. There were many pieces of this type in the Coleman Quartet's repertoire in the early Sixties (*Free, Forerunner, Cross Breeding, Enfant,* etc.). The method of taking such asymmetrical lines as starting points was later adopted by many free-jazz musicians.

A second type of Ornette Coleman composition — actually *the* type in the early Sixties — is represented by *Congeniality,* among others. The model on which the piece is based recalls, in its many contrasting ideas, some of Charles Mingus's compositions. It has since been widely imitated; in fact the "Coleman theme," like the "Parker theme" before it, became a technical term. When other musicians write a "Coleman theme" it somehow usually resembles *Congeniality.*

The notation in Example 24 can give only an approximate idea of the theme's timing. Passages 4 and 4 a are the only ones accompanied by a steady beat; in 1, 2, 1 a and 1 b the rhythm of the melody is accentuated by the drums; passages marked 3 are in a free

---

13) Nat Hentoff seems to have miscounted; in the record notes, he writes that this is a ten-bar piece.

tempo. The form of the piece, A - B 1 - A - B 2, has no consequences for the improvisations that follow.

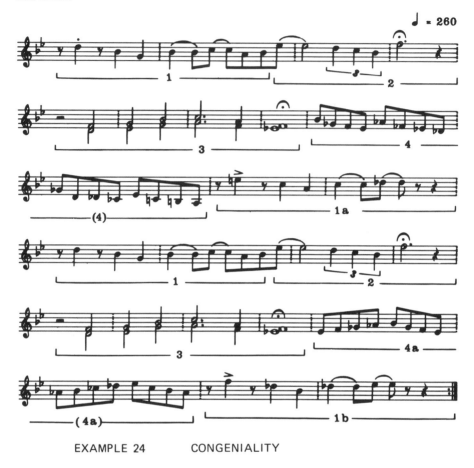

EXAMPLE 24   CONGENIALITY

The most striking feature of this piece, however, is its contrasting rhythms, which create several strata of feeling:

(1)   a jumping off-beat rhythm
(2)   leads continuously
(3)   to a lamenting passage in thirds and long note values,
(4)   which suddenly gives way to hectic eighth-note runs.

The expression emanating from this sequence of rhythms is neither happy, nor sad, nor hectic, but all three together. It is up to the improviser to choose from the reservoir of emotional content. *Congeniality*, therefore, is a free-jazz theme in the truest sense of the word.

In his notes to *Change of the Century* (recorded in October 1959), Ornette Coleman writes: "Perhaps the most important new element in our music is our conception of free group improvisation." Considering the time it was written, this sentence should be appraised as a plan whose realization had to wait a few more years. To be sure, Coleman's music — as we have demonstrated — was at that time already *free* from norms previously held to be inviolable. But the dominating role of the *soloist* and the resultant auxiliary role of the *accompanists* were not given up. The bassist had been liberated from playing chord progressions (at least after Charles Haden joined the group), but he and the drummer still had to play the beat. The universally common sequence of composed ensembles and improvised solos was only rarely broken by a faint-hearted free collective improvisation. Compared to Mingus's group improvisations, Coleman's first steps toward real *group* work were still quite hesitant.

This all radically changed in December 1960 with *Free Jazz,* whose title named a whole musical era. To record *Free Jazz,* two full quartets gathered in the studio of Atlantic Records: with Coleman were Don Cherry, Charles Haden and drummers Billy Higgins and Ed Blackwell (all members of his groups), plus Eric Dolphy on bass clarinet, trumpeter Freddie Hubbard, and bassist Scott la Faro. These eight musicians carried Coleman's conception of "free group improvisation" to a totality such as had never been heard before in jazz.

In terms of "freedom" as understood in 1960, the outer framework of this 36-minute piece is infinitesimal. Single complexes, each led by a different "soloist," are linked by transitional ensemble passages. Some of the ensembles are written out and have the character of Coleman's typical lines. Others are partially improvised structures which Coleman somewhat misleadingly calls "harmonic unison" (from Williams, Atl. 1364); here the players are provided with tonal material whose timing is not fixed, a procedure which was to be highly important as a composition technique in the later development of free jazz.

The tonal centre is obviously agreed upon too, as is the tempo which is adhered to from start to finish. There is also an allotting of roles: Charles Haden and Ed Blackwell are responsible for the fundamental rhythm, which is constantly challenged and consciously "endangered" by Scott la Faro and Billy Higgins.

The music played on the basis of these agreements depends for coherence almost exclusively on the players' readiness to interact. With a traditional framework, an uninspired collective improvisation with no interactions between the players at all might be hard to take, but would surely not end in a musical catastrophe. The same unrelated simultaneity in the boundlessness of free jazz could only end in chaos. Coleman and his musicians must have been aware of this danger. They obviated it by a method that had already given shape to Coleman's solo improvisations: *motivic chain-associations.* In *Free Jazz* these are evolved by the group as a whole, not by just a single improviser. Ideas introduced by the "soloist" of a given section are spontaneously paraphrased by the other players, developed further, and handed back to the originator in altered form. The short passage in Example 25 shows how a motive presented by Coleman is taken up by Cherry and counterpointed by Dolphy (Hubbard is not playing at this point). This process builds a network of interactions; by creating contrast, by imitation and continuation, it constantly renews from within the flow of musical ideas.

EXAMPLE 25   FREE JAZZ

Despite an abundance of motivic interaction, the overall character of *Free Jazz* must be called static rather than dynamic. Only rarely do emotional climaxes occur, and there is hardly any differentiation of expression. The wealth of musical ideas and the continuous exchange of thoughts take place on an unvarying expressive level. Now and then there are passages in which folksong-like phrases by Ornette Coleman suggest a kind of bucolic peacefulness (*cf.* Examples 20 a and 20 b); and Eric Dolphy's rumbling, vocalized bass clarinet sound adds an occasional humorous touch. But these passages are both short and relatively incidental.

Ten years after, one can only speculate about the causes of this emotional — not musical — sameness. Perhaps Coleman and his musicians were too occupied articulating a newly acquired vocabulary and conquering a musical *terra incognita,* to devise a palette of moods and temperaments in the process. It may also be that Coleman set out to create a statical, homogeneous whole, his main point being the integration of individual ideas to form an interlocking collective. His later music, especially his compositions for chamber ensembles inspired by the New Music idiom of the West, would seem to support the latter hypothesis[14].

It cannot be said for certain whether in *Free Jazz* Ornette Coleman had in mind the new directions in collective improvisation evolved by Charles Mingus. Although Mingus's music is a great deal more in line with the traditional axioms of jazz than Coleman's, the conceptions of the two have much in common. And even if the musical end products of those conceptions are quite different — a result both of the initial material and dissimilar

---

14)   See, for example, Coleman's *Forms and Sounds for Woodwinds.*

temperaments of the two musicians — one tendency bearing on the evolution of free jazz is present in both: the move away from individual monologuizing soloists toward a kind of collective conversation. In this respect, *Free Jazz* must be regarded as one of the most important milestones in the development of new forms of jazz.

Free Jazz remained without consequences for Ornette Coleman. He did not continue to put his faith in a large collective, as one might have expected. Instead, he made a few more records with a quartet, and then went alone on his way, with a group of infinitesimal proportions for a single wind player. After a two-year voluntary inner exile during which Coleman — in his own words — wanted to find himself (from van Peebles 1965), he re-emerged on the jazz scene.

For his 1965 engagement at New York's "Village Vanguard" he worked with bassist David Izenzon and drummer Charles Moffet. This trio put Coleman's conception of free group improvisation into practice, with a consistency that outstripped even *Free Jazz*. On that record, the pulsing beat still governs the rhythmic flow; it is never absent. In the Coleman Trio, it becomes a creative means to be either employed or omitted, a formative element and source of emotional content. Coleman's fellow artists, Moffet and Izenzon, are blessed with very keen reflexes. Charles Moffet, with whom Coleman had already played in his home town of Fort Worth, is an eclectic in the positive sense; in his playing he incorporates the driving beat of the great big-band drummers of the swing epoch[15], as well as the achievements of the new generation from Tony Williams to Milford Graves. His work with Coleman often recalls the Mingus - Richmond team, for whom "feeling each other out" (*cf.* p. 38) plays such an important role. Moffet "feels" what Coleman plays, and in this way emphasizes the rhythmic-melodic impulses coming from Coleman, not only by accentuating, but also by anticipating them

Bassist David Izenzon makes considerable use — especially in his bowing work — of the technical vocabulary of European avantgarde music. With spiccato, harmonics and glissandos, he expands the sound potential of his instrument in a way that was all but unknown in jazz before. In this respect, Izenzon's bass playing had a pronounced stylistic influence on free jazz. He does not, as a rule, provide only a foundation for Coleman's music, but serves as a supplement whose expressive power and nuances decisively add to the impact of the music.

In the years following *Free Jazz*, Coleman's saxophone style was remarkably consistent. Although the overall character of his music was bound to alter with his various groups, the essentials of his improvising — as we have described them above — remained intact whether he worked with drummers like his ten-year-old son Ornette Denardo (who, understandably, was utterly untroubled by traditional constraints), or Elvin Jones, the real inaugurator of new percussion playing.

If there was a change in his sax playing at this time, it was above all the increased precision of his technique.

---

15) The French jazz critic Alain Gerber (1966) compared him to Big Sid Catlett.

Instrumental technique has always been a favourite talking point for jazz critics; it was not any different in the epoch of free jazz. The question posed is that of technical "perfection" as a criterion of the quality of an artist's music. Clearly, a musician's creativity is relatively independent of his manual dexterity. There are enough examples, in all walks of art, of technical brilliance alone causing nothing but boredom. On the other hand, whether or not musical ideas can be articulated is surely determined to a great extent by the presence or absence of a technical vocabulary suitable to those ideas. The question is not *less* or *more* technique, but the *subjective* adequacy of it. When the musical idea gives rise to and shapes its own technical vocabulary, there is no danger. But when the expression of an idea is determined by the available vocabulary (or rather by its limitations), there is a danger of self-deception, because what is articulated is assumed to be the original idea.

Unlike his unquestioning apologists, Ornette Coleman in the late Fifties obviously considered his technical equipment inadequate. This emerges (as indicated above) from the post-"Five Spot" recordings, in which he overcame many of his initial handicaps. It is further manifested in the records made by his trio in the latter half of the Sixties. Here Coleman's saxophone playing is virtuoso — in the positive sense. A short passage transcribed from his piece *The Riddle* can serve as an illustration (Example 26). The notation should be regarded as a poor substitute for the aural impression. In these eighth-note chains, every eighth is clearly articulated — at a tempo of ♩ = 360[16].

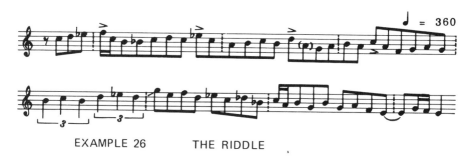

EXAMPLE 26   THE RIDDLE

In the same example, we see how Coleman gives a rhythmic tension to the melodic flow, even in an extreme tempo: by accentuation, eighth-note groups of various lengths are established — an implicit six-count metre at first, then a metre of fours.

Coleman's virtuosity is positive in that it never becomes an end in itself. Even now that he is capable of doing it, he does not put on a pyrotechnic display at the cost of musical substance. On the contrary, in his improvisations on alto during the latter half of the Sixties, he leans increasingly toward relatively simple structures. Example 27, an excerpt

---

16) In principle, this melodic sequence is not too difficult to play on the alto; it does not involve the octave key (Coleman goes up again after the f) and lies "in the fingers." But we must remember there are twelve notes to a second in the given tempo, without the slightest hint of glissando.

EXAMPLE 27   LONG TIME NO SEE

from a Coleman solo in *Long Time No See*, shows several important aspects of his post-1965 saxophone playing. Recorded in 1969 or 1970 under circumstances described at the end of this chapter, the piece points to D as the tonal centre of its thematic material. Coleman begins by basing his solo on B flat at the start, but then shifts to secondary centres as the melody becomes increasingly chromatic (see the last three staves of the example).

The characteristic features of this passage can be summarized as follows:

a) relatively simple intervallic structure; diatonic, song-like melody with frequent sequences;

b) numerous motivic associations, especially at the beginning;

c) punctuation in the form of long sustained tones that are strongly accentuated;

d) great importance attached to rests; some of them are surely reactions to rhythmic interjections from drummer Ed Blackwell, who took part in the recording.

The simplicity of Ornette Coleman's alto sax improvisations — like the one just discussed — does not mean a reduced creative capacity, and has nothing to do with primitivism or banality. It is the expression of an inner balance, a poise, which brings an element of relaxation even in the most hectic musical context.

When he returned to the New York jazz scene in January 1965, Ornette Coleman — to everybody's surprise — played two more instruments, violin and trumpet. The sensation this caused for the public and the jazz press was not due to the fact *that* he played them, but to *how* he played them. Coleman's violin playing had nothing in common with Joe Venuti's; his trumpet playing was totally unlike Dizzy Gillespie's. In Coleman's hands, both instruments — traditionally, they have always had an elite air about them — were refunctioned into "sound-tools." The trumpet and the violin are melody instruments par excellence. Coleman treated them as producers of sounds, rhythms and emotions.

His violin playing is notable above all for its rhythmic intensity; Coleman's point is not melodic lines, but sound-structures and rhythms. His playing frequently has a distinctly percussive character, with extremely rapid repeated tones and double-stop triplets sounding like drum-rolls. As for the trumpet, Coleman prefers it in the high register. Here too, there are scorching runs of driving intensity which fuse into a single drawn sound, sharp accents, glissandos and blurred scraps of sound without any melodic identity.

It is noteworthy that Coleman uses both instruments predominantly in very fast, dynamic pieces. His alto playing is marked by its calmness, but on trumpet and violin he creates tremendous excitement. Significantly, pieces like *Falling Stars, Snowflakes and Sunshine,* and *Sound Gravitation* have no themes in the traditional sense, no identifiable melodies. They are compositions in sound that grow from the spontaneous interaction of three musicians; in them, the traditional division between melody and percussion instruments is effaced. For Coleman, one instrument serves to complement the other. Just as trumpets and timpani, fifes and drums, belonged together in medieval European music, or guitar and harmonica in American country blues, trumpet and violin form a unit in Coleman's music, acting as a stylistic antithesis of his saxophone playing. In one piece, Coleman often changes from violin to trumpet, or vice versa, after very short passages; brief motives proposed by the violin are extended by bass and drums, and lead to the sound-cascades from the trumpet.

Interestingly enough, Coleman took up his new instruments at a time when the alto appeared to present no more problems for him. Anyone who may have assumed then that, as happened in his sax playing, his treatment of the new instruments would after a time become more conventional, was disappointed. In Coleman's violin playing, we can in fact see a fundamentally new conception of musical formation. This idea is expressed by the English jazz writer Victor Schonfield in his notes to *An Evening with Ornette Coleman,* an album recorded in London: "Whereas the overriding impression of Coleman's alto is of his conscious control of the instrument and the improvisation, that of his violin (and to a lesser extent his trumpet) is of the abdication of conscious control, and a reliance on pure chance. The vaulting ambition of the traditional artist, standing back from his work in order to plan the next move, is replaced by the humility of a newer kind of artist, who stands back so as to allow something larger than his mind can conceive to emerge. The results are at once less intellectual and more complicated, less clear but more communicative, in fact more truly lifelike."

In later years Coleman began to eliminate the trumpet as a mere sound-producer, treating it — in line with its traditional function — as a melody instrument. At such moments his playing reminds the listener very much of his saxophone improvisations: rhythmically simple phrases freely placed in the flow of the music, and sequences whose folkloristic style contrasts with the driving rhythm of the bass and drums. These "melodic" twists are rare, however. Usually, Coleman interpolates them as enclaves of repose in emotion-charged passages, whose intensity is briefly suspended just short of the bursting-point.

After his trio broke up at the end of the Sixties, things again grew quiet for Ornette Coleman. His antipathy toward the prevailing system of exploitation that rules the jazz business, and his unshakable determination not to sell his music short (*cf.* Wilmer 1971a) led him for the second time into isolation. He now goes on tour or appears in clubs only rarely. The musicians he works with on those occasions are all friends from the old days, before jazz criticism painted him a revolutionary: bassist Charles Haden, tenor saxophonist Dewey Redman (a fellow high-school student in Fort Worth), and drummer Ed Blackwell, whom Coleman first met in New Orleans during his rhythm-and-blues years, and who later played in the Ornette Coleman Quartet.

A Coleman record issued in 1970 was recorded in one of the warehouses of Prince Street, New York, where Coleman lives. In a way, the title is symptomatic of Coleman's situation, as well as that of his audience and fellow musicians: *Ornette Live at Prince Street: Friends and Neighbors.*

Chapter 4

CECIL TAYLOR

"Call Ornette the shepherd and Cecil the seer." In these words the tenor saxophonist and poet Archie Shepp characterized the two musicians who are at once the true initiators of free jazz and its musical and psychological antipodes (Shepp 1966). One side of the coin is the "shepherd" Ornette Coleman, with a new and almost folkloristic simplicity of expression whose roots — for all Coleman's abrogation of traditional norms — go back to the blues, the bed-rock of jazz. The other side is the "seer" Cecil Taylor, whose music is marked by unremitting tension between emotionality and a constructionistic complexity that is due in part to assimilating contemporary European and American New Music tendencies into the language of free jazz. The fact that the two speak such fundamentally divergent dialects of that language can be traced to psychological differences, but even more to the contrasting social and musical milieus that gave Coleman and Taylor their primary musical impressions and experiences. Coleman grew up in conditions of extreme poverty in the black ghettos of Fort Worth. His "apprenticeship" began at fifteen in the wild atmosphere of nightclubs and in the tents of travelling minstrel shows. For him, at that time, blues was not just one kind of music, it was the *only* music.

Cecil Taylor, on the other hand, had a relatively protected childhood in New York. His family belonged to the black middle class, and in their home a piano was as much a natural status symbol as it was for their white neighbours. Musical training was encouraged — in any direction but jazz, for that sort of career was regarded as undesirable. As a boy, Cecil Taylor's musical horizon was occupied more by European impressionist composers than by Ellington. His early acquaintance with blues was mostly hearsay; his father, who came from the South, used to talk about it[1].

Cecil Taylor was born on March 15, 1933, in Long Island, New York. He started taking piano lessons at the age of five. A few years later he also began to study percussion, with a timpanist who at that time was playing under Toscanini; we can ascribe some significance to this fact in view of Taylor's later stylistic evolution. In 1951, he went to Boston where he studied for three years at the New England Conservatory: piano, solfège, theory and composition. There he came into closer contact with the works of Schoenberg, Berg and Webern. But it was the music of the "classic" modern masters, Bartók and Stravinsky, that apparently had a more direct appeal to Taylor than the

---

1) Cecil Taylor's biographical data are taken chiefly from A. B. Spellman (1967).

twelve-tone techniques of the Viennese School. At the same time, however, the influence of jazz began to make itself felt. Living in Boston at this time was a group of prominent jazzmen, like pianists Jackie Byard and Dick Twardzik, trumpeter Joe Gordon, and saxophonists Gigi Gryce, Charlie Mariano, Sam Rivers and Serge Chaloff. Taylor heard them all, in clubs and at sessions. He went to guest appearances by the innovators of bebop, Dizzy Gillespie, Charlie Parker and Bud Powell. As his inclination toward jazz increased, his interest in the routine of academic learning began to fade, and his days at the Conservatory were numbered.

In the late Forties, Taylor had already heard the orchestras of Count Basie, Jimmie Lunceford and Duke Ellington in New York. Although Ellington's music, in particular, then made a lasting impression on him, he was fascinated by two other pianists: Dave Brubeck and Lennie Tristano. Looking back, it may seem strange that Cecil Taylor should have felt attracted to the detached coolness of Tristano's music and the pompous exuberance of Brubeck. Both those musicians, however, had a background similar to Taylor's, and both tried to modify the harmonic and formal aspects of jazz by incorporating "European" stylistic features. Both of them, to be sure, showed a certain emotional sterility, but this was probably secondary for Taylor at this point, since he had not been able to get close to the music of Thelonious Monk, Bud Powell, or any other bebop musician. Taylor says about his first encounter with Brubeck: "When Brubeck opened in 1951 in New York I was very impressed with the depth and texture of his harmony, which had more notes in it than anyone else's that I had ever heard. It also had a rhythmical movement that I found exciting . . . I was digging Stravinsky, and Brubeck had been studying with Milhaud. But because of my involvement with Stravinsky, and because I knew Milhaud, I could hear what Brubeck was doing" (from Spellman 1967, p. 61). And about Tristano: "(His) ideas interested me because he was able to construct a solo on the piano, and I guess that has a lot to do with why I dug Brubeck too. Brubeck was the other half of Tristano; Tristano had the line thing and Brubeck had the harmonic density that I was looking for, and that gave a balance" (loc. cit., p. 62).

These two contrasting principles — Tristano's lines (with little or no tonal reference) and Brubeck's harmonic density — became the decisive factors in Cecil Taylor's music, as did the constructionistic element common to both Tristano and Brubeck. Without considering direct influences (i. e., models), we can assume that Taylor heard his own ideas confirmed in the playing of Tristano and Brubeck, ideas whose realization he could not yet envision because of his preoccupation with "Occidental" ways of musical thinking. Taylor doubtless had in mind, like Brubeck and Tristano, the integration of European avantgarde musical elements into a jazz context. He later said that his problem was to consciously utilize the energies and techniques of European composers, to blend them with the traditional music of the American Negro, and in this way to create a new energy (from Spellman 1967, p. 28).

Cecil Taylor continues to accept European influences as components of his music even today; but he soon turned away from Brubeck and Tristano. Listening to pianists of the

Bud Powell school, like Horace Silver and Walter Bishop, he came to the conclusion that there were two kinds of jazz, white and black: "I went to Birdland one night to hear Brubeck playing opposite Horace Silver, and I noticed Brubeck imitating Horace. Then came Bird (Parker) with Percy (Heath) and Milt (Jackson), and man, like they demolished Brubeck . . . Well, that ended Brubeck for me. And it ended my emotional involvement with his music and my intellectual involvement also" (from Spellman 1967, p. 63).

Subsequently, his European musical background was pushed aside during his stay at the Conservatory, with considerable aid from Boston jazzmen. The process was not without programmatic overtones, as Cecil Taylor's turning to his black musical heritage was more emphatically expressed in his words than de facto in his music, at least at the start. Nevertheless, this process was of great importance to his whole stylistic development; European elements gradually ceased to dominate and were completely integrated in what was, to be sure, a very novel conception of jazz.

Cecil Taylor's career during the past twenty years has been marked by ups and downs that are only too typical of the free-jazz movement. Musical maturation, the acquisition of a personal language, was accompanied by an utter lack of financial success. Most of the groups Taylor formed in the Fifties broke up without ever having had one engagement worth mentioning. Not until 1957, after his first record, *Jazz Advance,* was he able to get a regular job at the "Five Spot." And even though Taylor's music had come to have a reasonably large following in New York, this engagement was short — as were all those that followed it. Between jobs, Taylor had to take on all kinds of makeshift work as a cook, record salesman, dishwasher, and so on. "I've had to simulate the working jazzman's progress. I've had to create situations of growth — or rather, situations were created by the way in which I live," is Taylor's comment on these years (from Hentoff 1965). Buell Neidlinger, bassist in Taylor's group for some time, sketches the situation in this way: "Trying to make a living playing with Cecil is absolutely unbelievable, because there is no economic advantage to playing music like that. It's completely unsalable in the nightclubs because of the fact that each composition lasts, or could last, an hour and a half. Bar owners aren't interested in this, because if there's one thing they hate to see it's a bunch of people sitting around openmouthed with their brains absolutely paralyzed by the music, unable to call for the waiter. They want to sell drinks. But when Cecil's playing, people are likely to tell the waiter to shut up and be still" (from Spellman 1967, p. 8).

Misfortune dogged not only Taylor's club jobs, but his record-making too. Since 1956 just ten LP's of Taylor's music have appeared. The record-producing establishment's lack of confidence in the salability of his music is illustrated by the fact that a record made under his direction for United Artists in 1958 was later put on the market under the title *Coltrane Time.*

In the music recorded by Cecil Taylor in the late Fifties, there is the kind of conflict between two musical languages that makes tradition-minded jazz enthusiasts ask "Is this really jazz?" What prompted that question was not the same considerations that led die-hard defenders of the "old order" to fling the epithet "anti-jazz" at the music of Ornette Coleman and John Coltrane. Ten years later, now that the initial surprise of Taylor's harmonic, formal and technical innovations has worn off and the strangeness of certain elements no longer conceals the musical totality, we can see what *else* was different in his music: the rhythm.

Until the end of the Fifties, one of the criteria that decided whether music was to be called jazz or not, had always been the phenomenon of swing. We need not go into this magic ingredient of jazz again, its relativity and its dependence on both epoch and individual style (*cf.* p. 32). But it is apparent in the earliest recordings of Cecil Taylor that, by any traditional definition, he does not swing. Instead of a "flowing" rhythm, achieved by tiny deviations from the beat and by the superimposition of even and uneven rhythms, there is a certain rhythmic rigidity in Taylor's music. The contrast of *tension* and *relaxation,* characteristic not only of traditional jazz, but also of the music of Coltrane and Coleman, is missing. Taylor replaces it by an alternation of *tension* and *stagnation.* Whereas jazz musicians normally tend to accentuate *before* the beat, Cecil Taylor at that time (*i. e.* when his music was still based on a constant metrical pulse) played *on* or *behind* the beat more than anyone else. Example 28 is a short excerpt from Taylor's 1958 trio recording, *Of What.* If we disregard its melodic and harmonic content, we will find that the regularity of its accentuation on strong beats recalls the motoric rhythm of Bach toccatas.

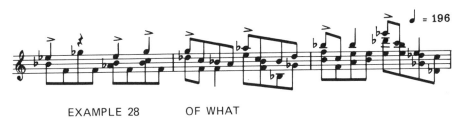

EXAMPLE 28   OF WHAT

As time went on, Taylor compensated the "stagnating" motion (also found in Brubeck's music) by a kind of playing whose dynamic impetus arose not from off-beat phrasing but from combining the parameters of time, intensity and pitch, thereby creating a new musical quality, *energy.* Borrowed from physics, this term is frequently misused as a meaningless catchword for anything that suggests "power." Let's look closer at this term. Energy is not equivalent to intensity (measured in decibels), as some of my jazz-practitioner countrymen, champions of a misunderstood freedom in jazz, often assume. Energy is, more than anything else, a variable of time. It creates motion or results from motion; it means a process in which the dynamic level is just *one* variable, and by no means a constant. We need not continue analogies to physics here. Suffice it to say that the kinetic impulses emanating from Cecil Taylor's music are based on the rise and fall of energy. Many of his accompaniment patterns, as well as the structure of his solos, are marked by progressions as in the graphic notation of Example 29.

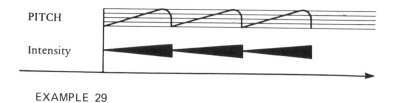

PITCH

Intensity

EXAMPLE 29

Swing in the traditional sense — the essential rhythmic element of jazz — ceases to exist when musicians play in a free tempo that has no clear metrical identity. For swing is produced by "creating a conflict between the fundamental rhythm and the rhythm of the melody" (Slawe 1948, p. 19), even when the fundamental rhythm can only be "sensed," that is, has been removed from an "objective" level of perception to a "subjective" level of feeling. This kind of conflict, which arises on the one hand from "off-beat phrasing"[2] and on the other from a superimposition of even and uneven rhythms, is very often missing in the recordings of Cecil Taylor's early groups. But already in the latter half of the Fifties, Taylor was trying to forestall the latent danger of rigidity in his music by creating a kind of energetic tension. However, the musicians playing with Taylor (principally bassist Buell Neidlinger and drummer Dennis Charles), usually made a point of accenting a steady beat. More often than not, this gave a peculiar "cramp" to the rhythm, rather as if one were trying to mix Stravinsky with a jazz rhythm section. Especially bizarre in this respect are the pieces of Taylor's third recording session *(The Hard Driving Jazz)*, which took place in the autumn of 1958, with hardbop trumpeter Kenny Dorham, John Coltrane (who was still playing in a relatively conventional way), bassist Chuck Israels and drummer Louis Hayes. Here the clash of musical conceptions — and not just rhythmical ones — is so pronounced that the product can hardly have been very gratifying for anyone involved. And as the session went on the strain apparently spread from music to personalities. About his differences with Dorham, for instance, Taylor later said: "By the second tune, 'Caravan', Kenny started attacking my playing, and this of course killed any excitement that may have been possible in the date" (from Spellman 1967, p. 69). *The Hard Driving Jazz* not only demonstrates that Taylor is dependent, to a special degree, on his fellow musicians' willingness to cooperate. It also indicates another important aspect of his further musical development: getting away from a constant beat and achieving a manner of playing, free from rhythmic constraint.

---

2) *Cf.* Alfons M. Dauer (1961, p. 110). J. E. Berendt's attack (1968, p. 150) on the "scientists who have no feeling for swing themselves" proceeds from a misunderstanding, namely that "off-beat" means an "accentuation 'away from the beat' on weak beats of the bar that are usually unaccentuated in European music." In fact, however, "off-beat" does not mean | ♩ ♩ ♩ ♩ |, but ♪♫♫♫♪ |; it is not a "macro-displacement" of accents, but a "micro-shift" of the melody rhythm against the beat.

This means more to Cecil Taylor than simply the addition of a new stylistic resource. As his music evolved, it became an absolute necessity.

The polarity of two dominating kinetic forces — swing and energy — is of essential significance for the whole evolution of free jazz. This polarity gave rise to two fundamentally different modes of creation, two "schools" whose distinctive stylistic features go far beyond different approaches to rhythm. In connection with free-jazz alto saxophonists, Archie Shepp (1966) speaks of "post-Ornette players" and "energy-sound players." What he obviously had in mind was the difference between melodic and a-melodic, *i. e.* timbric, variation. But of course these two kinds of playing also imply two different attitudes toward rhythm. In Coleman and his "school," the old swing is integrated into a new context. Cecil Taylor, on the other hand, does not refashion swing by placing it in a new setting, but replaces it entirely by a new quality, energy.

Any classification of "schools," or stylistic directions in jazz, cannot claim to be more than an orientation aid. This applies here, and in succeeding remarks, when a differentiation is made between musicians for whom energy is paramount and those for whom swing is. Swing and energy, as the concrete forms of opposing attitudes toward rhythm, are headings and not pigeon-holes. Which one is relevant for a given musician must be tested on that musician's playing; furthermore, reciprocal influences and stylistic overlapping tend to weaken their validity.

Finding his way to a kind of music in which energy is the decisive element was a laborious process for Cecil Taylor. Toward the end of the Fifties, most of his other formative principles — we will come back to them later — had consolidated into a personal language: his conception of group improvisation, the formal organization of his pieces, his treatment of tonality. The problem of rhythm, however, was still largely unsolved. The key to the puzzle lay in the interaction between Taylor and his drummer (as we can see from a comparison of two records made in 1960 and 1961). *Air* and *Lazy Afternoon,* recorded in 1960 with tenor saxophonist Archie Shepp, bassist Buell Neidlinger and drummer Dennis Charles, have the same rhythmic rigidity that marks most of Taylor's earlier recordings, despite sensitive cooperation between Taylor and Shepp. Dennis Charles's metronomical hi-hat conflicts with Taylor's eruptive dynamism; passages in free rhythm are blocked by the drummer, not supported. We do not wish to cast Charles in the role of a villain who, so to speak, clipped his master's wings. Difficulties in finding the same wave-length were not all on one side. With the possible exception of Dannie Richmond, hardly any percussionist at the time could have communicated with Taylor on a rhythmic basis.

But Cecil Taylor's music needs precisely this kind of communication and profits immensely from it. This is evident in *Pots, Bulbs,* and *Mixed,* recorded in 1961. With Taylor are Archie Shepp, Jimmy Lyons (the alto player who later worked permanently with Taylor), bassist Henry Grimes, and finally Taylor's new drummer, Sunny Murray. Murray had begun to rehearse with Taylor at a time when he himself was not yet committed to a definite style; thus he was relatively untroubled by traditional percussion techniques and — perhaps for that very reason — adapted very quickly to Taylor's conception of rhythm. He is probably the first drummer in jazz who was able — while largely negating metre — to develop urgent, dynamic chains of impulses, and in this way gave Taylor's music the support it needed.

It may seem paradoxical that precisely by getting away from a steady beat (then one of the sine qua nons of jazz), Cecil Taylor's music took on a much more strongly pronounced jazz character than before. But this proves that the essence of jazz depends more on the intensity of rhythmic communication in a group than on the basis of that communication. For Taylor (who may always have felt limited by a steady beat, who either would not or could not do anything with its immanent possibilities), the intuitive reactions offered him by Sunny Murray are a continuous source of energy. The rhythm created by the interaction of the two is marked by an undulating rise and fall in energy; the element of "stagnation" is compensated for by a constant propulsion. And although Taylor, in these recordings with Murray, is further removed from the conventions of traditional jazz than ever before, he arrives at one of jazz's very own ingredients, which in its rhythmic intensity, however, goes far beyond what jazz theory had called, until that time, *drive*.

Cecil Taylor is so aware of the significance of rhythmic communication for his music that during the last ten years he has had only two steady drummers. Andrew Cyrille, who followed Sunny Murray in 1964 and is still with the group at this writing, proceeds from the same conception of metrically free rhythm. He is Murray's equal in vitality and possibly surpasses him in precision.

To try to give a verbal impression of Murray's and Cyrille's playing would be a rather fruitless exercise. A transcription is almost impossible, since the drums are covered by the other instruments, and would not be very enlightening anyway, since accents that seem to be placed without rhyme or reason when heard as isolated phenomena, disclose their musical sense only when heard in the total context. When any predictability of rhythmic formulas is abandoned, except for those laid down by an arrangement, the intuitive interactions between all the instruments of a group will necessarily be intensified. These interactions, and not just the drummer's rhythms, forge those chains of impulses whose links, though they may be of irregular length, do suggest a dynamic order. That order can perhaps best be visualized if we compare the beat of traditional jazz to walking, or to the even strides of a long-distance runner; while the rhythm of the Cecil Taylor group is like the alternating strides and leaps of a hurdler, with the hurdles placed at unequal intervals.

Closely associated with the question of rhythm in Cecil Taylor's music — and in free jazz in general — is the matter of tempo. If we say that tempo, as it came to be defined in traditional music, presupposes a constant or nearly constant metre, then Taylor's music after 1961 has no "objective" tempo. If, however, one understands tempo — in accordance with the findings of modern musical psychology — as "impulse density" (*i. e.* the frequency of musical impulses per time unit), one arrives at one of the phenomena that cause a subjective feeling of tempo in free jazz: the relative density of impulse series creates the impression of different tempi. But there is a second variable, which is probably more important on the whole: above and beyond the impulse density[3], *accentuation* is instrumental in giving an impression of tempo. It is not the regularity of accents that counts, but their frequency in time. Here too, we must realize that changes in impulse density and accent frequency, and thus in the subjective tempo, are not the result of actions in the bass and drums only (as they are in Charles Mingus's accelerandos, for instance), but arise from the interactions of all the players. With this in mind, it will be obvious that superimpositions of different tempi on several tempo planes will often occur. On a number of Cecil Taylor recordings, it can be noticed that there is a high degree of correlation between the tempo arising from rhythmic impulse-chains and the element of *energy*. To put it more precisely, Taylor's music loses its jazz quality (for which — among other things — the "energetic" element is essential) below a certain "subjective" tempo threshold: when neither swing nor energy determines the rhythmic progress, his music approaches very closely the avantgarde music of the West.

Example 30 is the introduction to *Enter Evening,* recorded in 1966. Here four melody instruments (oboe, trumpet, alto and piano) play unaccompanied lines of different lengths, in an utterly free rhythm[4]. When even an intimation of a common rhythmic basis is dispensed with, kinetic energy is totally reduced and there is a subjective indeterminacy, like that occasionally encountered in serial music — with the considerable difference that the objective rhythm of the latter (fixed in written note values) is organized to the nth degree. Examples like this show how blurred the boundaries between free jazz and European avantgarde music have become.

EXAMPLE 30   ENTER EVENING

---

3) Sometimes called "information density," *cf.* Behne (1971).

4) In transcribing the rhythms in this example, the time values were measured precisely. When it came to putting them into our system of notation, however, tolerances had to be allowed for the sake of readability; otherwise, the tiny deviations would have made it necessary to break down the rhythm into 64th notes at least.

For a time, listeners to Cecil Taylor's music were hardly aware of its rhythmic aspect, or the consequences of abandoning swing. Their attention was attracted to other things which thanks to their newness were more obviously at odds with traditional jazz. As early as the Fifties, one of the most prominent features of Taylor's playing was a harmonic language in which functional relationships are, if not abandoned, at least heavily veiled. The reason was not so much that Taylor enriched functional harmonic progressions by adding dissonances (there had already been an abundance of that in bebop), but that he jeopardized the functional identity of his chords by their very density.

From "harmonic density," which had once fascinated Taylor in Brubeck's music, it was a logical step to clusters. A cluster can be defined as a pile or stack of tones, created by simultaneously striking all or most of the chromatic steps within a certain area[5]. There is no perception of single pitches in clusters; the impression is of diffuse sounds differentiated by compass and register. In New Music, clusters are mainly used in tone-colour compositions as stationary sound-fields that are given "an internal vitality by means of written-in patterns of motion" (Dibelius 1966, p. 320). In Cecil Taylor's music, however, their primary function is the intensification of energy. As a rule, Taylor's clusters are not sustained sounds, but short, sharp tone-blocks hammered in extremely rapid succession like arpeggios and covering several piano registers. The percussive nature of his playing here becomes very evident.

Jazz critics attached an importance to the clusters in Taylor's music that was out of all proportion to their number, probably because they represented a radical departure from the traditional aesthetic norms of jazz. Clusters alone do not make a style, but are one stylistic feature among many (something Taylor's imitators often overlook); and many things that sound like clusters prove, when listened to more critically, to be chords in close position with a clearly defined intervallic structure (but not, of course, oriented on triadic harmony)[6].

Cecil Taylor's music has often been called atonal, and it probably is — if the superlative be permitted — the most atonal in early free jazz. But all things are relative, and precisely with regards to tonality, European musical terms can be applied only in a very limited sense to free jazz (Berendt 1968, p. 33), unless one wishes to undo the dichotomy of the concepts "tonal" and "atonal" by putting a sliding scale between them. As concerns Taylor's music, there are certainly moments when no tonal reference can be noticed. These are usually passages in which a conception of tone-colour variation is dominant, or in which percussive figures serve to intensify the energy. Taylor uses atonality

---

5) *Cf.* Mauricio Kagel (1959).

6) The "chord scraps" Cecil Taylor puts under the solos of John Coltrane and Kenny Dorham in *Hard Driving Jazz* are not clusters, as Manfred Miller thinks, but chords; they even adhere to standard patterns, but their function is obscured by dissonances and close positions (*cf.* Miller 1970).

not for its own sake because "you can't play tonal anymore" but as a means of structural differentiation. On the other hand, there are melodies in his compositions whose tonal character is quite obvious, as for example the thematic material of *Conquistador* (recorded in 1966), a piece in which improvisations are played on alternating tonal centres. (*Cf.* also Example 28, in which F functions as a point of reference.)

Taylor's "multi-track" harmonic language is most apparent in the melodic lines' relationship to the chords underlying them. The chords — which may be clusters hit with the left fist — do not act as a harmonic-rhythmic *accompaniment* to the melody as in traditional piano playing, but as an independent entity whose intensity occasionally overrides that of the upper part. Frequently, the interval structure of the melodic lines is full of tonal patterns (whole-tone scales, broken chords, scales, etc.), while the chords opposed to them have, in addition to their predominantly rhythmic function, the effect of coloration.

From this manner of using the left hand, which has nothing more to do with traditional accompanying, Taylor also drew consequences for his ensemble work. We notice even in early recordings, such as those of the Fifties, that he does not back the solos by soprano saxophonist Steve Lacy or vibraphonist Earl Griffith by "feeding" them chords, as was customary, but carries on a constant dialogue with his musicians. As background (if it can still be called that) Taylor plays everything that occurs in his solos, too: extremely fast chromatic runs, wide arpeggios across several octaves, two-handed swelling and receding tremolos, changing to sharp staccato chords that hack the continuity of the "soloist's" melodic lines. This kind of accompaniment, which in no way resembles the "comping" of traditional jazz piano playing, has frequently been criticized as lack of discipline. Whitney Balliett, a commentator who from the start was very positive toward Taylor's music, asks rhetorically why Taylor bothers with other musicians at all, when his accompaniment is usually nothing more than a continuation of his solos (Balliett 1968, p. 236). And Cita Carno said that by playing so *much,* Taylor is an overly busy, bad accompanist (from Spellman 1967, p. 39). The point, however (and this becomes evident especially in his later playing, with more cooperative musicians), is that Taylor has in mind a new conception of jazz piano playing, which goes beyond the traditional division of roles into soloist and accompanist. The "orchestral treatment" of the piano, which he often speaks about, precludes merely laying down the chords. Taylor "feeds" his soloists all right, but he feeds them with rhythmic energy, not with a chordal background.

It may seem paradoxical that energy, the basic element in Cecil Taylor's music (at any rate since about 1961), always goes hand in hand with a strong element of construction which one would assume must sooner be anti-energetic in its effect. Taylor has pointed out in numerous interviews that his chief concern is to create *forms* that govern the energy, to arrive at a kind of music with "improvisation, content and shape becoming one" (from Spellman 1967, p. 38). "My music is constructionistic, that is, it is based on the conscious working-out of a given material" (from Noames 1965a).

The dangers lurking in jazz that predominantly depends on construction are generally known. The music of Dave Brubeck, the Third Stream experiments of John Lewis and J. J. Johnson, Stan Kenton's "Artistries in . . . " are aural evidence of what can happen when construction is stressed at the expense of emotion and spontaneity. Taylor was obviously aware of these dangers. He averted them by bringing his musicians increasingly into the process of construction, like Mingus and Ellington before him. Around 1959, he went over to singing his compositions for the players, explaining the progress of the form, dynamic gradations, etc. Taylor's alto saxophonist Jimmy Lyons describes this procedure: "Sometimes Cecil writes his charts out, sometimes not. I dig it more when he doesn't. I don't know how to say this, but we get like a singing thing going when he teaches us the tunes off the piano. It has to do with the way Cecil accompanies. He has scales, patterns, and tunes that he uses, and the soloist is supposed to use these things. But you can take it out. If you go into your own thing, Cecil will follow you there. But you have to know where the tune is supposed to go, and if you take it there another way than the way Cecil outlines it, then that's cool with Cecil. That's the main thing I've learned with Cecil, the music has to come from within and not from any charts" (from Spellman 1967, p. 44).

For Cecil Taylor, renouncing the principle of an unchanging fixed form is more than just a demonstrative gesture in the direction of his "conservatory" background. The appearance of his kind of "collective composition," at the time that aleatoric techniques were on the rise in European New Music, is surely a coincidence. Taylor's move meant two things: a reference back to the tradition of jazz, and the conscious vitalization of his music by a fusion of construction and spontaneous action. "I had found out that you get more from the musicians if you teach them the tune by ear, if they have to listen for changes instead of reading them off the page, which again has something to do with the whole jazz tradition, with how the cats in New Orleans at the turn of the century made their tunes" (from Spellman 1967, p. 70).

It was clear very early in Cecil Taylor's musical development that the formula "theme-improvisation-theme" had no validity for him. Just as transitions between solos and collective improvisations were already fluid in the recordings with Steve Lacy and Earl Griffith, there is often no dividing line between the end of the theme and the beginning of the improvisation. But to the same degree that external boundaries (bar patterns, sequence of solos, etc.) start to fade, internal formal associations are set up by register changes, dynamic gradations, and variations in the rhythm, kinetic pace and instrumentation. In the process, a striking correspondence between detail and overall form is attained: the rapid sequences of increasing and decreasing energy (Example 29), by which Taylor achieves a new kind of drive in his solos and accompaniments, is projected in similar "undulations" that recur in the larger context, creating formal entities. "Macro-structure and micro-structure obey the same laws. And precisely this gives rise to a new concept of musical organization" (Dibelius 1966, p. 97).

In his record notes to *Unit Structures,* Taylor gives some slightly metaphorical hints as to the formal breakdown of his pieces. There are three contrasting blocks: *Anacrusis, Plain* and *Area.* The title of the first is taken from antique prosody, and means "up-beat"; this part defines above all the emotional level of the "collective compositions." Taylor did the same sort of thing in *Conquistador,* for instance, where a thrusting piano cadenza (aptly called a "pianistic field holler" by the American jazz critic Bill Quinn [1968]) announces the energetic mood of the piece to come. In *Enter Evening,* unaccompanied, free polyphonic lines give a preview of a relaxed piece whose outstanding feature is a play of sounds rather than rhythmic intensity (*cf.* Example 30).

The purpose of *Anacrusis,* then, is to lay down a general "programme" rather than to provide material for improvisatory elaboration. That happens in the section called *Plain.* There the actual thematic (motivic) material is evolved, predetermined structures are stated, juxtaposed, and reshaped in the process of improvisation. New melodic and rhythmic patterns grow out of given patterns, "content, quality and change growth in addition to direction found" (Taylor). In the third part, *Area,* "intuition and given material mix group interaction." An "unknown totality, made whole thru self analysic (improvisation), the conscious manipulation of known material" (Taylor). The realization of this method of spontaneous formal construction in Cecil Taylor's compositions proves to be extremely flexible. What happens is not that traditional formal schemes are replaced by others whose novelty lies only in an unorthodox terminology; the formal disposition of *Anacrusis, Plain* and *Area* does not create boundaries, but directions, not predictable structures, but progressive developments.

As with rhythmic communication on the basis of energy, whether or not a spontaneous construction of form in Cecil Taylor's groups is successful depends on the musicians with whom he plays. At the beginning, in the Fifties, he may often have had difficulty finding musicians who could follow his lead in bringing about a fusion of constructive planning and improvisatory creativity. During the Sixties, however, the reservoir of free-jazz musicians was substantially larger and constantly growing. With some of the best players of the day, Taylor was successful in evolving a form of ensemble playing that came to have an enormous influence on many free-jazz groups and also on improvising ensembles in the so-called serious field. For this and other reasons it is ironic that at a time when Cecil Taylor's music attained the highest possible degree of formal conciseness and emotional power, only two recordings of it reached the market: *Unit Structures* and *Conquistador,* both made in 1966 for Blue Note[7]. Each of these records has such a wide variety of forms and structures, such a wealth of musical achievement, that to analyze any one piece would illustrate only some dimensions of Taylor's music. Such reservations notwithstanding, we will try to trace some of Taylor's most essential procedures, taking the title piece of *Unit Structures* as an example.

With Taylor on this recording are the following players: alto saxophonist Jimmy Lyons, who had already worked with him for many years; drummer Andrew Cyrille; alto

---

7) On a third recording in June 1968, Taylor appears as soloist with the Jazz Composers' Orchestra.

saxophonist Ken McIntyre, who plays bass clarinet in this piece; trumpeter Eddie Gale Stevens, Jr.; and bassists Henry Grimes and Alan Silva.

The most important soloists on the recording are — apart from Taylor himself — saxophonists Lyons and McIntyre. Lyons is something of an outsider in free jazz, because his playing usually sounds like a successful transformation of Charlie Parker's musical idiom into a new context. While taking full advantage of the freedom Taylor's music offers him, Lyons achieves a rhythmic and melodic continuity typical of bebop musicians. McIntyre's musical background is as variegated as his stylistic potential. Like Cecil Taylor, he was trained at the New England Conservatory, then worked as a music teacher in New York, while establishing a reputation as a jazzman and composer in clubs. Like the late Eric Dolphy, for whom he once worked as sideman, McIntyre plays a whole arsenal of woodwind instruments. Archie Shepp called him an "energy-player" (1966), but his work here, in its duality of energetic sound blowing and melodic lyricism, goes far beyond this narrow classification.

As its name indicates, *Unit Structures* evolves from short self-contained models (structural units), some of which last just a few seconds. Their formation and gradual dissociation comprise the first part of the piece. This is followed by *Area* — freely and in part soloistically improvised — where according to Taylor the known material is formed into a whole.

The written "protocol" of *Unit Structures* below, illustrated by musical examples, tries to give a survey of what happens in the piece, the formal details, and how structural differentiation is obtained.

Anacrusis:[8]

0:00 The drummer sketches out a simple pattern on the tom-tom; shortly after, Taylor begins by placing strange sounding chords against this pattern (he is probably playing *inside* the piano), thus creating from the start a strong element of rhythmic tension.

0:13 Alto saxophone and trumpet enter, accentuating freely at first, then proceeding to long sustained tones; Taylor's and Cyrille's background remains rhythmically constant, but the dynamic intensity of piano and drums increases.

0:23 Bass clarinet and basses (arco) enter successively, forming with the others a stationary chord whose function is mainly coloristic. Glissandos on one bass start some internal motion going, and the chord is finally dissolved when the wind instruments recede and one bass begins to play shrill, sliding successions of sounds in the highest register — above the constantly increasing diffuse rhythms of Taylor and Cyrille. Already at this point it becomes evident that the basses are assigned different roles: one plays pizzicato in the low register, the other arco in the high register, mostly sounds without any melodic function.

---

8) To show the time relationships in the piece, the point at which each section begins is indicated.

0:57   Taylor establishes an initial melodic pattern, a simple five-tone minor scale on F sharp, with a rhythm that, for Taylor, is astonishingly uncomplicated (Example 31a).

EXAMPLE 31a   UNIT STRUCTURES

1:02   Jimmy Lyons takes up the phrase, transposing it a minor third down and varying its rhythm (Example 31b).

EXAMPLE 31b   UNIT STRUCTURES

At the same time Taylor, McIntyre and the bassists play polyphonic, strongly accentuated lines in free tempo. Lyons repeats the pattern while the density of sound increases. The accentuations of the other players crumble away, ending in slurred pizzicatos by one bassist.

1:32   Lyons and McIntyre, unaccompanied and in unison, present a passage with a thematic function; as the piece goes on it is used several times as a means of formal articulation (Example 31c). The "theme" is a series of short motives played

EXAMPLE 31c   UNIT STRUCTURES

in unison and separated by rhythmic interjections from the drummer or interrupted by short polyphonic passages. As a literal repeat later in the piece shows, every detail of this unit is precisely fixed. Since the two horns are playing in free tempo without a governing, pulsing beat, their unison is never quite "right."[9] The whole thing recalls certain Ornette Coleman compositions; their angular make-up possibly may have inspired Taylor.

2:00   The theme ends with a sustained sound in the horns and a drum-roll from Cyrille. After a short pause, Taylor sets up a fast "tempo" by playing just a few down-

9) "Heterophonic" unison playing of this kind is found earlier in the free-tempo compositions recorded by Thelonious Monk with his "Town Hall Orchestra," for example *Crepuscule with Nellie*.

ward-moving notes. The rest join in, at first with conflicting rhythmic accents, and then find a common rhythmic denominator. The driving rhythm of this structural unit presents a marked contrast to the free tempo of the "theme." Its asymmetry points to the typical Taylor "energy curve" (Example 31 d).

1,5 sec.

EXAMPLE 31d   UNIT STRUCTURES

2:17   The horns start a new unit, a twice-repeated falling line in "quasi-unison" (Example 31 e) isorhythmically accentuated by the drummer. Against the melody's rhythm, Taylor plays clusters that rise like an arpeggio.

2 sec.

EXAMPLE 31e   UNIT STRUCTURES

2:26   Taylor begins the transformation of the previous material (Example 31 f). The direction taken by the horns (rising, signal-like broken chords) is, as it were, reversed. The sound-structure is altered by a bass playing *arco sul ponticello*.

3 sec.

EXAMPLE 31f   UNIT STRUCTURES

2:33   Five units follow in which fragments of the previously used material are worked out. Within the units, which are separated by pauses, a dissociation process becomes increasingly evident, that is, the sections come to have fewer and fewer signs of a fixed order and there is a tendency to collective improvisation, with one of the players (usually Taylor himself) leading the way. Each unit lasts only about 10 seconds.

3:14   Taylor lines out a quick triple metre which is taken up by the group (Example 31g). After a few seconds, however, he drops the initially clearly accentuated beat and goes on to a hectic, irregular rhythm.

1,5 sec.

EXAMPLE 31g   UNIT STRUCTURES

80

3:23　The gradual reduction of structural clarity is followed by a unit in which Ken McIntyre starts a pattern that leans toward a beat; its melodic-rhythmic contours recall Monk's composition *Epistrophy* (Example 31h).

2,5 sec.

EXAMPLE 31h　　　UNIT STRUCTURES

3:37　Cyrille matches McIntyre's rhythm with eighths on the hi-hat. The tempo is accelerated to the point where the structure's clarity dissolves and the tempo impression is destroyed.

3:55　Jimmy Lyons takes up the descending melodic motive evolved by him in the previous unit, thus defining the shape of a new unit.

4:05　Taylor plays a kind of inversion of the passage proposed by Lyons; this in turn is copied by Lyons. The others contribute polyphonic lines in frée tempo.

4:17　A call-and-response pattern starts, with Taylor doing the "calling" and Lyons and McIntyre answering. This passage was obviously worked out in advance, or at least the melodic line was determined.

4:37　At Taylor's instigation, there is a change to a quick triple rhythm, played principally by the rhythm section.

4:50　A melodic fragment derived from the thematic motive and played in unison by Lyons and McIntyre brings the formal complex *Plain 1* to an end (Example 31i).

8 sec.

EXAMPLE 31i　　　UNIT STRUCTURES

During the horns' final sustained notes, Taylor creates motion with a driving rhythmic pattern whose accentuations establish the tempo of the improvisations that follow.

Area 1

5:00　Now come large formal units which in traditional jazz would be called solos. Although Cecil Taylor speaks about "soloists" in the sleeve notes, these units are not so much solos in the real sense as they are collective improvisations by Taylor, *one* wind player, the bassists and drummer (in contrast to the passages involving two or three wind players), Taylor "as catalyst, feeding material to soloists in all registers, encompassing single noted lines, diads, chord clusters, activated silence" (Taylor).

The first such "solo" is played by Ken McIntyre on bass clarinet. He begins with broad melodic spans, above an extremely agitated rhythmic foundation. Two tempo levels are thus immediatedly created: one melodic and the other rhythmic. Later the melodic spans are compressed into rapid runs through all the many bass clarinet registers, until McIntyre finally begins to behave like the "energy-player" Archie Shepp said he was. Melodies give way to strident sounds and trills without any pitch function.

7:38   The next solo, by Jimmy Lyons, has a diatonic structure that makes a marked contrast to Taylor's expanded tonality. As opposed to McIntyre, whose rhythmic conception is attuned to Taylor's asymmetrical energy waves, Lyons's rhythm is clearly rooted in the feeling of swing.

Plain 2

The solos by McIntyre and Lyons lead to a new group of structural units, some of which are derived from motivic material used in *Plain 1,* while others are formed from new motives that arise spontaneously from interactions between the players.

10:23   Taylor takes up a rhythmic pattern from the "theme" (Example 31 k).

5 sec.

EXAMPLE 31 k   UNIT STRUCTURES

A collectively improvised passage is evolved from it, in which trumpeter Eddie Gale Stevens takes over the lead (Example 31 l) in a lyric, melodic vein; again two tempo levels are the result.

6 sec.

EXAMPLE 31 l   UNIT STRUCTURES

10:53   Four units follow (separated by pauses), their progress guided primarily by Taylor. Here too, elements of dissociation are prominent.

11:30   Before the theme is repeated, there is a passage that seems rather out of place in the total context. It sounds like part of a solo by Jimmy Lyons[10]. The theme itself is a literal repeat of the one in *Plain 1*; as in that section, it ends with a drum-roll by Cyrille. With a rhythm pattern similar to the one he used after the first presentation of the theme, Taylor leads into the trumpet solo.

---

10)   The tape may have been subsequently spliced at this point.

Area 2

12:30   To start off his solo, Gale Stevens goes back to the "lyric" melody he played in *Plain 2* (Example 31 I) and evolves sustained melodic lines from it. Very soon, however, he is swept along by the energetic drive of the rhythm section, and alternates between high held notes (to which he gives a squeezed sound by depressing the valves only halfway) and sharp accents. In comparison to that of the other musicians, his playing seems somewhat confused.

14:41   Taylor starts his solo in a free tempo; then, with call-and-response patterns of clusters and runs, he gradually establishes a tempo that is taken up by the drummer. His improvisations, too, are not a solo in the usual sense, but are the product of constant interaction between all four participating instruments. Again the different bass roles — high and bowed, low and plucked — come into play. In the course of this unit, Taylor's playing becomes increasingly compact. Runs in the right hand are combined with rolling basses, producing polyphonic figures and merging into clusters which are played in arpeggio fashion and at close time intervals. These end in widely-spaced tremolos that swell and recede.

17:00   Jimmy Lyons takes up a phrase derived from the five-tone scale presented by Taylor at the beginning of the piece (Example 31 a). The other instruments join in, freely improvising. The whole thing unravels in heterophonic scraps of melody that gradually fade out.

What Taylor does in *Unit Structures* illustrates several things that are of great importance to free jazz as a whole. Beneath the emotional impact of his music, which is what the listener primarily responds to, is an intricate network of formal relationships. These inner formative aspects — created by composition and agreement, as well as by spontaneous interaction on the part of the players — are utterly independent of traditional schematic demarcations and thus have only a low degree of predictability for the listener. Manfred Miller (1970) correctly states that a first unprepared encounter with Taylor's music usually causes complete confusion. And especially at live performances by his group one meets, again and again, listeners who are willing but irritated. Overwhelmed by the energy and intensity of the music, they are rarely able to immediately grasp the inner structures. But it is precisely the formative details — which become apparent only after several listenings — that set Taylor's music apart from that of his many cluster-clumping emulators. By demonstrating that spontaneity and constructionism need not be mutually exclusive, Taylor shows that the freedom of free jazz does not mean the complete abstention from every kind of musical organization. Freedom lies, first and foremost, in the opportunity to make a conscious choice from boundless material. Further, the idea is to shape this material in such a way that the end result is not only a psychogram of the musicians involved, but a musical structure, balancing in equal measure emotion and intellect, energy and form.

Chapter 5

JOHN COLTRANE 1965 - 1967

"New York is where everything happens." Words like these, a siren song for jazzmen ever since the Roaring Twenties, took on a new currency in the early Sixties. Countless musicians from all parts of the USA flocked to New York, where the struggle for a living was the toughest and where the avantgarde in particular could scarcely hope to find a financial footing. They came nevertheless, to participate in new jazz where it was happening. Many gave up and returned home, others disappeared in the metropolitan jungle. Those who held out formed a closely-knit community. They settled in down-at-the-heel East Village, lived on part-time work, and played for fun in their lofts or for little pay in the cafes of the quarter, where it was at least possible for them to make *their* kind of music.

With this uncertain situation as a backdrop, a situation in which life was anything but rosy, even for stars like Ornette Coleman and Cecil Taylor, there occurred in the mid-Sixties three significant events. The first was a four-day festival devoted exclusively to new trends in jazz, the "October Revolution in Jazz" as its initiator, trumpeter Bill Dixon, called it. The second was a benefit concert for the "Black Arts Repertory Theater-School," programmatically titled "New Black Music." The third was a recording called *Ascension,* for which John Coltrane gathered around him for the first time a group of young musicians, most of whom were all but unknown outside the New York free-jazz circle.

On the surface, these three events appear to have nothing whatever to do with one another, but there was an invisible bond uniting them all: the will of New York musicians to join together, to organize, to achieve as a collective what they could not achieve as individuals.

The "October Revolution in Jazz" took place in early October 1964 in the "Cellar Cafe" not far from Broadway — a festival in a small coffee-house. For four long days and nights, some twenty different groups played, including countless musicians, known and unknown; players who never became more than local successes (which was not necessarily their fault), and jazzmen whose music was later to become familiar the world over. Among the latter were saxophonists John Tchicai and Giuseppi Logan, trumpeters Dewey Johnson and Mike Mantler, pianists Paul Bley and Burton Greene, trombonist Roswell Rudd, bassists Louis Worrell and Alan Silva, and drummer Milford Graves.

The musical spectrum ranged from Jimmy Giuffre's solo clarinet to the "Space Music" of the Sun Ra Orchestra; from the structural-formalistic to the ecstatic-unruly-seemingly formless. There were tunes that swung (in the old sense), and there were a-metrical, tempo-free pieces[1].

With his festival Bill Dixon was able to show, first of all, that there was an enormous pool of musicians in New York who deserved a hearing, and second, that there was a (predominantly young) public which was just as fed up with ossified musical norms — and with the commercial hustle of established jazz clubs too — as were the musicians themselves. The "October Revolution" did nothing to relieve the financial insecurity of free jazz musicians at first. But it did indicate how musicians could take the initiative into their own hands and secure for themselves what the establishment — content to earn on Brubeck and Peterson — denied them.

"New Black Music," the concert arranged in March 1965 under the guidance of writer and jazz critic LeRoi Jones, was put together partly as a manifestation of a new black nationalism; therefore it has a place in the social history of free jazz. Although it was not as all-encompassing as Bill Dixon's "October Revolution" (whose principle of selection was intentionally very liberal), the concert nevertheless displayed a wide range of musical types[2]. Alongside the music of a group led by Archie Shepp (blues-conscious, but a radical departure from traditional jazz models) stood the improvisations of brothers Albert and Donald Ayler (in a paradoxical way folkloristic and chaotic at once). The expanded hard bop of the Charles Tolliver Quintet co-existed with the so-called space music of the "Sun Ra - Myth Science Arkestra." Of particular significance, however, was the appearance of John Coltrane, who until then had been an outsider for the New York free-jazz community. He found himself in that position not only because of his evolutionary attitude toward jazz — in contrast to the revolutionary behaviour of younger musicians — but also because of his commercial success. The fact that Coltrane was prepared to play under the heading of "New Black Music" was taken as a good omen. Not only did he thereby demonstrate his solidarity with the socially underprivileged musicians of the New York circle, but the music he played was not one iota less uncompromising than that of the younger musicians, while it surpassed theirs in perfection and maturity. The movement had found in Coltrane a "super-ego" of sorts, as a number of titles dedicated to him by musicians like Archie Shepp, Marion Brown and Albert Ayler testify.

If the consequences of the first two events were social-psychological, they were soon followed by musical ones. Three months after Jones's concert, on June 25, 1965, an approximately three-quarter-hour piece, *Ascension*, was created in the Impulse studios. Taking part with the John Coltrane Quartet was a group of young musicians from the New York circle: Dewey Johnson and Freddie Hubbard on trumpet; Marion Brown and

---

1) Morgenstern and Williams (1964) give a detailed report.

2) Live recordings of the concert appear on Impulse A-90 under the "neutralized" title *The New Wave in Jazz*.

John Tchicai, alto saxophones; John Coltrane, Pharoah Sanders and Archie Shepp on tenors; McCoy Tyner, piano; the bassists Art Davis and Jimmy Garrison; and Elvin Jones on drums.

From the list of players alone, it is clear that this session meant a great deal more than just another free-jazz recording. But what is really special about *Ascension* goes beyond the personnel of the group and the length of the piece. "This is possibly the most powerful human sound ever recorded." With this sentence, jazz theorist and critic Bill Mathieu began his review of *Ascension* in *Down Beat* (1966). His words are just as valid today as they were in the mid-Sixties, a significant reflection of the emotional impact *Ascension* had on listeners at the time.

Even while *Ascension* was being made, that is, during the recording session, the musicians must have been aware that they were involved in an experience of total communication, and that the product could never match that experience completely. Marion Brown said later: "We did two takes, and they both had that kind of thing in them that makes people scream. The people who were in the studio *were* screaming" (from Spellman, Impulse A-95). Here we arrive at a problem that looms ever larger as free jazz develops: being in on the act of creation, the "now," becomes at least as significant as the "after," the musical end-product. Whether or not the acoustical result heard as the record rotates on the turntable transcends the event of total communication is, likely as not, of secondary interest to the musicians themselves. Nevertheless, one of the most apparent features for the listener in *Ascension* is its extraordinary emotionality. But this very intensity may obscure the fact that in the piece are thoroughly traditional elements, and where one might assume that everyone is playing exactly what he pleases, there is, in fact, a definite musical organization.

Two takes of *Ascension* were made on that 25th of June. They appeared successively on Impulse, unfortunately under the same number. (One version is now available on Impulse A-95, the other on His Masters Voice/EMI CSD 3543). While these recordings hardly differ in formal structure and even less in their emotional content, they obviously do differ in their micro-structures and still more in the solo improvisations, as is to be expected from music that is chiefly improvised. A direct and detailed comparison of the two versions, as instructive as it would certainly be, would exceed the scope of this book. But even from a superficial aural comparison, the listener will recognize what was pre-arranged in this improvised music and what was not; identical passages in both versions hardly came about spontaneously.

In analysing this piece, I refer only to the take issued by HMV (it is presumably the second). My reason for doing so is that various components important for *Ascension* —

and perhaps for free jazz as a whole — are more clearly evident than in the other version, whose musical quality is otherwise on a par[3].

As many observers have pointed out, *Ascension*'s construction has certain parallels to that of Ornette Coleman's 1960 double quartet recording, *Free Jazz (cf.* p. 59). In both pieces, the formal framework is an alternation of collective improvisations and solos, and in both there is a minimum of pre-set material and a maximum of spontaneous, free creation. But although the two show a similar radicality in their renunciation of traditional norms (and can thus claim a similar trigger effect on the development of jazz in the ensuing years), their internal structure and their emotional content represent two fundamentally different dialects of the same language. I will return later to the parallels and divergencies between these two recordings, whose consequences are probably the most important and far reaching in the evolution of free jazz.

In *Ascension,* the formal disposition into collective improvisations and solos has a second framework superimposed on it, which is a source of structural differentiation, especially during ensemble passages. It consists of systematic changes of modal levels, and occurs with only slight deviations in all eight collective improvisations. The beginning is an Aeolian mode on B flat; a change to D Phrygian is usually coupled with a change of rhythmic structure; the closing sections of the collective blocks are in F Phrygian and lead into the solos that follow; these as a rule begin again in B flat Aeolian. The logic of this structural principle is evident in the tonal material of the modes: F Phrygian and B flat Aeolian contain identical tonal material, and differ only in their point of reference, the fundamental tone of the mode (Example 32). This ambiguity in the scales

F Phrygian   B flat Aeolian

EXAMPLE 32

makes transitions from collective improvisations to solos fluid, at least in terms of the modal framework, and the soloist can break away from the ensemble easily.

The modality of *Ascension* is, to be sure, of another kind than the modality of Coltrane's earlier pieces, like *Favorite Things, Olé* or *India.* In many parts of the piece, modal scales "show through," rather than being palpably present. Alongside collectively improvised passages, in which the modal material is clearly emphasized (in part by broken chords in the horns), creating a distinct modal basis, there are passages in which dissonant com-

---

3) The two versions can be identified from the sequence of solos which, contrary to the details in the sleeve notes (the same in both versions), differ in one particular; the order of solos on HMV is Coltrane, Hubbard, Sanders, Johnson, Shepp, Tchicai, Brown and Tyner, which agrees with the sleeve notes; on Impulse, however, the solos of Shepp and Brown are interchanged, and Elvin Jones's solo is missing.

plexes only allow guesswork at a modal focus. Finally, there are solos in which a modal coloration is present nowhere except in the accompanying basses and piano.

I do not want to make it appear that modal playing, whatever forms it may take in *Ascension,* is the essential element responsible for the general character of the music, for there are certainly more important components to which *Ascension* owes its significance in the history of free jazz. It does seem necessary, however, to point out that for all the spontaneity of the piece, not only intuition and empathy are at work, but that other things help determine its musical progress.

The changing of modes during collective improvisation always means more than just a move to new tonal material. At these points, structural differentiation is created on all levels at once:

a) an alteration of the rhythmic basis, *e. g.* by transition from freely accentuated, a-metrical passages to passages in which a beat is emphasized; or

b) a change of motion in the melodic parts, *e. g.* by transition from long static sounds to descending melodic lines or ornamental runs; or

c) variation in the timbre composite by change of register and dynamics.

Thus modality, and even more the mode changes, have in *Ascension* a distinctly formal, structural function.

Such an organization — however elementary it may be — naturally needs a certain amount of steering, especially when, as in *Ascension,* organization occurs spontaneously, *i. e.,* is not subject to any schematic breakdown with a fixed timing. Usually the "steersman" is John Coltrane. He gives signals for changing modes by holding tones related to the modal level toward which the music is moving (frequently by suspensions to the mode in question, *e. g.,* A flat before B flat Aeolian). In the collective improvisations, changes thus initiated are then usually defined by complete scales or scale fragments — played as a rule by Freddie Hubbard — and stabilized by chord patterns from pianist McCoy Tyner.

The melodic nucleus of *Ascension,* a short motive played by John Coltrane to open the first collective improvisation, doubtless has a symbolic character; the similarity to the main theme of Coltrane's suite *A Love Supreme* cannot be missed (Example 33a, b). As

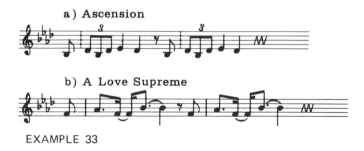

a) Ascension

b) A Love Supreme

EXAMPLE 33

concerns the development of the piece, however, this "leading motive" has only a secondary function. The principal model used to steer the group improvisations consists of descending lines which both define the mode and create a distinct body of *sound.* These lines, often scale fragments or broken chords drawn from the modal framework, are obviously pre-arranged only as to the general course they take, but not as to their melodic shape or exactly where they occur.

Thus a large number of rhythmically independent lines are set against one another by seven wind instruments, with the resultant overlappings. This superimposition produces rapidly moving sound-fields whose rhythmic differentiation is provided as a rule by the rhythm section, rather than coming from within. When seven independent melodic-rhythmic lines coincide, the relationships between them lose clarity, fusing into a field of sound enlivened by irregular accentuations. On the other hand, there are passages in *Ascension* in which individual musicians, by incessantly repeating short rhythmic motives, create a driving, drilling rhythm whose impulses — when taken up by the other improvisers — not seldom awaken associations with the energetic rhythms of Cecil Taylor's groups.

In view of the variety and density of sound and the occasionally dissonant cutting edge of these group improvisations, it is evident that their elements, namely what the various musicians play, are less "revolutionary" melodically than the sum of those parts. Whereas in the group improvisations of Coleman's *Free Jazz,* the melody of every player has a clearly-drawn horizontal intervallic structure (the result of motivic give-and-take between the musicians); the horn lines in *Ascension,* taken singly, are relatively simple in shape. Runs composed of seconds and thirds, like those in Example 34, are by no means rare. (The example is a phrase played by trumpeter Freddie Hubbard in the fourth collective improvisation, which follows Pharoah Sanders's solo.)

EXAMPLE 34   ASCENSION

Here we can lay hold of one of the essential differences between Coleman's *Free Jazz* and Coltrane's *Ascension.* In the collective improvisations of *Free Jazz,* the contributions of each and every improviser have a certain melodic life of their own; motivic connections and dove-tailing of the various parts create a polyphonic web of interactions. In *Ascension,* on the other hand, the parts contribute above all to the formation of changing sound-structures, in which the individual usually has only a secondary importance. Quite plainly, the central idea is not to produce a network of interwoven independent melodic lines, but dense sound complexes.

Melody-plus-motives on the one hand; tone-colour structures on the other; the antithesis these two principles represent gives rise to problems that go far beyond the immediate comparison of *Free Jazz* and *Ascension*. We have already mentioned in another connection (*cf.* p. 71) the tags established by Archie Shepp to distinguish between melodic and energetic playing ("Coleman player" and "energy-sound player"). These categories were originally intended only to describe *individual* stylistic features. In the group improvisations of *Free Jazz* and *Ascension* respectively, they are transposed to a large ensemble, and in this form point the way for many free-jazz groups in the years to come. The increasing trend in collective improvisation (especially in larger groups) toward playing with tone colour and away from motivic improvisation, is probably due in some measure to the extraordinary effect *Ascension* had on late Sixties' jazz.

In *Ascension* itself, the antithetical ideals of motivic and tone-colour organization can be heard in the playing of individual musicians. The dense sound of the group improvisations hardly permits such individual stylistic traits to stand out, but in the solos at least two different formative principles clearly come to the fore.

Pharoah Sanders, for example, plays hardly any lines that have a recognizable melodic context. Predominant in his improvising are multiple sounds — some sustained, some given a speechlike cadence — all without clearly definable pitches. Breaking up these sounds are extremely fast runs through the range of the saxophone. But the runs must not be taken as melodic elements either. Their purpose is kinetic. Sanders is simply gathering momentum for the next round of sounds.

The solos by Archie Shepp and, to a lesser extent, Marion Brown, are likewise deliberately a-melodic for long stretches. In Shepp's playing, scarcely one tone has a definitely fixed pitch, or ends as it began. His glissandos, his "smeared" and stretched tones, with a vibrato that calls to mind the raw tenor players of the Thirties, are spans of sound rather than melodies. And when melodic fragments do turn up, there is no continuity of development.

There is a certain linear flow now and then in Marion Brown's solo, but here too, the experiments with sound are uppermost. Unlike the real multiple sounds Sanders gets by fingerings and embouchure, what Brown produces are more often "fake" multiple sounds. These are extremely fast tremolos or trills played as successive intervals, but give the impression of composite sounds in somewhat the same manner as the separate shots of a film are seen by the viewer as a continuous action.

The concept of instrumental tone colour playing manifest in the solos of Sanders, Shepp and Brown agrees with the overall character of the group improvisations in *Ascension*. This makes the solos of the other two saxophonists, John Tchicai and John Coltrane, stand out more sharply.

The essential features of John Tchicai's improvising can be gathered from the opening passages of his solo (Example 35). Tchicai begins with a variant of the *A Love Supreme* motive, introduced by Coltrane at the start of the piece. He repeats the motive over and

90

over (A), and then gradually gets away from it by interpolating short, explosive glissandos (B) and blurred chromatic runs (C). A sequential transposition of the motive (D), similar to Coltrane's procedure in *A Love Supreme* (Example 14, p. 33), ends with a return to the initial position (E) and finally leads to a freer section, in which Tchicai makes use of various tone colour possibilities — but much less than Sanders or Shepp. His playing remains motivic during the rest of the improvisation; free passages return again and again to the point of departure, the motive from *A Love Supreme*. In this respect, the motive has a completely different meaning for Tchicai than, for instance, Ornette Coleman. Melodic and rhythmic patterns for Coleman usually serve to release motivic chains that are constantly self-renewing; they set the wheels in motion. For Tchicai, the motive derived from the theme has more the function of an anchor, serving as a fixed point of reference throughout his whole improvisation.

EXAMPLE 35   ASCENSION

Just as structurally clear as Tchicai's solo, but of greater emotional power, the improvisation by Coltrane unites the two conceptions we have mentioned, that of tone colour and that of melody-and-motive. The most significant characteristics of Coltrane's solo can be seen in Examples 36 and 37.

EXAMPLE 36   ASCENSION

♩ = 215

sounds →

EXAMPLE 37   ASCENSION

While the first collective improvisation is still going on, Coltrane enters with a repeated figure, whose function is not so much melodic or motivic, as it is rhythmic ("bars" 1 - 15). Accentuated in threes, the eighth-note chains run contrary to the fundamental rhythm (there is a steady beat here). At the very beginning of his solo, then, two rhythmic levels are established, their accent collisions engendering a strongly propellant effect[4]. The rhythmic tension of these against-the-beat eighth-note chains dissolves in a change of register (bar 17), with Coltrane playing overblown multiple sounds up to an altitude of b flat^2 [5]. Then the change of mode (from B flat Aeolian to D Phrygian) brings a caesura. The change is introduced by Coltrane with a run descending to the lower octave (bar 24), and is stabilized by a held A (bar 25). This, incidentally, is the only modal caesura in *Ascension* executed by a *soloist* during his improvisation. As a rule, changes of mode are left to the initiative of McCoy Tyner, and in most solos there are no mode changes at all. With the new modal basis, Coltrane changes the motion pattern of his solo, too. Again he introduces a rhythmic figure opposed to the rhythm; but in contrast to the earlier pattern, this one triggers a further motivic development (beginning in bar 28). In the last part of this example, Coltrane reaches a form of improvisation that may be called "self-dialogue" (bars 37-45). This is a rapid succession of related phrases in the highest and lowest register of the instrument. The dialogue nature of this segment is aurally self-evident. Its presence is an indication of Coltrane's intention to expand the potential of his instrument. In addition to extending its range by overblowing in the highest register and by special fingering and embouchure techniques[6] — thereby producing multiple sound textures, as Sanders does — there is at this point a kind of simulated polyphony, in which a single instrument appears to take on the role of two.

Coltrane's solo ends (Example 37) with a complete synthesis of tone colour and melodic-motivic work: short broken chords (familiar to us from Coltrane's "pre-modal" period) aim at a rising succession of pitches which at the same time increasingly lose the identity of single tones and become sounds. The three-octave downward leap at the end of the solo leads into the succeeding collective improvisation, A flat having the function of a suspension to B flat Aeolian.

These brief analyses of a few solos are by no means intended solely as insights into typical improvisational features of the musicians involved. In that respect, *Ascension* is a bad example for many reasons. But the various phenomena we have described do permit some generalizations about tendencies in free-jazz improvisation, its expressive characteristics and techniques.

1. A new type of group improvisation emerges in which melodic-motivic evolution gives way to the moulding of a total sound. For Ornette Coleman *(Free Jazz)*, the various parts have an "intellectual" influence on one another, resulting in a collective "conversation"; for Cecil Taylor the collective is mainly led by *one* player who acts in accordance with constructionist principles; in *Ascension,* however, the macro-structures of the total sound are more important than the micro-structures of the parts.

---

4) There is something similar in Ornette Coleman's solo on *Forerunner,* Example 22, p. 55.

5) The tone constitution of these multiple sounds can hardly be analyzed; in the music, they are marked by square note-heads or wavy lines.

6) *Cf.* especially Bartolozzi 1967.

2. In solos, there is a gradual emancipation of timbre from pitch that leads to a-melodic structures primarily delineated by changes in colour and register. This kind of playing expresses an emotionalism heightened to the ultimate degree (Shepp, Sanders).

3. On a par with emotionalism is a melodic-motivic improvisation, which takes its cue from the playing of Ornette Coleman. The fundamental approach in this kind of improvising is constructional rather than emotional (Tchicai).

4. A synthesis of the two phenomena is evident in a style of improvising that embraces both *emotion* and *construction* (Coltrane). Into a context that is melodic-motivic, all possibilities of tone coloration are incorporated, partly as a constructive device — when they serve as a means of formal articulation — and partly to provide for emotional intensification.

These stylistic features are not labels to be attached to this or that musician, in order to identify his style. Shepp, Sanders and Brown cannot be spoken of as "sound-players" *only*. Tchicai does not follow *only* constructionist principles, any more than Coltrane *always* strives for a synthesis of the two. The solos of these musicians illustrate stylistic criteria, some of which were in the making long before *Ascension.* Here, however, they are strikingly evident, and they continue to occupy one's attention throughout the further development of free jazz. But they are representative of the musicians concerned, only with reservations.

So far, next to nothing has been said about the trumpet players in *Ascension,* Freddie Hubbard and Dewey Johnson. This was not without reason, for the role of the trumpet here — and in free jazz in general — is in fact problematic. Unlike saxophonists, trumpeters have virtually no means of denaturing and expanding the tone colour of their instrument. The growl tones played by Hubbard on other recordings are in the "anything-in-a-pinch" category and have little musical point. Saxophonists found a source of new impulses by extending the compass of their instrument into the overblowing register, but this means nothing at all to the trumpet since, like all the members of the brass family, it is an overblowing instrument anyway. Free-jazz trumpeters therefore get no new inspiration from the dizzying peaks scaled by Cat Anderson and other high-note "whistlers." Even less successful were experiments with so-called underblowing. Tones below the normal fundamentals can be produced on the trumpet, but they proved, as a rule, too unwieldy to give any real enrichment to the sound. It is indicative of the situation that Don Ellis turned to the quarter-tone trumpet, and to many kinds of electronically-produced, artificial "sound effects." Don Cherry's and Lester Bowie's multi-instrumentalism may in part derive from the same reason.

The urge to explore tone colour, one of the most important sources of stylistic innovation, presents more or less insoluble problems for free-jazz trumpeters. Therefore, it is understandable that the solos of Freddie Hubbard and Dewey Johnson sound a little confused and lacking in direction. In the powerful sound-fabric of group improvisations in *Ascension,* their parts do make an important coloristic contribution to the sum total. But compared to the emotional power of the saxophonists' solo excursions, they are pale. To give the trumpet a place in free jazz — while retaining its traditional sound — another musical context was needed, as we shall see in the chapters on Don Cherry and the Art Ensemble of Chicago.

The real musical significance of *Ascension* for the further course of jazz history lies in part in its chronological position. Coming five years after Ornette Coleman's *Free Jazz,* it signals a second phase of free collective improvisation: the chamber-music dialogue between musicians, which was Coleman's principal aim, is succeeded by orchestral sound structures. No longer does the whole take its meaning from the constituent elements. Just the reverse: the elements now cannot be understood except by reference to the whole.

For Coltrane, *Ascension* was both a look back and a look ahead, both derivation and advancement. By using the older modality as an underpinning, Coltrane gave himself a firm footing in a *terra incognita* toward which he was pushed by the young free-jazz musicians surrounding him. That he took that stride in company, leaving his soloist isolation to appear as *primus inter pares* in a big group, is an act with a great deal more than purely musical significance. By doing so, Coltrane declared his loyalty to a new generation of free-jazz musicians, for whom he had already become a kind of father figure in the mid-Sixties. His backing of musicians like Archie Shepp and Pharoah Sanders (he helped them get jobs and recording dates) gives the collective improvisations in *Ascension* a social import.

The most obvious outgrowth of John Coltrane's association with the young New York jazz avantgarde .was the personnel of his group during the period after *Ascension.* Before *Ascension,* the Coltrane Quartet — with pianist McCoy Tyner, Elvin Jones on drums and Jimmy Garrison on bass -- had been something of an institution, comparable in its stability to John Lewis's Modern Jazz Quartet. After 1965, tenor saxophonist Pharoah Sanders, who was in on *Ascension,* played more and more frequently with Coltrane. Occasionally, as in the recording of *Kulu Se Mama,* Coltrane called in several drummers; and finally his old comrades-in-arms, McCoy Tyner and Elvin Jones, left the group. Their places were taken by John Coltrane's wife, harpist and pianist Alice McLeod Coltrane, and the drummer Rashied Ali. All these personnel changes made a difference in the general character of Coltrane's music. Without causing a fundamental stylistic upheaval (Coltrane was always Coltrane), several highly important musical modifications occurred in these years. Coltrane's stylistic evolution had led from a phase of experimentation with vertical, harmonic development in the early Sixties, to a modal linearity. Now came a third phase, which would have to be called — in simplified terms — *sound exploration.* The title *Om,* which Coltrane recorded with Sanders in October 1965, has, in addition to its religious and philosophical implications, a further import, which can be taken as a clue to Coltrane's musical conception: as Coltrane says, the Hindustani word *Om* means, among other things, "All possible sounds that man can make vocally" (from Hentoff, Impulse 9120).

Although the phase of sound exploration was triggered by *Ascension,* it went a great deal further in its consequences. As sound came to be the decisive principle, older categories of musical organization lost importance. Modality, for instance, was hardly used anymore; the exception, *My Favorite Things* (a piece that is inextricably involved with Coltrane's career), proves the rule.

The share of John Coltrane's new collaborators in this transformation was, of course, not inconsiderable, but it must not be over-estimated either. It would seem that certain changes are "due" at a certain time, and often need only a suitable trigger to set them off. Even so, alongside *Ascension* (which may be said to have provided the spark) saxophonist Pharoah Sanders had an important role. In the recordings that followed *Ascension* he became more and more a "sound-player." As an analysis of these recordings shows, it was not so much Coltrane's individual style that altered, but the overall character of his music, due to reciprocal effects within the group. And that overall character was determined in some measure by Sanders's improvisations, sound-conscious and at that time downright "anti-melodic." This is apparent in several collective improvisations, for example, in *Manifestation,* where John Coltrane plays logogram-length motives, with strong rhythmic accentuation against Sanders's sustained, screaming harmonics. Another example is found in *Meditation,* where Sanders "screams," while Coltrane "sings." This duality of musical idioms was already present in *Ascension;* it is just as typical of the recordings made in the following years. One principle may dominate — as sound does here — but it is never to the total exclusion of everything else.

Now and then, the question is raised about the role of pianist McCoy Tyner and drummer Elvin Jones in Coltrane's music during the last year they worked together. Was it really the case, as is sometimes claimed, that Coltrane parted company with them because they fell short of his requirements, because they kept their master "earth-bound," hindering his "flights of genius?"

McCoy Tyner, a member of Coltrane's group from 1960 on, was never (and is not now) considered a true free-jazz musician; in many respects this is doubtlessly correct. A comparison with Cecil Taylor is too close at hand. By creating a prototype of free-jazz piano playing, Taylor set a standard by which all other pianists were measured. And yet it was precisely the kind of playing developed by McCoy Tyner, above all his comping, that made possible the improvisatory freedom for which many musicians were looking. By having to fulfil the traditional servant role that has always been the lot of pianists to big stars, Tyner perfected that function. Transplanting Coltrane's modal, linear conception to the piano, he achieved the harmonic indeterminacy that at once left sufficient leeway for the improvisers and yet provided them with a stable groundwork. Like Cecil Taylor, McCoy Tyner negated traditional patterns of functional harmony. But while Taylor's way was a sweeping liberation of dissonance and an avoidance of any association with traditional harmony, McCoy Tyner's modally coloured changes always aimed at a certain traditional "beauty of sound." (This is presumably what makes Tyner suspect for many dyed-in-the-wool free-jazz addicts.)

In *Ascension,* Tyner is still able to flawlessly suit his playing to the musical totality. He makes mode changes when they are suggested by the progress of the collective improvisations, or by soloists improvising in a melodic-motivic manner. On the other hand, he supplies a neutral groundwork open to any moves when the improvising is a-melodic and thus a-modal. But in *Om,* just a few months later, and in *Kulu Se Mama* which followed — that is, at the moment Coltrane begins to move away from modal improvisation — Tyner is on precarious ground. His solo in *Om* contains clusters and single lines strung along in a relatively disconnected way, and the "dialogues" between the right and left hand, introduced by Cecil Taylor with such extraordinary percussive clarity, sound rather confused as played by Tyner. To a certain extent, then, he combines traditional and progressive playing on these recordings. What comes out, however, is not a synthesis, but a conglomerate. Elements stand side by side rather than being fused.

These remarks should not be understood as a "negative appreciation." McCoy Tyner had already found his definitive personal style before 1965 (as he later demonstrated on trio recordings under his own name). Was he unable to follow Coltrane on what was probably his most radical move, or did he simply refuse to? A moot point that has nothing to do with his own musical qualities. Perhaps Tyner's mistake was only that he stayed a bit too long in Coltrane's group.

McCoy Tyner's successor, Alice Coltrane, is not more "modern" in her playing than he was, whatever the word "modern" is supposed to mean. To be sure, the chords she places against the improvisations of the horns are in general less definite in their harmonic relationships. By omitting thirds, they tend to sound "emptier" and thus vaguer (and as far as that goes, "less") than McCoy Tyner's. On the other hand, the chord changes she uses for ballad themes like *Expression* or *Ogunde* prove to have the simplest harmonic functions imaginable. In the same way, her solos frequently show utterly traditional features, especially when she plays single lines with hardly any rhythmic differentiation on linear — not modal — chord progressions or quasi pedal-point sounds.

Alice Coltrane is not a "hard" pianist who drives the music with rhythmic accentuations. Rather than treating the piano as a percussion instrument, a role which the piano has often been assigned in free jazz since Cecil Taylor, she uses the instrument more for coloration and to create a foundation of sound. Arpeggios, tremolo chords and copious use of the pedal may be derived from her harpist training. And although her playing, thanks to pedalling habits, sometimes threatens to become bombastic, it may be that the predominance of sound and resonance, produced by over-pedalling, makes her fit so smoothly into the group.

The function of the rhythm section in the post-1965 Coltrane groups (or rather the function of what is traditionally called the rhythm section) must likewise be seen in terms of the new attitude toward sound. The presence of several drummers in *Kulu Se Mama* and *Meditation* — both recorded in November 1965 — brought an important change in the rhythmic structure; it gains in tone colour and loses in clarity. In place of the sharply accentuated rhythm of Elvin Jones alone, there is now an abundance of accentuations, superimposed on one another and in part cancelling one another out. In place of *chains of impulses,* in which the beat, if not directly perceptible, is at least felt, there are rhythmically fluid *accent levels* from which — in unpredictable sequence and density — single intensity maxima break out.

This kind of rhythm still gives an impression of tempo, especially in fast motion, but one that is a great deal more diffuse than, for example, in *Ascension.* In slow pieces, however, the function of percussion is reduced almost exclusively to coloristic effects. By playing predominantly on cymbals with long-lived resonance, static, high sound-fields are created as a contrast to low chord tremolos on the piano. It may be that this attitude toward rhythm ran counter to Elvin Jones's ideas. His later work in a trio with tenor saxophonist Joe Farell and bassist Reggie Workman (who had played for Coltrane) shows that he still wanted a driving, sharply accentuated rhythm, and that he was not willing to sacrifice the old beat — as he understood and practised it — for a new freedom. What Elvin Jones's rhythmic strength means for Coltrane's music can perhaps be heard best on Coltrane's last record, *Expression,* where the new drummer, Rashied Ali, is left to his own devices. Ali may play more unconventionally than Jones, and he may suit Coltrane's new conception better, but he certainly does not surpass Jones's vitality.

Exploration of tone colour in John Coltrane's post-1965 music takes place on two levels: one is, so to speak, internal, and consists of a redefinition of various traditional means; the other is external, the integration of new sounds into the musical idiom of the group. We have already looked at the first aspect, whose results can be seen in the new functions assigned to the percussion instruments and the piano, the new sounds drawn from the saxophone (multiple sounds, overblowing, etc.), and the formation of tightly interlaced sound-fields in the collective improvisations. The outcome of the second aspect was the use of a new group of instruments: in *Om* a zanza (the so-called African thumb piano) is heard at the beginning, and later there are bells, a gong and finally, the tinkling of cowbells. All these percussion sounds have little or no rhythmic purpose; the point is purely to add colour. This goes so far that the gong strokes during McCoy Tyner's solo actually destroy rather than accentuate the rhythmic flow. Less exotic instruments are also used for sound exploration. In *Om* and *Reverend King,* Coltrane plays bass clarinet; in *Manifestation,* Pharoah Sanders plays piccolo, and *To Be* has a flute duet by Sanders and Coltrane. The motto of *Om,* "All sounds that man can make," points the way in every respect.

In the late Fifties, jazz critic Ira Gitler coined the term "sheets of sound" for John Coltrane's style of improvising; it has been used a great deal ever since. At the time, Coltrane was playing extremely fast broken chords and scales in a way that must have struck his listeners' ears as strange. Even so, "sheets of sound" hardly applied to what was happening musically. The reason Coltrane's broken chords and scales seemed like sheets, like surfaces in which details cannot be caught hold of, may have had something to do with what listeners were accustomed to, for the ability of the ear to solve complex sounds grows with training and exposure. Coltrane's improvising at the time, however, hardly aimed at creating sheets of sound (or "sound surfaces" as they are commonly known in New Music), but rather — in line with his harmonic investigations — at the coordination of as many intervals as possible into a single chord. What could not be foreseen in 1958 was that the improvisations of Coltrane and Sanders in the latter half of the Sixties would give the term "sheets of sound" a new currency and — at last — its real significance. When Sanders, in *Meditation* for example, plays an extremely dense tremolo that ends with a descending run, the subjective impression is that of an insoluble sound that can be described only as a vertical and horizontal occurrence (*i. e.,* in terms of compass and duration) and not as individual tones. This pattern, which occurs frequently in Sanders's improvisations, is not comprehended aurally as a tremolo — that is how it would be written in traditional notation — but definitely as a "sheet of sound."

Similarly, Coltrane plays "runs" in the fast sections of *Expression* (for example) or in the breakneck duet with drummer Rashied Ali in *Offering,* in which individual tones can hardly be distinguished; they merge into shapes, into sound contours. If ever the term "sheets of sound" was justified, it is here.

While sound-playing is the one overriding feature of Pharoah Sanders's improvisation at this time (a procedure that is not always without its problems, at any rate for the listener), John Coltrane develops a much broader range of expressive means and stylistic attributes. It cannot be directly ascertained that after 1965 he arrived at a way of improvising that was new from the ground up. What he did was to draw on his rich reservoir of musical experience and incorporate into his style everything he had worked out in past years, adjusting it to an altered frame of reference. Nevertheless, several patterns do take shape which can be regarded as especially typical of Coltrane's post-1965 style.

In my remarks on *Ascension,* I drew attention to a new kind of instrumental expansion, which I called "self-dialogue." This procedure now takes on increasing weight. In almost all of Coltrane's pieces, there is at one time or another a passage in which he strings together a quick succession of related phrases, two, and sometimes three octaves apart. Examples are found in *Meditation, Expression, Manifestation, Offering* and *Reverend King.* One especially impressive instance from his solo in *Offering* appears in Example 38. (The rhythmic values are only approximate, because of the free tempo.) These "dialogues" — an ingredient, incidentally, of Cecil Taylor's piano playing and later often used by Archie Shepp — hark back to one of the most traditional elements of jazz, however new and strange it may appear in Coltrane's music. They are highly compressed, logogram call-and-response patterns, such as occurred in the earliest forms of religious Afro-American music, or — to go back further yet — in African music. Not least for this reason, they would seem to be symptomatic of free jazz as a whole.

Another characteristic of Coltrane's post-1965 improvisation is his frequent use of sequences. Now, sequences as a means of melodic-motivic organization are nothing new in jazz. Coltrane also had used them before (for example in *A Love Supreme*). But while

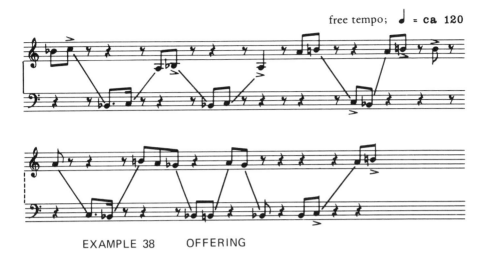

EXAMPLE 38   OFFERING

a melody based on sequences usually runs the risk of sounding like an etude (and thus becoming a bore, especially when used to excess), Coltrane gets just the opposite effect. His sequences almost always rise, and very rarely fall. As a rule, he begins in the low register with what is often only a short phrase, and then leads (or rather drives) it upward with immense persistence, via many a roundabout phrase and with a steady rise in dynamics, until it ends at last in shrill overblown sounds. It may be the persistence that gives these sequences a new — and in a way, an extra-musical — quality. If "striving toward a higher level of existence," suggested by Coltrane's titles and texts, has any programmatic expression in his musical content, then it is here, in these insistent and obstinate sequences, whose emotionalism goes far beyond what can be formally notated.

One highly important factor in Coltrane's music after 1965 is the thematic material he uses. In just two of the recordings of this period issued at this writing does he fall back on pieces from his old repertoire: *Naima* and *My Favorite Things,* both recorded during a club date at New York's "Village Vanguard" on May 28, 1966 (he already had his new rhythm section). A comparison of the different versions of these two titles is all one needs, to realize the influence of the six years in between on Coltrane's musical development. *Naima,* a ballad of such surpassing melodic beauty that Coltrane was content to play just the theme without the slightest variation on the earlier recording, now becomes a launching pad for tension-charged improvisations. Points of contact between them and the original material are established in sporadic fragments of the theme, and hardly at all by harmonic references to the chord progressions. This is a kind of melodic-motivic improvisation that does not take place within the time-boundaries of the theme; those boundaries are stretched or shrunk as prompted by the flow of musical ideas.

In *My Favorite Things,* one of Coltrane's most tradition-conscious recordings from this period (thanks to its modal basis and triple metre — even if the latter is largely broken up), the new musical idiom is unveiled while the theme is being presented. Example 39 shows how Coltrane, disregarding the harmonic foundation, interpolates an ornamental run (bars 10-13) that soars freely over the beat and sounds as though he were impatiently breaking out of the constricting waltz pattern.

EXAMPLE 39   MY FAVORITE THINGS

A prominent place in Coltrane's repertoire — if not the most prominent of all — is occupied in these years by what I would like to call "rubato ballads." In line with customary jazz terminology, these are slow pieces, which Coltrane plays principally in a free tempo, their outward features frequently recalling the freely fashioned lead-out cadenzas of traditional ballads. The majority of the compositions recorded by Coltrane from 1965 to 1967 belong in this category, among them *Reverend King* (dedicated to Martin Luther King), all the thematic material of *Expression (Ogunde, To Be* and *Offering),* and most of the themes used in the suite *Meditations.*

Coltrane's rubato ballads have a predecessor in *Spiritual,* which he recorded with Eric Dolphy in 1961. This too is a sustained melody played with a metrically free accentuation over a harmonic groundwork. In *Spiritual,* however, a distinct caesura is made after the presentation of the theme, separating the free-tempo composition from the improvisations, which are on a steady beat. In Coltrane's late ballads, on the other hand, the transitions are fluid. The wide-ranging melodic spans of these pieces slide imperceptibly into flowing melismatic lines, which are heightened in motion and intensity until they reach an imaginary point of culmination, after which they return just as continuously to the quiescent pole of the theme from which they came. The beginning of *Ogunde* (Example 40), a record made in March 1967, shows the start of that process.

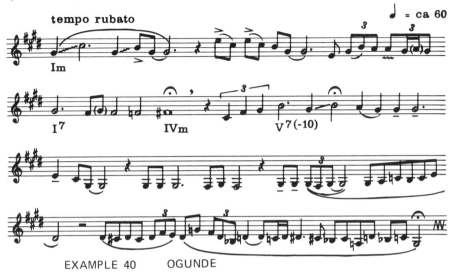

EXAMPLE 40   OGUNDE

Usually, these compositions are based on a functional harmonic framework, which is frequently a very simple one limited to changes between tonic, subdominant and dominant. This "old-fashioned" frame, which is generally confirmed by the melody and very firmly emphasized in arpeggiated chords by Alice Coltrane, continuously disintegrates in the course of development. To the extent that motion and density of sound are intensified, the tonal system of references loses ground, until only vague relationships to a tonal centre remain at the point of emotional culmination.

In pieces of this kind, there is a form of musical creation that is new to jazz. For not only is the traditional distinction between ballads and up-tempo pieces set aside, but also the expressive implications of the two. Coltrane's rubato ballads are never oriented toward just one of two opposite poles, toward "calm" or "activity." On the contrary, they all have a variety of levels. In these pieces meditation and action, mourning and fury, poise and agitation, are not incompatible, but are different images of the same thing, with roots in Coltrane's spiritual strength.

Without question, it would be wrong to reduce this music to its programmatic content, even though that is suggested by the words of the spoken or sung introductions, and by titles like *Love, Compassion, Serenity,* etc. To what extent verbal avowals can be translated into music, and to what extent they can filter into the consciousness of an uninitiated listener *through* the music, is a matter which need not be discussed in detail here. We can be sure, however, that recordings like *Expression* and *Meditations* reflect (over and above their purely musical aspects), something of Coltrane's "message," no matter how clouded the reflection and how non-specific its meaning may be. Paradoxically, Coltrane's message of "peace" and "love" is not seldom expressed in an apparently chaotic musical context, which could be taken as an indication of the times in which he sought to make that message known.

John Coltrane died on July 17, 1967, at the age of forty. Like hardly any other musician of his generation, he accomplished the evolution from post-bop to free jazz with a remarkable consistency, step by step and in his own personal way. His music never kept abreast of the most topical free-jazz trend, which is to say that it was never as "in" or as "far out" (or whatever terms avantgarde apologists use) as that of his most revolutionary colleagues. Therefore, it may seem all the more surprising that he had such a strong influence on the second generation of free jazz. But the broad appeal of his music was obviously due less to its relative newness, and more to its emotional force.

The traces of Coltrane's music go far beyond his death. Much the same thing happened to him as had happened to Charlie Parker, in that a "Coltrane school of saxophone playing" has formed over the past few years, even if its adepts are less slavish in imitating their model than was the case during bebop and afterward with the musicians of the Parker succession.

Among Coltrane's countless emulators are some who limit themselves to copying catchy patterns which, torn from their context, are generally awkward and void of sense. But there are also a number of musicians who — familiar with Coltrane's musical idiom — have transformed it into a language of their own, building on his music as a whole and not just borrowing effective details. Without wishing to install new stylistic pigeon-holes, a few of the players can be named in whose music Coltrane was and is a definite influence. Belonging to that group are tenor saxophonists Wayne Shorter, Charles Lloyd, Joe Farell and Pharoah Sanders, and in Europe Carsten Meinert (Denmark), Gerd Dudek (Germany), Leschek Zadlo (Poland), and finally the English baritone and soprano saxophonist John Surman. This selection may seem arbitrary (it is admittedly too narrow), but it does show the broad range of styles and expressive means that Coltrane's music has inspired. For each of the musicians mentioned speaks (leaving the matter of quality aside) what is without question his *own* personal musical dialect; and yet there is a bond that unites them all — the language of John Coltrane.

Chapter 6

ARCHIE SHEPP

Tenor saxophonist, composer, poet, actor, dramatist, social worker and high-school teacher, Archie Shepp is not one of those well-behaved people who modestly goes on playing his music and leaves the talking to the critics. Far from it. He is vociferous about social abuses and pillories racial discrimination when and where he sees it, a circumstance that has led to Shepp's outlook on life being discussed more often, and in more detail, than his music. It is quite true that to dismiss Shepp's verbal furor as unimportant would be doing him wrong. Shepp *is* angry, and he has a right to be. The notion of *l'art pour l'art,* with music shut up in a capsule and carefully set apart from general conduct and attitudes, is inconceivable to him. But although aggression, ferocity and irony have a share in his work, to imagine that anger is its only motive force is to block one's under-standing of this music. For one must not overlook the somewhat crotchety humour in his improvising and his compositions alike, the subtle emotion that distinguishes his interpretations of Ellington ballads, and the earthy strength — optimistic, not destructive — of his blues improvisations.

Archie Shepp was born in Fort Lauderdale, Florida, in 1937. He was introduced to music by his father, who earned a living playing the banjo in various local Dixieland groups. In 1944, the family moved to Philadelphia, and there, at the age of fifteen, Shepp began playing the tenor. Very soon he came into contact with the young hard bop musicians of Philadelphia, among them trumpeter Lee Morgan, who was then fourteen. While still in school, Shepp and Morgan played occasional jobs with a rhythm-and-blues band named "Carl Rogers and His Jolly Stompers"[1].

In 1959, after finishing his studies in literature and dramatics at Goddard College in Vermont, Shepp went to New York. There, playing badly paid jobs in Greenwich Village cafes, he had what was probably the decisive encounter for his further musical career. Through bassist Buell Neidlinger he met Cecil Taylor and joined his group. With Taylor, he played the stage music to Jack Gelber's "Connection" for several months, and took part in his first recording, *The World of Cecil Taylor,* in October 1960. In Philadelphia, Shepp had learned from Lee Morgan how to play changes, that is, to break

---

1) LeRoi Jones (1965) correctly points out that rhythm-and-blues bands came to be of increasing importance for many young musicians of the newer jazz styles. R+B jobs not only kept musicians like Coltrane, Coleman, Shepp and others financially above water, but gave them a firm blues foun-dation at the same time.

up chords and draw significant melodic phrases from functional chord progressions. Taylor now showed him a new frame of reference that went beyond functional harmony, with tonal centres and melodic-rhythmic patterns playing a predominant role. The two recordings Shepp made with Cecil Taylor (*Into the Hot* followed in October 1961) show him still very much under the influence of John Coltrane, whose playing — according to Shepp himself — was the first big source of inspiration for his own stylistic development (Jones 1965). Like Coltrane then, Shepp played arpeggiated chords; in combination with the harmonic groundwork provided by Taylor, however, they have a completely different effect than the arpeggios in Coltrane's pieces like *Giant Steps* or *Count Down*. But it is also evident as early as the modal piece *Lazy Afternoon,* recorded in 1960, that Shepp's strength lies not so much in melodic linearity as envisioned by Coltrane, but rather in shaping short, compressed phrases which — consciously or unconsciously — seem more inspired by Sonny Rollins's motivic variation of brief musical ideas than by Coltrane's evolution of broad melodic spans.

Although Shepp may not yet have found an individual musical idiom in the early Sixties, some technical and expressive features can be heard — especially in the records made during the second session with Cecil Taylor — which later became unmistakable characteristics of his improvisation. In his solos on *Bulbs* and *Mixed,* Shepp plays with the kind of hard-edged tone that a few years earlier had led musicians like Coltrane and Rollins to be tagged "hard tenorists." But Shepp also reminds one of the extroverted swing saxophonists of the Thirties, with a wide vibrato and a full — and slightly breathy — tone, a sound in which growl and shout effects do not appear extraneous, but rather serve to heighten emotion in a quite natural way.

What is especially conspicuous is Shepp's way of attacking (or rather punching) a tone. As we know, there is in jazz hardly any legato in the European sense. As a matter of principle there is a percussive element in jazz tone production, even in the wind instruments; usually, almost every tone is tongued[2] but without necessarily being played staccato. Shepp carries this phenomenon even further. Rather than just casually tonguing notes, he blurts them out, presumably controlling them with the palate. This produces a kind of staccato that is much more dynamically differentiated and flexible than the normal wind staccato familiar to us from European instrumental playing, or as used (with modifications) by the saxophone players of the late Twenties. There is in fact no term to denote Shepp's articulation, unless we are prepared to take the apparently self-contradictory "staccatoed legato." Like most of the sound phenomena of jazz, this one eludes verbal definition; perhaps a graphic illustration can come closer (Example 41).

This manner of articulation seems to be important above all for Shepp's subsequent development. Later, not only is each individual tone produced that way, but "staccatoed

---

2) Schuller (1968, p. 8) attributes this phenomenon to the origins of jazz in African music, in which each musical utterance is determined primarily by the rhythm, particularly the percussion rhythm.

legato" also marks his phrasing as a whole, particularly in very fast tone sequences (*cf.* p. 117 f.). "Staccatoed legato," however, is but one side of the coin. From the start,

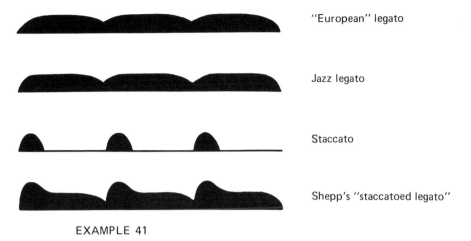

"European" legato

Jazz legato

Staccato

Shepp's "staccatoed legato"

EXAMPLE 41

there is another prominent feature of Shepp's playing that is the exact opposite, namely slurred tones, with whole sequences of tones glissandoed. In such slurs, definite and definable pitches are perceptible only at the beginning and end of a phrase. This phenomenon also calls to mind associations with older jazz traditions, when off-pitch playing was used consciously as a means of expression, and was thus one of the basic characteristics of jazz.

As mentioned, these attributes of Shepp's playing are present, as it were, in embryo in the Taylor recordings, and were not yet fully developed. Only in later years do they come into their own. For the time being, the impression is mainly that of a young musician searching out his way in a terrain that is as yet unfamiliar, taking as a guide his R+B experience plus perceptions gained from listening to Coltrane's music, and trying to measure up to what was presumably, at the time, the least immediately accessible direction of jazz. If Shepp's attempts to accommodate himself to Taylor's style sound somewhat uncertain at this point, it is perhaps understandable.

In 1962, Shepp left Cecil Taylor's group and formed his own quartet with trumpeter and composer Bill Dixon, who was later one of the founders of the "Jazz Composers Guild." Among the things the two had in common was the ambition to play a kind of music unburdened by traditional constraints and yet retaining to a great extent the essence of older jazz styles. Shepp also shared with Dixon the Marxist conception of the artist's function in society (Carles 1965). Jobs for the new group were few and far between, but Shepp and Dixon nevertheless somehow managed to record an LP for one of the few progressive companies, Savoy, in December 1962. That recording gives us some information on the musical conception of the group and on Archie Shepp's stylistic evolution.

In several ways the quartet recalls the early Ornette Coleman groups. First, there is no piano. Second, in the general compositional and formal frame of reference and even in certain details of Shepp's improvisations, there is not much difficulty recognizing Coleman as the model; indicatively, Coleman's composition *Peace* is in the Shepp-Dixon repertoire. Third, as with Coleman, the tunes act principally as emotional triggers and not as determinants of harmony and form. The players improvise on a tonal centre (*Peace* and *Quartet*), or on a relatively flexible modal groundwork *(Trio)*. In both cases a steady swinging beat is present at all times, with no recognizable symptoms of rhythmic dissociation. Shepp's solos have a greater amount of motivic connections than those in his recordings with Cecil Taylor. Again as in Coleman, they give progression of ideas to his improvisations, which otherwise frequently sound somewhat static. Possibly this emphasis on motivic work is directly traceable to the influence of Ornette Coleman[3]. But Shepp is more erratic. Motivic connections develop in his playing with less consistency and continuity than in Coleman's. Shepp's penchant for short, eruptive phrases leads him often to string together unrelated melodic fragments rather than cultivate coherent motivic chains, as Coleman did. In passages like the beginning of Shepp's improvisation in *Quartet* (Example 42), the melodic flow is broken into atoms. The rhythmically

EXAMPLE 42   QUARTET

accentuating twist of these staccatoed single tones, as well as their sound (which no notation can reproduce) and the dynamism with which Shepp intones them, are the things that predominate. It is in passages of this type that Shepp's articulation, which we have discussed above, is particularly effective.

---

3) Later, Shepp repeatedly spoke about the strong impression that Ornette Coleman's improvising made on him: "The early work of Ornette Coleman has been invaluable to me . . . " (Shepp, Impulse 9134).

On this Shepp-Dixon LP one striking interpretation stands apart from all the others: the rendition of a hit tune from Leonard Bernstein's "West Side Story." Actually, the fact that Shepp and Dixon took, of all things, *Somewhere* as a basis for improvisation is not at all surprising. (Many jazz greats have shown a special liking — at which some of their listeners have shaken their heads in disbelief — for rather hackneyed tunes. We need only recall Miles Davis's *Some Day My Prince Will Come,* Monk's *Just a Gigolo,* or Coleman's *Embraceable You.*) What *is* astounding is what Shepp and Dixon do with *Somewhere.* They play the tune nice and straight, without giving it the remotest semblance of a jazz piece by rhythmic recasting. The result is heightened banality, with a strong touch of irony. This underplayed humour becomes even more evident in Shepp's chorus. Sticking very closely to the thematic material in his improvisation, he adds occasional growl flourishes which take the mickey out of the tune, while at the same time confirming its insignificance.

The Shepp-Dixon Quartet lasted until 1963. That year Archie Shepp founded, with trumpeter Don Cherry and alto saxophonist John Tchicai, the *New York Contemporary Five* (NYCF), a group which despite its likewise short lease on life, has considerable historical significance. Forming a "steady" group in the economically disillusioning setting of New York free jazz took a large degree of idealism[4]. Over and above this, there was a social-psychological aspect that set the NYCF apart from the star-plus-sidemen ensembles of the time: its triumvirate of co-leaders. Far from being a purely theoretical structure, the democratic co-existence of three different temperaments (Cherry, Tchicai and Shepp) had a favourable effect on the group's musical variety.

Don Cherry, who had co-founded the Ornette Coleman Quartet, is musically the senior member of the NYCF. His playing is more relaxed and has more self-assurance than it does under Coleman. And especially Cherry's own contributions to the group's repertoire *(Sound Barrier* and *Consequences)* show a side of him that could never have become prominent under the composer Ornette Coleman.

John Tchicai is a Dane of African extraction. We have already met him in connection with Coltrane's *Ascension,* on which recording his highly developed melodic playing stands out from the other saxophonists' sound-blowing (*cf.* p. 90). Tchicai's role in the NYCF is obviously that of a stylistic counter-force to Archie Shepp. In contrast to Shepp's extrovert and rhetorical style of improvising, a cooler (not colder), spun-out linearity prevails in Tchicai. His tone is less round, his phrasing more fluid. That John Tchicai gives Charlie Parker and Lee Konitz as his first important models (Fox, Fontana 881013) is informative as to his own kind of playing.

Like the Shepp-Dixon Quartet, the NYCF takes the Ornette Coleman group of the late Fifties as the starting point for its own general musical conception. This means the

---

4) Significantly, the NYCF's most important records were made in Denmark.

negation of harmonic-metrical patterns. But it also means the retention of a steady, swinging basic rhythm and a quite conventional "theme-solo improvisation-theme" form. (Only rarely is there collective improvisation in the NYCF.) The absence of a piano, and the ensemble sound of the NYCF (high-register as a rule) evoke inevitable associations with the sharp-edged unison playing of the Coleman Quartet.

The real importance of the NYCF lay without question in the fact that as early as 1963 it assimilated various trends of new jazz and at the same time did not hesitate to reach back to older models. With a combination of these elements — and without sacrificing its own stylistic identity — it thereby laid the corner-stone of what might be called the *mainstream of free jazz.* The music of the NYCF may be eclectic in many respects, but it is eclectic in just as productive a way as the music of Charles Mingus was a few years earlier.

One of the most obvious signs of the group's variability is its repertoire. The thematic material written by Shepp, Cherry and Tchicai is carefully planned, and it is not treated merely as a peg on which to hang solo improvisations. The repertoire as a whole is, one might say, Janus-faced: one face looks back, the other forward toward a continuing development of knowledge gained from the jazz tradition. Besides the Lee Konitz title *Ezz-thetic* (surely brought in by John Tchicai), there are Ornette Coleman's *When Will the Blues Leave* and Monk's *Crepuscule With Nellie,* a piece which in its rhythmic-melodic contours is a "free-jazz composition," dating back to a time long before free jazz was even dreamed of. Apart from this non-member material, what is really interesting about the repertoire of the NYCF is the original compositions written for it by Shepp, Tchicai and Cherry. Here, as in the improvisations, the principal source of variety is the contrasting musical backgrounds of the three. Don Cherry's compositions are still very much in the vein of Ornette Coleman's hectic, angular lines. John Tchicai's *For Helved,* on the other hand, has a balanced, calmly flowing linear quality, which makes it sound like a cool-jazz theme projected into free jazz. The pieces furthest removed from traditional patterns are those by Archie Shepp. To be sure, he writes — among other things — tunes patterned on Coleman's lines, like *Rufus* for example, which the group recorded several times. But already in this composition there is a tendency away from the model of Coleman; *Rufus* does not really consist of lines, but — analogous to Shepp's own style of improvising — of discontinuous melodic fragments. Here, too, there is a conscious atomization of the phrase.

An entirely different aspect of compositional organization is present in Shepp's piece *Funeral,* a lament for the civil rights worker Medgar Evers, who was murdered in 1963. The emphasis here is on distinct, *cantabile* melody and a very subtly shaded play of tone colour. Sound-blowing, usually employed to intensify activity, serves — in the collectively improvised introduction by Shepp and Tchicai — to create finely differentiated layers of sound, which contrast with the broad melodic spans in the main part of the composition. With its restrained lyricism, this piece reveals a hitherto unknown side of Archie Shepp, one which later comes more into its own, especially in his ballad interpretations.

Two Shepp pieces recorded in January 1964 at the last session of the NYCF show that his compositional conception is by no means static. Like the features of his improvising, it follows a gradual evolution. The titles *Where Poppies Bloom* and *Like a Blessed Lamb* are marked by polyphonic voicings in the ensemble passages, by changes of tempo and rhythm, and by dynamic differentiation. Without being in any way imitative, they contain echoes of Ellington and Mingus, overlaid on one side by the tonally disoriented sound of the Cecil Taylor groups *(Into the Hot!)* and on the other, by a coarse folksiness, a quality also occasionally present in later Shepp compositions.

When the New York Contemporary Five broke up in the spring of 1964, John Coltrane arranged for Archie Shepp to make some records for Impulse. These proved to be a challenge to Shepp's talents as an arranger and composer. From then on he worked on two tracks. With his steady group, usually a quartet (his partners were first vibraphonist Bobby Hutcherson and later trombonist Roswell Rudd), Shepp did his day-to-day work, played club dates and occasional concerts. Kept small for reasons of economy, these groups concentrated on spontaneous, imrpovisatory creation. For his Impulse sessions, however, Shepp frequently used larger ensembles too, specially put together for studio work. Here Shepp the composer-arranger took over. To make the albums *Four for Trane, Fire Music* and *Mama Too Tight,* a number of Shepp's friends among New York musicians gathered in the studio: saxophonists Marion Brown and John Tchicai, trumpeters Ted Curson, Alan Shorter and Tommy Turrentime, trombonists Grachan Moncur III and Roswell Rudd, bassists Reggie Workman, Reggie Johnson and Charles Haden, and drummers Charles Moffet, Joe Chambers and Beaver Harris. Hand in hand with the variability of the ensembles in size and make-up went a steady increase in Shepp's compositional command and versatility.

The first LP of the series, *Four for Trane,* a musical bow to Shepp's great friend and well-wisher, is primarily a demonstration of Shepp's work as an arranger. As it happens, however, the four Coltrane themes chosen by Shepp *(Mr. Syms, Cousin Mary, Syeeda's Song Flute* and *Naima)* do not take very well to arrangement for a larger group. These tunes are basically simple, and to be really effective they need the forced tempo at which Coltrane plays them on the LP *Giant Steps.* Shepp slows them down and enriches them harmonically by thicker homophonic settings; thus they lose not only the driving intensity Coltrane gives them, but also their compelling simplicity. The best arrangement is perhaps Roswell Rudd's setting of *Naima;* in an Ellington-Mingus vein, the piece becomes a suite, changes of rhythm and tempo giving it a great variety of emotional content.

It is, of course, possible that in listening to these arrangements of Coltrane themes 'the memory of the original is too fresh, to the detriment of the new settings. The most thoroughly convincing piece on this LP is, significantly, Shepp's own *Rufus.*

Shepp's importance as a composer becomes evident in the albums *Fire Music* and *Mama Too Tight,* recorded in 1965/66. Both in their formal structure and execution, *Hambone, Los Olvidados, A Portrait of Robert Thompson* and *Basheer* go far beyond the conception developed by the NYCF. Although the compositional techniques vary from piece to piece (and sometimes within a piece), although each tune has its own specific expressive content, several principles of Shepp's style are common them all.

If the titles written in 1964 for the NYCF *(Blessed Lamb* and *Poppies)* were reminiscent of Ellington, Shepp's compositions now are still more so, but they have even stronger associations with Mingus. It is not so much that Shepp imitates melodic, rhythmic or compositional models; what he does adopt is a verbally indefinable general emotional attitude, as well as formal features connected with the structure of the pieces as a whole.

As in Mingus's music, Shepp's themes are no longer isolated from the improvisations. Solos and collective improvisations are fitted into a compositional superstructure that permits differentiation without disintegration. Almost without exception, Shepp's compositions for his studio groups are like suites in which various (and sometimes extremely heterogeneous) means of expression are opposed and intertwined. It often happens that collectively improvised, tonally free and extraordinarily agitated passages end in melodically balanced and modally constructed themes. Homophonic sections, with bass and drums accentuating the melody rhythm synchronously with the horns, crumble into discontinuous fragments. Abrupt tempo changes or continuous reduction of kinetic density lead to complete stagnation, out of which a new thematic entity arises.

From this enumeration of formal features, one might be justified in concluding that Archie Shepp's group conception and the desire for differentiation visible in it closely parallel the music of Cecil Taylor. But one soon comes across a fundamental difference: the heterogeneous *technical* means employed by Shepp are overlaid by a stratum of *historic-stylistic* materials. When Cecil Taylor uses similar methods to arrive at a synthesis of seemingly divergent musical means, he always remains himself. In Shepp's music, however, the frame of reference is transformed (frequently in the course of a single piece) by a reversion to one or another historical jazz style. In this respect, Archie Shepp is closer to Mingus than is any other free-jazz musician.

What Shepp gains in the way of retrospective stylistic elements is most conspicuous in the way he treats marches and blues, and in the riffs which, more or less forgotten since the swing era (except for a brief new lease on life in Mingus), are revived in *Hambone* and *Mama Too Tight,* and later, for example, in *Damn If I Know.* It does not come as a surprise to discover that Shepp's riffs are less easy to take, more angular and — true to his own nature — more scurrilous than those of the swing bands.

While riffs have the primary function in Shepp's group conception of stimulating the soloist (Shepp himself profits greatly from that sort of background), there are doubtless programmatic overtones to the marches and blues. In his notes to *Mama Too Tight* Shepp writes: "It was my intention to couple in this album, the poignance of the blues and the jubilant irreverence of a marching band returning from a funeral. It is my interpretation of a slave and neo-slave experience; rather like the feeling of being subjected to a 'haunt.'"

And in fact Shepp's marches, for all their surface gaiety, do have something haunted about them. They are neither slick and polished like the blues marches of the hard boppers, nor do they have the cantilena (alienated as it may be) of Ayler's marches. Shepp's marches are gay and malicious at once. They suddenly break into a calm ballad *(Prelude to a Kiss)* and go on to unravel in chaotic-sounding collective improvisations.

Along with the adoption and transformation of historical elements of jazz, Archie Shepp attempts to bring the music of the immediate present — whether it belongs to jazz or not — into the context of free jazz. One example is his use of rhythm-and-blues formulas and techniques, another is the mixture of his music with African (or Africanized) rhythms. Although both grow out of the same conscious emphasis on an Afro-American heritage, the results are anything but similar. R+B compositions like the title tune of *Mama Too Tight* (1966) or the rock waltz *Sorry 'bout That* (1967) usually have an unburdened gaiety that gets its special Sheppian humour by parodistic exaggeration of trite patterns.

The incorporation of African rhythms, on the other hand, which reaches its first peak in *Magic of Juju* (recorded in 1967), is definitely not meant parodistically, nor does it sound that way. What the five drummers — Beaver Harris, Norman Connor, Ed Blackwell, Frank Charles and Dennis Charles — play behind Shepp's long solo are not African rhythms in the authentic sense, for the laws of cross rhythms and polyrhythms on which African music is based are in fact very strict, and leave the individual participants much less freedom than is apparent to the casual Western listener. Presumably, Shepp's Afro-American drummers are not out to follow to the letter this (only seemingly paradoxical) mixture of stringent rhythmic discipline and propellant vitality. Still, they achieve in their own way one of the most essential ingredients of African music, namely a quasi-hypnotic state of tension. In this sense, *Magic of Juju* has more the nature of a ritual, to which the principle of *l'art pour l'art* cannot really be applied.

Shepp's composing, his formal organization and his choice of traditional material (the latter in large measure ideologically motivated) are all of considerable importance in understanding his music. But they represent, as we have said, just one side of it. The other is Shepp the improviser, who fills with life the formulas established by Shepp the composer. In its tendency to assimilate the most varied influences, his improvising in the early Sixties resembles his composing. But in the course of time, and perhaps precisely because of that assimilation process, a number of characteristic stylistic features evolved that make Shepp one of the most individual and original saxophonists in free jazz.

Shepp's development as an improviser can easily be followed by looking at the various small groups he led after the New York Contemporary Five broke up in 1965. His partner in the first of those groups was vibraphonist Bobby Hutcherson. Working with Hutcherson required of Shepp a certain adjustment to the tenuous sound of the vibraphone and thus some modification of his rather robust manner of playing. Compared to his solos on a groundwork of horn riffs in *Four for Trane* and *Fire Music,* Shepp's playing is a great deal more restrained, his tone production more subtle and his dynamic gradations more differentiated. The many collective improvisations profit from Shepp's adjustment to his surroundings. Since he holds back, the individual lines blend in a dense polyphonic web, without losing transparency. (The clarity of contours is all the more conspicuous when we remember that just four days before Archie Shepp and Bobby Hutcherson made their first recording at the Newport Festival, Shepp took part in John Coltrane's *Ascension,* which was guided by a completely different conception, the evolution of motivic relationships being consciously dispensed with in favour of block-shaped sound complexes.)

The Shepp-Hutcherson group recorded two titles in August 1968 which departed — each in its own way — from what people were accustomed to hear Shepp play. The pieces in question are Shepp's composition *On this Night* and Ellington's *In a Sentimental Mood.* In *On this Night,* Shepp finds himself in the vicinity of Euro-American contemporary music. Accompanied by Shepp at the piano, Christine Spencer, who is obviously "classically" trained, sings the setting of a political poem by Archie Shepp. The "song" leads to a freely improvised passage which ends in a slow 12-bar blues with a traditional flavour. The piece finishes with a repeat of the song, accompanied by floating harmonics played by Shepp on tenor.

There is little point in applying the yardstick of stylistic purity to music like this. Still, one cannot help thinking that a synthesis of diverse musical idioms is attempted which, in the final analysis, is not successful. In the vocal parts of the piece, jazz elements are mostly eliminated, if one discounts Shepp's unavoidably jazzy articulation in the last section. Even so, there is as little of 20th-century music in them as there is of jazz in Stravinsky's "L'histoire du soldat."

Opposed to the vocal sections is the blues as a non-integrated, separate and self-contained block. Shepp's attempt to bridge the two musical levels by a free improvised interlude à la Cecil Taylor is obviously not very effective. The synthesis proclaimed by Shepp (Hentoff, Impulse A 97) does not materialize. Instead, conflicting musical traditions are juxtaposed rather than — as in Cecil Taylor — fused into a new entity.

Archie Shepp presumably was well aware of the gap existing between European and Afro-American music. This attempt to combine the two had no further consequences in his recorded music at any rate.

At the same session with Bobby Hutcherson, Shepp played Ellington's *In a Sentimental Mood.* This was the first of a long series of highly individual ballad interpretations "in modo antico." The manner in which Shepp plays these "historic" ballads shows definite signs of stylistic regression. The spirit of the Thirties had always moulded Shepp's tone production. In the ballads he also conformed to the phrasing and timing of the grand old saxophonists of the swing era. Johnny Hodges's glissandos up to the highest registers of the instrument, the low, voluminous and very breathy "bent" tones of Ben Webster — all awaken to new life in Shepp's ballads.

Ellington's pieces (*Prelude to a Kiss* and *Sophisticated Lady* followed later) are obviously not treated by Shepp as thematic material to be recast as it were in his own image, which was the customary post-Parker way of doing things in modern jazz. Shepp does just the opposite. Influenced by the material, he modifies his own personal free-jazz idiom, but not to the extent of giving up its fundamental tone qualities. And that would seem to be the important point. He accepts harmonic models long considered obsolete, and slips into the straitjacket of metrical patterns. He plays lyrically (or if you will, romantically) in a manner that contrasts markedly with his "angry" image. There is no trace of the irony he had brought to bear, a few years earlier, on Bernstein's *Somewhere* and the bossa nova tune popularized by Brasilian vocalist Astrud Gilberto, *The Girl from Ipanema.*

It can, of course, be said that there is an indefinable something left over in Shepp's ballad interpretations once their debt to tradition is deducted, something not pre-fabricated by Hodges, Webster or Lucky Thompson, but "typically Shepp." But this cannot disguise the fact that since 1965 (at the latest) Shepp has spoken what are basically two musical languages whose grammar and syntax have hardly anything in common. The degree to which Shepp's ballads go counter to the stream of contemporary trends becomes clear when we recall that at about the same time, both Coleman and Coltrane were evolving models of ballad playing absolutely in keeping with the language of free jazz (*e. g.,* Coleman's *Sadness* and Coltrane's *Ogunde*).

The other members of Shepp's group have a strong influence on his own playing. This is apparent when we turn to his music after 1966. That year he reshuffled his group, bringing in two exceptionally extroverted musicians, trombonist Roswell Rudd and drummer Beaver Harris. Earlier, with Bobby Hutcherson, Shepp's style had taken on a certain restraint and balance. In the new group the predominant elements are vitality and energy.

Among New York free-jazz musicians, trombonist Roswell Rudd is rather an outsider, who owes his initial musical training neither to the hotbeds of experimentation in Greenwich Village cafes nor to a rhythm-and-blues band, the testing ground of many of his contemporaries. Rudd's musical forbears were the Dixieland musicians around Eddie Condon. With John Tchicai he evolved in 1964, within the short-lived New York Art Quartet, a group conception whose decisive factor was free collective improvisation, without any metrical or harmonic restrictions. In the same year, he took part in Shepp's recording *Four for Trane.*

Apart from Grachan Moncur III, who later often worked as second trombonist in Shepp's group, Roswell Rudd was one of the few trombone players who was then able to escape the overwhelming influence of the standard set by J. J. Johnson. The way in which Rudd transforms, with a tone that fairly crackles, the vitality of old jazz into a free-jazz idiom must have been of considerable inspiration for Archie Shepp, whose mind likewise runs on two stylistic tracks.

One of the most important and illuminating documents of this group's music is a live recording of a San Francisco club date in February 1966[5]. Playing with Shepp and Rudd are Beaver Harris and bassists Donald Garrett and Lewis Worrell. Like Rudd, the latter had been a member of the New York Art Quartet. This recording, made at the Bothland Club (and lasting more than an hour), reflects, on the one hand, the fundamental technical procedures of the group — repertoire, musical organization and execution — and, on the other hand, the various inward aspects of Archie Shepp's changing styles of improvisation. We hear one of those sardonic poems by Shepp *(The Wedding)* in which, with a dadaistic, disguised voice, he takes the rites and customs of the bourgeois wedding as his target. We hear one of his archaized ballad interpretations (again Ellington's *In a Sentimental Mood*), and a relaxed swinging piece on a constant, but curiously indeterminate, beat like Miles Davis's drummer Tony Williams used to play *(Wherever the June Bugs Go)*. And finally, we hear for the first time one of Shepp's "marathon" pieces *(Three for a Quarter — One for a Dime)*, to which jazz critics subsequently developed a pronounced allergy.

In the group with Hutcherson, collective improvisation had already had a substantial part. Now it moves even more into the foreground, for in Rudd, Shepp has a partner and opposite number whose intensity often provokes him into what can be called an eruptive way of playing. What is remarkable about the noisy dialogues between Shepp and Rudd is that they seem to come about planlessly when one of the two begins casually to join in the other's solo. As the dialogue continues, the "intruder" advances from a supporting player to an equal partner, until he retires and leaves the field again to the soloist.

The transformation that takes place in Shepp's improvisation during his collaboration with Rudd is marked by two very different (actually antagonistic) features. One is an increasing *melodic continuity;* the other is a renunciation of just that continuity, in favour of *kinetic clusters* that are sharply set off from one another. The first feature is the outcome of a gradual process. In the quartet with Bill Dixon and in the NYCF, one of Shepp's most obvious improvisational traits was the negation of melodic phrases, or the splintering of lines into tiny particles that were "shouted" (Example 42). In the recordings of his studio groups *(Fire Music, Four for Trane)* and even more in the quartet with Hutcherson, there was already a tendency to create longer units and to develop a certain melodic flow. This becomes stronger in the group with Rudd, and is especially apparent when Shepp plays at a medium-fast tempo. Example 43 is the beginning of his solo in *Wherever June Bugs Go.* His phrasing is more relaxed than ever before, and swings in the traditional sense of the word.

---

5) Issued on two LPs under the titles *Live in San Francisco* and *Three for a Quarter — One for a Dime.*

EXAMPLE 43   WHEREVER JUNE BUGS GO

Parallel to his reintroduction of melody and swing, Shepp evolves a second type of improvisation whose musical and affective qualities are utterly different. The most prominent ingredient of this playing, which can be considered as an alternative to Shepp's "melodic" style, is a string of "phrases" almost equal in length, intensity and kinetic density. These vehement bursts last one to two seconds at a constant fortissimo and break off abruptly. It is evident, however, that these "phrases" are no longer phrases in the traditional musical sense, for the elements comprising them do not form a melodic line, that is, a succession of distinct and perceptible pitches. There are two reasons for this: first, the extremely high speed (up to 15 units per second); second, Archie Shepp's "slurred" articulation. Together they make it all but impossible for the ear to distinguish individual melodic particles.

As described here, this may recall the "sheets of sound" John Coltrane developed in the last years of his life (*cf.* p. 99). The outward shape of these Sheppian "phrases," however, is completely different from Coltrane's. They are less plane-like, more compact, and — since they are almost all very brief — more stereotyped. To bring in another geometrical comparison, they are periodically recurring *sound-blocks* in which the impression of "sounds" is created not by playing multiphonics (as Coltrane or Sanders), but by an excess of internal kinetic density. Shepp uses these sound-blocks with relatively little regard for the kind of piece being played. They occur most often in fast, dynamic passages with free accentuation in the rhythm group, such as in *Three for a Quarter — One for a Dime* or *One for the Trane* (recorded in Donaueschingen). But they also turn up in *Magic of Juju*, a piece in the manner of African music, and in the introduction to the ballad *In a Sentimental Mood.*

Although individual elements of tone successions, when they cannot be perceived as such, have no musical significance, it is still interesting to discover what happens *inside* Shepp's sound-blocks. With a transcription, we can put them under a microscope. This can be done only by employing several technical tools, and can be only approximately accurate, especially as regards the rhythmic values[6]. In Example 44a, we reproduce four of a total of 61 successive sound-blocks from the introduction to *In a Sentimental Mood*. (They are "blocks" 15-18 and were chosen at random.) For further clarification, the time-intensity diagrams of the transcribed sound-blocks are given in Example 44b, recorded with the help of a level writer.

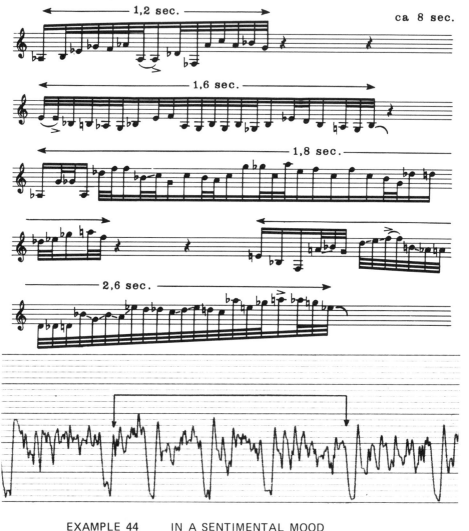

EXAMPLE 44   IN A SENTIMENTAL MOOD

6) Using a frequency counter and the so-called tempophone, the fundamental frequency of each and every tone was measured, with the tape stopped and the tone-head rotating.

The example shows that Shepp starts, as a rule, from strongly accentuated "anchor tones," which recur frequently during the improvisation. In the present case, those tones are A flat in the first and third sound-block, and E in the second and fourth. (A whole series of other passages in the introduction begin with the same tones.) A variant of the anchor *tones* in *Sentimental Mood* are the anchor *phrases* Shepp uses elsewhere. As a point of reference and a trigger for his sound-blocks, he plays a short riff motive (often just three or four notes) in the lowest register, thus achieving a kind of call-and-response pattern.

Variation in the sound-blocks is attained, not by altering their interval structure but in external contours, as shown in the direction the blocks take and the register in which they occur. The first block in our example undulates between the low and middle registers. The second moves exclusively in the low register, while the third jumps from low register to high, etc. Naturally, variation of this kind is soon exhausted, and the listener, who does not analyze but only perceives what can be perceived, might arrive at the conclusion that when Shepp improvises in this way, everything that happens is the same. Accordingly, the rock critic Alan Heinemann may be justified when he writes in *Down Beat* of *Three for a Quarter* (1969) that one can place the needle anywhere one likes, since there is never any difference. From *his* point of view, that may indeed be the case. The constant repetition of musical structures which have the same effect, leads without question to a high degree of predictability. The question is, however, whether predictability, which in the final analysis is the result of an intellectual process in the listener, is really an adequate standard of valuation here. The way Shepp plays his sound improvisations, visually accentuating each block by energetic rotating movements of his body, would seem to indicate that the point is expression and the conveyance of an emotionality raised to the "n^{th} degree," rather than the presentation of meaningful music for intellectual gratification. The reciprocal effect of a visual dynamism and musical energy gives a total impression of enormous intensity, which is not weakened but strengthened by the repetition of particles identical in effect. In the end, whether the listener is bored because — like the critic quoted above — he "always hears the same thing," or whether the psychic element of ecstasy immanent in Shepp's sound-blocks gets across to him, will mostly depend on what he wants, is accustomed to hearing, and on his readiness to go along emotionally.

The problematic nature of Shepp's sound-blocks can be taken as symptomatic of free jazz as a whole. After 1966 they are for Shepp a very important source of expression, but certainly not the only one[7]. In a way, they represent an opposite pole to his melody-conscious, swinging style (illustrated in Example 43), as well as to his "modo antico" ballad interpretations. Just as there are many strata in his compositional conception, divergent formative principles also evolve in Shepp's improvising; signifying various levels of consciousness, they demand to be heard in various ways.

---

7) In the review mentioned above, Heinemann calls Shepp "Johnny-one-mood," which says rather more against that critic's powers of discernment than against Shepp.

During the time Shepp played with Roswell Rudd, a certain consistency of conception established itself in his music. But his development at the end of the Sixties and the beginning of the Seventies is marked first and foremost by constant moves between old and new forms, between rhythm-and-blues and Africanisms, free jazz and Ellington. In the process, Shepp very often joins forces with musicians of the most diverse stylistic origins, and occasionally, it must be said, of uneven musical ability. The lists of players on the recordings he has made since 1968 suggest that the stylistic field of jazz his fellow musicians call home is relatively insignificant for him. He plays with hard bop veterans, with young avantgardists from the Chicago free-jazz circle, and with neo-blues musicians. Since there has always been great variability in Shepp's improvisation, it has been easy for him to adjust to all these changing groups and styles without giving up his own identity. Nevertheless, many of his recordings around 1970 give rise — for all their good qualities— to a nagging feeling that the increasing timelessness of his music is now accompanied by a certain aimlessness. Motivated by the idea of opening up the whole broad spectrum of Afro-American music for himself and his listeners, Shepp often gets bogged down in externals. No longer does he experiment with the various modes of expression, with a view to transforming and fusing them with one another. Instead, he takes existing models and places them side by side in their pure form, without making any attempt at a synthesis. Perhaps, however, this only seems to be caused by aimlessness and stagnation; it may very well result from Shepp's conviction that his duty as a musician must go beyond creative self-realization. If one accepts his statement that he finds comic strips valuable because ghetto children learn to read from them (Impulse 9134), then one will have a notion as to why Shepp plays rock compositions that are as far removed from contemporary jazz as Mickey Mouse is from James Joyce.

Chapter 7

ALBERT AYLER

"Never try to figure out what happens, because you would never get the true message"
(from Kofsky, Impulse 9165).

Albert Ayler's warning against trying to understand his music fits in very nicely indeed with much of what has been said and written about it. It would seem that the extraordinarily brusque way in which Ayler turned his back on the conventions of traditional jazz, plus what he himself has said and written about his music, closed the ears of his critics, friendly and hostile alike, to the musical facts. This is probably the best explanation of why reviews of Ayler's music deal with what it is all supposed to *mean,* and spend little time on telling what actually happened. With no other free-jazz musician (except perhaps Archie Shepp) have veritable mountains of philosophy and polemics been erected between the music and the listener, shutting out a view of the musically relevant factors. LeRoi Jones's unconditional apologetics, their argumentation deeply dyed by ideology, are just as much a peak of that mountain chain as are the thoughtless attacks by critics like Harvey Siders (1966), whose so-called criticism is interlaced with zoological references and crude insults. The split of jazz criticism into all-pro and all-contra, first evident in free jazz in connection with Ornette Coleman at the end of the Fifties, continued with still greater intensity in the mid-Sixties, with Albert Ayler's music as the object of the exercise. The schism in the ranks of professional observers caused by Ayler's music was not entirely a mischance, however. In many respects, that schism is in the music itself. "J'étais déchiré, tordu, j'avais mal — mal! et je jure que j'avais envie de grincer des dents mais j'étais en même temps envahi par un plaisir immense" (Gerber 1966 a). These are not the words of a schizophrenic, but of a serious jazz critic, and were written to describe his first confrontation with Ayler's *Ghosts.* A dualism of horror and euphoria like this is by no means *only* the listener's subjective reaction to his experience; as I will try to show, it is immanently present in Ayler's music.

Albert Ayler was born in Cleveland, Ohio, in 1936. Taught by his father, he began to play the alto at the age of seven. At sixteen, after a short period of study at the Cleveland Academy of Music, he became a professional musician, working in a blues group led by the harmonica player Little Walter. During Ayler's army service, part of which he spent in France, he changed to tenor. While stationed in France (1959-61) he occasionally played in Paris jazz clubs and visited Scandinavia where, not long after, he made his first recording.

Back in the USA, Ayler worked off and on with Cecil Taylor, joined the "Jazz Composers Guild" for a short time, and founded his first steady group in 1964 with bassist

Garry Peacock and drummer Sunny Murray, who had made a name for himself as a member of Taylor's group. With this trio, he made some of his most important records that same year, and went on a Scandinavian tour. During succeeding years, he played with his younger brother, trumpeter Donald Ayler, and various rhythm sections.

On November 25, 1970, Albert Ayler's body was pulled from New York City's East River. It was assumed that he committed suicide. But nobody knows.

Albert Ayler had less than ten years to mature as a musician. During that time roughly a dozen recordings of his music were issued. They form a curiously symmetrical arch of musical evolution, whose highest point — and turning point — was reached in 1964/65.

At the beginning are the recordings produced in 1962/63 in Scandinavia, marked by an unbridgeable gulf between the orthodox playing of the rhythm sections and Ayler's vision of a kind of music independent of traditional ties. Separating Ayler's part in these recordings from the total context (which is not easy), we can observe the beginnings of what later crystallized into several features of his personal style. His approach to intonation, the distorted paraphrases of melodic lines, and above all his highly individual vibrato-laden sound are first formed in these recordings. At the same time, however, we still hear a pronounced orientation toward hard bop models. This is expressed primarily by a curiously alienated way of using clichés such as we were accustomed to since the Fifties in the groups of Horace Silver, Art Blakey and others (especially conspicuous in Ayler's rendition of the blues *Billie's Bounce*). The main reason these stock phrases sound odd is that they are not integrated into the larger structure of Ayler's solos, but are inserted into his improvisations like quotations from another context. In *Billie's Bounce,* for example, each 12-bar chorus begins with melodic (or "etudesque") figures, like that in Example 45. These then abruptly change to fragmentary flourishes, which are placed against the harmonic foundation.

♩ = 210

EXAMPLE 45   BILLIE'S BOUNCE

The majority of the tunes on Ayler's early Scandinavian records are standards: *I'll Remember April, Softly As in a Morning Sunrise, Bye-bye Blackbird, Summertime,* etc. Ayler's way of deforming those tradition-ridden tunes, however, is so patently at cross purposes with the framework provided by his Swedish and Danish accompanists that the total result frequently sounds absurd. These recordings demonstrate that constituent parts of a musical whole can neither be exchanged nor isolated from one another. As it happens, what Ayler plays cannot, except in a few instances, be called free jazz (as the title of a later edition of the record — originally called *My Name is Albert Ayler* — rather irresponsibly claims). Ayler neither escapes the formal implications of the thematic material, nor is he able to consistently avoid the routine functional harmonic progressions served up with relentless regularity by his Scandinavian rhythm sections. Since he cannot relax the rigidity of the traditional framework, Ayler clearly tries to detach himself from it as much as possible. His most obvious method of accomplishing this is to deform the melodic line. He goes about it in a different way from Ornette Coleman, for instance, who a few years earlier had begun to deviate more or less casually from fixed interval sizes, later using those deviations consciously as a means of expression at exposed points in his improvisations. Ayler's approach is more direct: from the outset he made a principle of negating tempered pitch. Themes like *Bye-bye Blackbird* and *Green Dolphin Street* are retained only in outline, losing the clarity of the pitch relationships. A collision with the harmonic framework is inevitable. And especially when a comping pianist is playing a background of chords (as on *My Name is Albert Ayler*), the group's music often sounds hopelessly out of tune.

Not all the pieces on these records show the same discrepancy between the playing of Ayler and his rhythm sections that is present in the standards. The well-worn paths of traditional forms are deserted in *Free* (on *The First Recordings*) and *C. T.* (on *My Name*). Conventional frameworks are replaced by improvisations free of thematic, formal, rhythmic and harmonic constraints. And although the Scandinavian players are audibly unfamiliar with a musical terrain of this sort, these titles achieve the kind of inner balance that is lacking in the performances of the standards. Example 46 is an excerpt from Ayler's improvisation in *C. T.;* in certain particulars it is typical of these recordings. Here Ayler's playing is marked, on the one hand, by a pronounced discontinuity of phrasing (segments A), a result of (1) short flourishes, (2) single staccato tones, and (3) wide leaps. (Passages like this occasionally recall Archie Shepp's improvisations with the Shepp-Dixon Quartet; *cf.* p. 107). On the other hand, Ayler slurs succeeding tones to form continuous spans, with accents placed by growled "bent" tones (segment B).

EXAMPLE 46   C. T.

All in all, Ayler's improvisations here seem somewhat more integrated into the total context; the lines and rhythms in the saxophone, bass and drums dovetail, supplement and influence one another. Although there are moments of stagnation in these pieces, when none of the musicians seems to know quite how to keep things going, and though they hardly approach the communicative intensity of Ayler's later trio recordings, they do unmistakably point ahead to what was to come.

The year 1964 in New York, following Ayler's Scandinavian trips, was one of his most productive, not only as to the number of records he made, but above all as regards their content. At the same time as the young guard of free jazz — Archie Shepp, John Tchicai, Marion Brown and others — was primarily concerned with finding its own identity in terms of the standards established by the founding fathers, Albert Ayler achieved the most radical (and probably the most shocking) renunciation of the conventions of jazz — and in a certain way of the nascent conventions of free jazz.

It is evident from the four records issued in 1964 that what Ayler was then playing was not merely a continuation or further evolution of what Coleman had introduced in the late Fifties. It is something entirely different[1]. The ever greater degree of freedom in improvising is not what actually makes Ayler's music unique. The source of that difference is the coupling of radicality with a regression to the simplest musical forms. A description of Ayler's music, then, inevitably ends in "on the one hand" and "on the other hand."

On the one hand, Ayler continues the melodic deformation first noticeable in the Scandinavian recordings of 1962/63, playing what could be called waves of overblown tones that have no definite pitch, but appear as contours or *sound-spans.* On the other hand, his music — especially its themes — is replete with melodiousness, an occasionally weird mixture of folksong cheerfulness and pathos.

On the one hand, Ayler's tenor sound in the low register is rough, with the brutal staccato harshness of a rhythm-and-blues player. On the other hand he tends to play in the upper register a relatively thin, alto-like sound, with a mawkish touch added by an extremely wide, fast vibrato.

On the one hand, his music lacks transparency, is hectic and void of relationships. On the other hand it has a transparency and simplicity that make even Ornette Coleman's "simplest" melodic phrases seem complicated.

One of the paradoxes of Albert Ayler's improvisation is that for all its unconventionality, it is not infrequently *motivic.* But Ayler's motivic improvisation is fundamentally dif-

---

1) As a curiosity we mention that Frank Kofsky reduces Ayler's playing to the following formula: "Ayler = 50 percent Coltrane + 20 percent Coleman + 30 percent X, X representing Ayler's own share" (Kofsky 1970, p. 178). How nice it would be if everything were that simple.

ferent from what we are accustomed to in Rollins, for instance, or later in Coleman. Ayler does not extract individual motives from the tune and work them out (like Rollins), nor does he connect a number of organically evolving motivic chains (like Coleman). His method is to paraphrase whole themes by "quoting" them note for note, distorting them by shifting or transposing the individual pitches, so that the original can be recognized only from the general outline. An especially striking example of this method is the version of *Ghosts* (one of many) which Ayler recorded with Don Cherry, Garry Peacock and Sunny Murray in September 1964 during a stay in Copenhagen. The theme of this piece consists mainly of a series of variants on one and the same model (which sounds as though it could have come straight from a folksong). Ayler's improvisation begins with a deformation of one of those variants. As Example 47 shows, he retains first and foremost the period structure of the theme and remains in the vicinity of the harmonic basis. The large leaps and the overt simplification of the melody rhythm make this kind of improvisatory elaboration seem not like a variation but like a deliberate caricature of the given material.

EXAMPLE 47   GHOSTS

This is without question an extreme example of Ayler's improvisation. It does not often happen that he stays that close to the thematic model. More frequently he improvises a-melodically in sound-spans, but those sound-spans also follow the period structure of the given theme (or another theme). This procedure hardly permits a verbal description; nor can it be illustrated by the usual methods of transcription, since Ayler's negation of fixed pitches makes impossible a direct (notatable) coordination of sound-spans and thematic structure. If, however, one listens to pieces like *The Wizzard, Spirits* or *Ghosts* (all on *Spiritual Unity*) repeatedly and with unwavering attention, one will almost necessarily arrive at the conclusion that in the seemingly total irregularity of Ayler's improvisations, there does exist an inner connection with the simple period construction of his themes. This becomes manifest above all in the contours, the direction and duration of the sound-spans.

48 Sek.

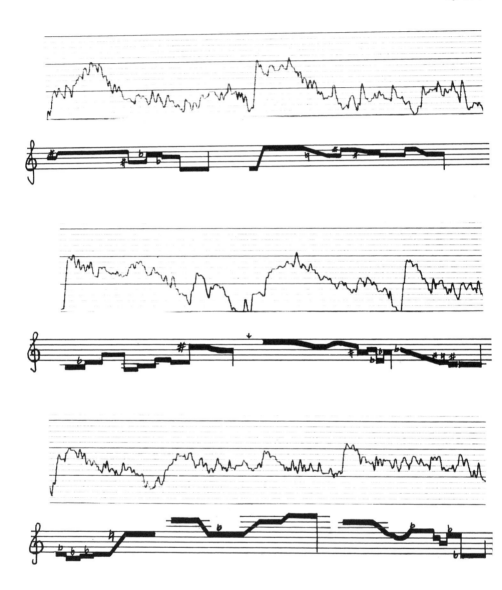

EXAMPLE 48   WITCHES AND DEVILS

One of Ayler's characteristic formative means is a high degree of dynamic differentiation, hardly to be found anywhere else in jazz in quite the same form. Ayler begins phrases (or sound-spans) fortissimo and then lets them subside gradually to pianissimo, until they end in whispered tones that are barely audible. (Much of Ayler's pathos, incidentally, issues from these gliding dynamics.) Example 48 is a short passage from his improvisation on *Witches and Devils,* together with an electro-acoustic registration of the levels, illustrating Ayler's dynamic differentiation.

(Certain inaccuracies of the level-writer registration must be allowed for; these arise because the machine records not only the dynamic curve of the saxophone sound, but also of the group sound. However, since Ayler dominates very strongly in this section, the intensities produced by the other instruments enter the picture only during Ayler's rests, that is, between his phrases.) This example, too, shows a distinct periodicity of phrasing, which in addition is distantly reminiscent of the call-and-response patterns of early jazz.

As has already been intimated, Albert Ayler's *themes* are a category of free-jazz composition all their own. Their most prominent feature is their simplicity. But unlike the music of Coleman, for example, it is not the simplicity of Black blues, but of an imaginary genre of folksongs, or folk dances, whose expression seems more Euro-American than Afro-American. And whereas Ornette Coleman, however simply he may write, always gives his "folksong" structures a surprising twist (*i. e.,* "alienates" them in one way or another), the folk character of Albert Ayler's themes is never impaired. Ayler himself says about these pieces: "I'd like to play something — like the beginning of *Ghosts* — that people can hum. And I want to play songs that I used to sing when I was real small. Folk melodies that all people would understand" (from Hentoff 1966). In another place he states: "We play folk from all over the world . . . Like very, very old tunes, you know, before I was even born, just come in my mind" (from Kofsky, Impulse 9165). This conscious archaizing of thematic material is musically reflected in Ayler's choice of the most elementary melodic, harmonic and rhythmic forms. In general, Ayler's melodies are strictly diatonic and are frequently triadic. Their rhythm is simple and by and large confirms (or helps establish) the metre, while their harmonic groundwork is limited to cadential patterns like I-IV-V-I.

Viewed as a whole, Ayler's 1964 recordings concentrate on three contrasting types of thematic material, to which a few others are later added. By far the greatest emphasis is placed on folk themes such as already mentioned. The model piece is *Ghosts.* Not only did Ayler record at least five different versions; it also appears like a leading motive in his improvisations on other pieces. (It turns up repeatedly in *Holy Holy,* for example, which was recorded in February 1964, before the first version of *Ghosts* appeared on record.)

The second type of thematic material is Ayler's ballads. These are sustained melodies played in a free tempo, and in many respects they can be regarded as forerunners of

127

Coltrane's post-1964 "rubato ballads." Unlike Ayler's folk themes, which usually have a dance-like gaiety, his ballads are charged with a considerable amount of pathos, often dangerously close to pomposity. A drastic example of this type is *Mothers*. Its sentimentality is due not only to the banality of the melody, but even more so to Ayler's elegiac phrasing and tone production.

The third type of Ayler composition (and relatively neutral in emotion) is shown in themes like *Holy Holy* and *The Wizzard,* which consist primarily of riff-like motives of great kinetic density.

The conflict into which the listener is plunged by Ayler's themes is created not so much by the themes themselves, but by the tension between the themes and the improvisations. In the themes, a reversion to archaic patterns leads to a maximum of predictability, so that ultimately "people can hum." In the improvisations, however, *that* kind of predictability at least is made absolutely impossible, due to the complete renunciation of conventions.

Although Albert Ayler is in the musical limelight on most of the records he made in 1964, the musicians he played with have a great deal of importance in terms of the musical sum total. They included trumpeters Norman Howard (on *Spirits*) and Don Cherry (on *Ghosts*); but their contribution is less decisive than that of Garry Peacock on bass and Sunny Murray on drums. Ayler's negation of fixed pitches finds a counterpart in Peacock's and Murray's negation of the beat. In no group at this time is so little heard of a steady beat, as in the trio and quartet recordings of the Ayler group. The absolute rhythmic freedom frequently leads to action on three independent rhythmic planes: Ayler improvises in long drawn-out sound-spans; Peacock hints at chains of impulses, irregular and yet swinging in a remote sense; Murray plays on cymbals with a very live resonance, creating colour rather than accentuation. Moreover, as can be heard on the second version of *Ghosts* (with Don Cherry), Sunny Murray has the nerve to suddenly stop, leaving the rhythmic progress to Peacock. This is remarkable when one recalls that drummers of this time usually seemed to be under a non-stop compulsion to drum. By sitting out, Murray proves that the emancipation of jazz percussion is not necessarily achieved by more action, but can just as well be attained by less.

Of the records Ayler made during 1964, the LP *New York Eye and Ear Control*[2],made on July 17, is a distinct exception. Why this record has attracted hardly any attention in jazz literature is difficult to imagine, for it is probably the most important link between the epoch-making collective improvisation *Free Jazz* by the Ornette Coleman double quartet, and John Coltrane's *Ascension*. Apart from that, it is — in my opinion — one of Ayler's very best recordings.

---

2) Originally recorded as film music for the film of the same name by the director Michael Snow.

New York Eye and Ear Control owes a large part of its success to the contrasting temperaments of the three musicians used by Albert Ayler in addition to his trio, namely, trumpeter Don Cherry, trombonist Roswell Rudd and alto saxophonist John Tchicai. Don Cherry improvises in broad melodic lines or places sharply accented staccato passages. Roswell Rudd interposes fragmentary flourishes in the highest register, or growl sounds and glissandos in the manner of the old tailgate trombonists. John Tchicai presents the polarity of a slightly "cool," linear style and offers motivic linkage by insistently repeating melodic patterns. All three inspire Albert Ayler to a breadth of expression which is too often missing in his improvisations with smaller groups. There is less limitation to his sound-span playing, more contrast, more punch and rhythmic accentuation, and with quick response Ayler takes motives from Cherry, Rudd and Tchicai, transforms them into his own musical idiom, and in turn gives a new direction to the flow of ideas.

Solo excursions play a secondary role on this LP. Only the first piece, a few minutes long, puts Don Cherry in the spotlight *(Don's Dawn)*. He plays a sustained, "peaceful" melody that may have had a programmatic purpose, *i. e.,* something to do with the film. The other two pieces, *Ay* and *Itt,* consist in the main of long collective improvisations. The single solos between them (usually very short) are merely transitional phases, which as a rule provide the motivic impulse for the next collective. Except for a short riff theme (identical to *Holy Holy*) played by Albert Ayler as the motivic trigger for *Itt,* the pieces are a-thematic and their form is obviously not planned in advance. The extraordinarily intensive give-and-take by the musicians themselves therefore becomes the only "control mechanism" governing the form. This may recall Coleman's *Free Jazz.* But its consequences go much further. In *Free Jazz*, despite a wealth of motivic variety, there is throughout a notable uniformity of kinetic density, rhythm, dynamics and consequently of emotional content. Unlike *Free Jazz*, there is a breadth of variation and differentiation on all musical levels in *Ay* and *Itt* that was attained earlier (if under different circumstances) in the suites of Charles Mingus, and after that in the "collective compositions" of Cecil Taylor.

There are many varieties of spontaneous structural differentiation in *Ay* and *Itt,* and they frequently overlap. In substance, they arise from motivic interaction. Each player in turn takes the initiative in breaking out of an incipient status quo in order to introduce a new, contrasting structural unit. Pulsing, hectic passages lead to slow lamenting sections threaded with glissandos. Staccato notes played independently of the rhythm by Cherry are imitated by the other horns to form a pointillistic network. Atonal passages governed by Ayler's sound-spans are pinned to a tonal centre by scale fragments and riff-like ostinatos from Tchicai. The players improvise on several emotional planes at once, finally coming together on a single plane, calm or agitated. Peacock and Murray add to this a constantly changing rhythmic groundwork that stretches from driving chains of impulses, via disintegrating a-rhythmic single accents, to a complete standstill.

Changes in the Ayler group in 1965/66 initially had only a slight influence on Albert Ayler's own playing, but they did affect the musical sum total in many ways. Drummer

Beaver Harris, who replaced Sunny Murray at the end of 1966, is an alumnus of the Archie Shepp circle. Harris's sound is less differentiated than Murray's, but his rhythm is more aggressive, and this was of great benefit to the Ayler group. Furthermore, Harris plays "lower-pitched" percussion than Sunny Murray, that is, he uses the drums and tom-toms more than the cymbals for accentuation. Murray tended to emphasize the prevailing "high-register" group sound with lots of cymbal; Harris gives that sound a contrasting level, or rather a foundation. This is even more the case with Milford Graves, who worked occasionally with the group in 1967.

Trumpeter Donald Ayler, who joined the group in the spring of 1965, adapts to his brother's "sound-span" improvising, but he does it in an undifferentiated and stereotyped way. Playing mostly in the middle register, with an exceptionally loud and sometimes bawling tone, he strings together extremely fast chromatic or diatonic runs to form phrases whose length seems to depend on his breath supply, and whose structure hardly ever varies. To the degree that he does away with the old clichés of trumpet playing in this manner, he establishes new clichés that are even more predictable than those from which he is trying to escape.

With the addition of Donald Ayler to the group, there is a distinct shift of emphasis toward ensemble playing. This, however, is not expressed in extensive collective improvisation but in an expansion of thematic material. It may be that the growth of that part of Ayler's music "that people can hum," contributed to the gradual growth of the group's popularity at this time. But hand in hand with it went an increasing triteness; this was the start of a decline that reached bottom with the records Ayler made for Impulse in the late Sixties.

Ayler's 1964 recordings conveyed the impression that the primary significance of his thematic material was in providing a relatively noncommittal frame for improvisations that starkly contrasted with it. With the September 1965 recording of *Spirits Rejoice* (if not before), one is forced to conclude that the thematic sector now occupies a rank at least equal (in quantity) to the improvisation sector. *Spirits Rejoice* starts with a march potpourri lasting four minutes, in which the same motives are repeated over and over. After this, Albert Ayler's one-minute solo sounds like a brief intermezzo that hurriedly returns to the signal motives of the march. "Marching songs" like *Spirits Rejoice, Truth is Marching In* or *Change has Come* seem to be even more European in their expressive content than the thematic material Ayler used for his 1964 recordings. However tenuous the distinction between "black" and "white" elements in jazz may seem, in connection with Ayler's music such a distinction forces itself on one again and again. Worn-out phrases like those in Example 49 evoke associations with the music of central European firemen's bands and not with the march music of New Orleans street-bands. Unlike their treatment in the marches of Archie Shepp, the formulas Ayler takes over from traditional military music are not integrated into an idiom consonant with the rest of the musical context, but stand isolated from it.

130

EXAMPLE 49   THE TRUTH IS MARCHING IN

The group's music acquired a further — and completely different — Occidental stylistic ingredient when Albert Ayler began working with cellist Joel Friedman and later with Belgian violinist Michel Simpson and harpsichordist Cal Cobbs. The polarity of march music and free-jazz improvisation became a triangle, with the addition of an element grounded in contemporary European music (with a throwback to Baroque pomp in Cal Cobbs's rolling harpsichord arpeggios). Here too, a synthesis of divergent musical idioms is mostly noticeable through its absence.

As regards Albert Ayler's improvisation after 1965, its substance remains — as we have said — initially unaffected by the changing membership of his group and the march-inspired themes. Now as before, periodic, overblown sound-spans and discontinuous staccato passages of changing length and intensity predominate. But there are also signs that the stylistic dividing line between themes and improvisation has begun to fade. More and more frequently, Ayler allows tonal phrases to creep into his solo improvisations, with broken triads playing a conspicuous role. One example of this is the excerpt from Ayler's ballad *For John Coltrane* (Example 50) in which he "improvises" for quite some time in a free tempo on a B flat major triad. As in his themes, regression to very simple formulas leads to an extreme *cantabile*; but here too, the border to banality is sometimes overstepped, because simplicity plus pathos is a dangerous mixture.

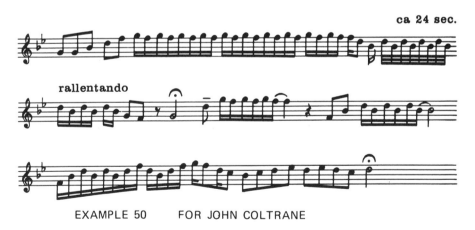

ca 24 sec.

rallentando

EXAMPLE 50   FOR JOHN COLTRANE

The spread of European influences in the music of Ayler's group, noticeable above all in the tunes and the instrumentation, came to a sudden halt in 1968/69 when Ayler turned to a genre on the borderline between jazz and urban Black folk music, *i. e.,* soul and rhythm-and-blues. In the introduction to the LP *New Grass* we hear Albert Ayler saying: "The music I have played in the past I know I have played in another place and a different time." *New Grass* and *Music is the Healing Force of the Universe* (recorded a year later) mark a turn to the simple structures, the stomping beat and the clichés of rhythm-and-blues, but also to the triviality and hardly bearable pomposity of pseudo-religious songs. There are moments on these records when Albert Ayler is greatly inspired by the rhythm-and-blues idiom he knew all too well from his Little Walter days. His lively tenor saxophone solo in *New Generation* (on *New Grass*) and his free bagpipe "duet" improvisations recorded by overdubbing in *Masonic Inborn* (on *Healing Force*), however, are isolated peaks in a plain of mediocrity.

It has frequently been pointed out that extra-musical factors were involved in both these records. Profit-minded producers bound Ayler to a kind of music that was easier for the broad public to understand[3]. Certainly, economic pressures, to which all jazz musicians are exposed under contracts to one of the larger record companies, may have played a role. But we should also bear in mind that Ayler's step in the direction of a medium more popular than free jazz may have been prompted by his desire to produce music that "people could hum."

The tragedy of Albert Ayler's musical evolution is that in trying to communicate with his listeners he wasted his strength on platitudes. He first replaced complexity by simplicity, and then simplicity by vacuity. In seeking to escape from the clichés he had himself created over the years, he reduced his musical language rather than expanded it.

---

3) *Cf. inter alia* "Un soir autour d'Ayler," a discussion by French critics and musicians published in *Jazz Magazine* 192 (September 1971) and 193 (October 1971). Bernhard Stollmann, for whose firm (ESP) Ayler made his first records in the USA, mentions that Ayler had to accept a clause in his contract with Impulse that obliged him to sing on his records (from Williams 1971).

Chapter 8

DON CHERRY

Trying to assign a musician to one or another stylistic region, school or tendency of jazz is often a futile pastime, for the boundaries erected between them for purposes of neat identification tend to be too inflexible. In the same way, the chronological point in the evolution of jazz at which historians place a musician is frequently little more than a crutch for rationalization. European musical history recognizes a distinction between early, middle and late periods in the work of a composer, which amounts to saying that a lifetime of creative work cannot be pinpointed by a single date or reduced to a decade. Even in the incomparably shorter history of jazz, there is evidence that the contents of carefully arranged "historical pigeonholes" need to be re-arranged after only a few years.

To speak of Don Cherry in connection with the "second generation" of free jazz may, from the viewpoint of the jazz historian, seem a chronological *faux pas*. Wasn't Cherry a member of the now legendary Ornette Coleman Quartet and thus one of the pioneers of free jazz? Wasn't he the very first jazz trumpeter to understand what improvising in a manner freed from traditional norms implied, and to act accordingly? This, of course, is true. And yet, one would probably misinterpret Cherry's function in the evolution of free jazz if one were to place him alongside innovators Ornette Coleman and Cecil Taylor. It was not Don Cherry who razed the barriers of the old formal and harmonic patterns at the end of the Fifties. He was around when it happened, but he was, one might say, more a conspirator than a ringleader. By this, I do not mean to diminish his stature (even if it sounds that way). The case of Don Cherry, like that of hardly any other free-jazz musician, shows that along with musical qualifications, socio-psychological factors and personality relationships within a group can influence the evolution of a musician and ultimately the effect he has on his musical surroundings. For years, Don Cherry was a trumpet player for somebody else: Ornette Coleman, Sonny Rollins, and — for a short time — Albert Ayler. Not until he took on the role of bandleader in the mid-Sixties (a quixotic venture in view of the then critical economic situation of free jazz) did it become apparent that he was not simply the trumpet-playing "sideman-in-waiting," but a creative individualist with a musical language all his own. The upshot: a little-noticed jazz veteran proceeded to introduce into the music of the second generation creative ideas that went far beyond what he had learned as a sideman with Coleman, ideas which had a decisive influence on the evolution of that music.

Don Cherry was born in 1936 in Oklahoma City and spent his youth in Los Angeles[1]. He first came into contact with jazz in a club where his father worked as a bartender, and

---

1) For Don Cherry's biographical data I am indebted to LeRoi Jones (1963).

that acquaintance deepened when his great-uncle, the wrestler and pianist Tiger Nelson, began to take him to the bars where he played. Cherry's actual musical training — like that of many jazzmen — began in a high-school band, where he learned to play almost all the brass instruments, including the unwieldy sousaphone. From about 1951 on, he worked with various musicians who were then living in Los Angeles, among them saxophonists James Clay, Wardell Gray and Dexter Gordon, drummer Billy Higgins, and trumpeter Art Farmer, in whose group he occasionally sat in as pianist. It was in this circle of musicians that Cherry later met Ornette Coleman. We need not describe the far-reaching consequences that meeting had.

In the group that Coleman and Cherry founded in 1957, the latter was really the sideman; Coleman's was the dominating personality. He composed those angular and — for the time — scurrilous-sounding pieces whose challenges the other members of the group were expected to live up to. He inspired them to leave the beaten track of hard bop, and showed them the path to take. In a certain sense, the role of Don Cherry in this formation was comparable to that of Miles Davis in Charlie Parker's quintet during the Forties (Jones 1963). There Parker set the standards, acting as the motive force to which Miles Davis reacted as well as he was then able to.

On the Coleman Quartet records of the late Fifties and early Sixties, Don Cherry's playing is a great deal more conventional than Coleman's. At times, Cherry's solos, full of arpeggios and played with a slightly "flawed" sound, recall the improvisations of Clifford Brown; but the influence of Miles Davis also seems to be present.

When Coleman's pieces have a harmonic framework, whether hard and fast or merely intimated, Cherry accepts it as a rule. A telling example of how Coleman and Cherry can arrive at contradictory interpretations of the same tune is *Tears Inside,* analyzed in the chapter on Coleman (*cf.* p. 48). As mentioned there, Ornette Coleman reduces the changes of that 12-bar blues to a tonal centre. Cherry, however, quite deliberately plays the changes, his melodic line closely following the chord progressions. Only later in Cherry's career does it become evident that referring to things that lie one or more stages back in his experience is not only the sign of a transitional period in which the vocabulary of a new language behaves according to the grammar of the old. The inclusion of traditional means in a new context turns out, in fact, to be one of the most important features of Cherry's music in his post-Coleman years too. Archie Shepp, one of the most perspicacious observers of the free-jazz scene, wrote about Don Cherry as late as 1966: "He knows that harmony teaches us certain lessons, that it is not so negligible as some people want to make us believe . . . If we discard certain rules consciously, being fully aware of their implications, even at times using those rules and implications to augment new ideas, we are not simply enslaving ourselves to the past: we are utilizing in the most intelligent way we can, all the artistic resources at our command. Cherry is in many ways the potential salvation of contemporary trumpet playing." One can read into these words a justification of the traditionalisms in Shepp's own music, but that hardly diminishes their accuracy.

EXAMPLE 51   THE FACE OF THE BASS

Around 1960, as Ornette Coleman's musical conception moved further away from the laws of traditional jazz and new principles began to take shape, the group became more and more unified in style. Don Cherry gradually adjusted to Ornette Coleman's manner of improvising. This is most noticeable in tunes of medium tempo, where Cherry's solos have the same tranquil simplicity as Coleman's but counterpose a certain dry humour to the latter's blues-like directness. Coleman's influences are reflected primarily in Cherry's rhythm and in his partial adoption of the principle of motivic chain-association. As a rule, Cherry's motivic chains evolve less consistently than Coleman's, but they are just as important as a means of governing the improvisation's progress.

Several significant elements of Cherry's improvising in the Coleman Quartet can be deduced from his solo in *Face of the Bass,* recorded in October 1959 (Example 51). Intended mainly as a feature for bassist Charles Haden, the piece has no ties to functional harmony; the tonal centre is B flat. Cherry begins with a melodic-rhythmic understatement; he plays repeated tones in eighths, tonally related to the B flat major chord (a). This passage which, it must be said, sounds somewhat poverty-stricken, leads to a relaxed, swinging conclusion followed by a rather long rest (b). Cherry's motivic work begins with phrase c 1. The motivic nucleus is the interval of a third, from the slightly "smeared" blue note a/a flat, to the relatively long sustained f. This interval, which can also be understood as a means of punctuation, is combined with phrase entrances that constantly change and expand, from a brief five-beat flourish (c1) to a nine-beat flowing melodic line (c3). In c4, the phrase is reduced to its original length; at the same time there is a shift to secondary tonal centres. With the consistency demonstrated in the motivic linkage of phrases c2-c5, Cherry later reverts (d2) to the cambiata motive he evolved in d1, combining it with an altered phrase ending.

A passage especially typical of Cherry's playing in general is segment e. The sequential motive is marked by wide leaps — these occur very often in Cherry's later playing — together with a rhythm that suggests a straight 4/4 while at the same time contradicting it by off-beat accents. If we put the rhythm of segment e into a metrical scheme (Example 52), we will notice something else too: a clear pattern construction. Thus the motivic links are not only melodic, but rhythmic as well.

EXAMPLE 52

Like Ornette Coleman's playing, Cherry's in these years is greatly dependent on tempo. While his improvisations in medium-fast to slow pieces have a remarkable angularity of line, but are at the same time extremely clear and transparent, Cherry sometimes gets confused in up-tempo pieces like *Rejoicing* and *Forerunner* and quite obviously fluffs.

One is tempted to dismiss this — as many commentators have — by referring to Cherry's technical insecurity at the time, and this to some extent may be justified. But there is more to it than that. Looking closer, we realize that in fact the problem lies elsewhere. Perfect technical control in extremely fast tempos was more or less risk-free as long as the improviser had to deal with standard changes that were familiar to him from years of working with them. To melodize them he could fall back on a whole supply of patterns he had learned or, as Berendt says (1956, p. 16) "improvised out," using them to overlay the changes. Teaching methods like Oliver Nelson's "Patterns for Saxophone" (1966) aim precisely in this direction.

As we all know, even the greatest musicians of traditional jazz, whose competence at spontaneous creativity is beyond question, do not always escape their own clichés in up-tempo pieces. This was not really their fault, for they were only paying tribute — consciously or unconsciously — to the circumstance that the human organism has natural limitations. This observation deserves a short digression.

If we think of improvisation as both a spontaneous and a conscious (i. e., controlled) translation of musical ideas into motor action (depressing piano keys, saxophone keys, trumpet valves), it will be clear that this procedure demands a certain amount of time, even if it is only a fraction of a second. The musician having to cope with ten notes per second[2] may find himself forced to reduce his "reaction time"; thus he will not think out musical ideas, but will fall back on ideas he has worked out at one time or another and committed to memory; these he translates into action[3]. This short-cut is frequently cut still shorter, when not the idea but the action itself is stored in the player's memory; in this case he plays what "lies under his fingers," since he has already played it countless times in one context or another, e. g. on a certain set of changes.

Now, what does all this have to do with Don Cherry? First of all, in the music of the Ornette Coleman Quartet — a "new-found-land" where the laws and habits of functional harmony do not apply — there is no use for patterns that had been worked out on that basis. Routine in playing changes, which Don Cherry had acquired by working with bop and hard-bop musicians in Los Angeles, is now not only useless, but a nuisance and, worse, an impediment. Therefore, the confusion into which Cherry is thrown by the prestissimo of *Rejoicing* is not necessarily caused by a faulty technical command of his instrument, but by having to break himself of habitual reactions, since they have no place in the new frame of reference.

---

2) This is roughly Charlie Parker's speed in his solo in *Koko* (= Cheerokee), where he improvises predominantly in long eighth-note lines at a tempo of $\downarrow$ = 300.

3) As an illustration we can take roughly parallel findings in the experimental psychology of learning: while a test person requires a reaction time of c. 0.5 seconds to name objects of everyday life shown to him, he needs up to 1.5 seconds for free associations, i. e., reactions involving a certain amount of creative thinking.

The fact that, as time went on, individual "improvised-out" patterns came into the playing of free-jazz musicians (whose attitude is pronouncedly anti-cliché) only shows how closely intertwined learning processes and spontaneous ideas are. Renunciation of extremely fast tempos and the virtuosity that goes with them (virtually a matter of principle in certain "schools" of free jazz like the Chicago AACM) may be due in part to the recognition that the time factor involved in improvising sets limits to spontaneity. But it is probably a renunciation of the proficiency principle in jazz too, i. e., of the standards by which a "good" musician is the one who is able to "improvise" in sixteenths on *I'll Remember April.*

After recording *Change of the Century* in May 1959, Don Cherry was heard more and more frequently on an instrument that is a curiosity in the history of jazz, a trumpet hardly 10 inches long. Cherry calls it an "Indian pocket trumpet," although it has nothing whatever to do with the classical instrumentation of Indian music. Aside from this instrument, Cherry mostly played cornet.

These two instruments must be taken into account in considering Don Cherry's highly individual sound, also to understand where the difference — above and beyond personal peculiarities of phrasing — lies between it and the sound of other free-jazz trumpeters like Bill Dixon, Dewey Johnson or Eddie Gale Stevens. Cherry's tone always sounds a bit "husky" and gruff. At times it recalls — absurd as it may seem — Wild Bill Davison, that very original cornetist among Chicago Dixieland musicians. One feature of Cherry's instruments, moreover, is that in the upper register they seem to sound higher than the actual pitch of the note played. When Don Cherry blows a c^3 it does not sound subjectively like a c^3 blown by Freddie Hubbard, but higher. The reason may lie in the different timbres of the trumpet and cornet, and also in the fact that the high register on the cornet demands a greater amount of physical energy than on the trumpet. That "plus" of energy — it is sensed rather than acoustically measurable — gives Don Cherry's accents in the top register, and his frequently blurred runs, a degree of tension and intensity which more than makes up for the lack of virtuoso smoothness and brilliance.

After more than four years with the Coleman Quartet, Don Cherry left, and with drummer Billy Higgins joined a group led by tenor saxophonist Sonny Rollins. Jazz critics took almost as little notice of him as before, but his playing underwent a distinct change in his new surroundings.

Musically a product of the bebop era, Sonny Rollins had always been an outsider in the hard bop of the Fifties. This was due in part to his habit of taking themes more or less where he found them, transforming them without hesitation into typical "Rollins pieces"[4]. His subtle humour was equally out of place in the musical practises of the time, as were his wilfully delayed rhythm and his habit of taking thematic motives apart and reassembling them with a persistence that sometimes made his improvisations appear as a musical jigsaw puzzle.

---

4) I would mention here especially his version of Weill's *Mack the Knife* and the cowboy song *I'm an Old Cowhand.*

At the end of the Fifties, Rollins turned his back on the jazz scene (as Ornette Coleman was to do at a later time) to work out something new without being pressured by club dates and recording sessions. In the early Sixties he turned to freer forms of jazz. The music of the group he formed with Don Cherry, Billy Higgins and bassist Bob Cranshaw (later replaced by Henry Grimes) is only sparsely documented on records. Nevertheless, the two albums issued by RCA give a good idea of Don Cherry's place and evolution in this group.

Unlike Coleman, for whom the composition of a tune was always very important, no matter how free the improvisations, Sonny Rollins was obviously not choosy about the quality of the thematic material he used. He picks standards like *I Could Write a Book* and *There'll Never be Another You* or older compositions of his own like *Oleo* or *Doxy*. But he doesn't seem to use them for their own sake, *i. e.* for their melodic or harmonic beauty, but just because they provide sufficient ground for improvisation. It sometimes happens that even while the tune is being introduced, it is dismembered beyond recognition and finally dropped entirely *(Oleo, Doxy),* to turn up again as fragments during what are usually very long pieces. Tempos and harmonic patterns are observed, but always form only a relatively neutral frame of reference which, in the spontaneous interplay between the musicians, can be abandoned at any time in favour of another.

Comparing the music of the Sonny Rollins group in 1962/63 with earlier records made by the Ornette Coleman Quartet, one recognizes that both groups play in a way that is free of hard and fast conventions, but that freedom is achieved in each case on different levels.

Coleman is consistent in eliminating the bonds of functional harmony and divisions into bar-patterns. But he holds fast to what could be called the traditional superstructure: the schematic order of theme, solo improvisation and theme, with the tempo remaining constant.

Rollins takes the opposite path. While the inner structures of his music, their melodic and harmonic content, are largely in line with the laws of Fifties' jazz, the overall form of his pieces is permanently open to spontaneous alteration.

Oleo, for instance, recorded in July 1962 at a club date in the "Village Vanguard,"is not a *piece* in the traditional sense, but has the marks of a spontaneously evolving *suite.* Following Rollins's lead in a process of continuous interaction, the group attains a variety of structure only rarely encountered in the free jazz of the early Sixties. In this respect, the music of the Rollins Quartet is closer to that of Charles Mingus than to Ornette Coleman. Like Mingus, Rollins does not eliminate traditional models in general, but calls them into question by playing with them, thus stripping them of their normative value.

This musical environment is not without consequences for Don Cherry's playing. On the one hand, he seems to be caught off balance now and then by Rollins's unpredictability in evolving his pieces, and by his habit of breaking in on his (Cherry's) solos. On the other hand, Cherry profits precisely from that lack of formal constraint. The informal way in which he and Rollins make music together forces him to be constantly on his guard, while at the same time being challenged to take the initiative himself, unless he wants to remain only an accompanist. Adjustment and accommodation, Cherry's tasks in much of his work with the Coleman Quartet, give way to a new self-assurance. For although Sonny Rollins usually takes the lead in initiating structural alterations, he proves as well to be receptive to every musical idea his colleagues suggest while the piece is in progress. There is a good example of this in the above-mentioned *Oleo*, where Don Cherry unexpectedly tosses a short phrase into Rollins's solo; taken up by Rollins, it gives his improvisation a new direction.

The Rollins-Cherry Quartet lasted a scant eight months. Looking back, it can be said that Cherry's collaboration with Rollins had a much more direct effect on his later musical development than did the succeeding two stages of his career, first as co-leader of the New York Contemporary Five and then with the Albert Ayler group, in which his position was rather that of a "playing guest." Working with Rollins laid the foundation for many things that continue to distinguish Don Cherry's music today. It is likely that one of the most important lessons he learned was that traditional models and improvisational freedom are by no means incompatible.

In 1963/64 Don Cherry was in Europe several times, first on tour with Sonny Rollins, later with Archie Shepp and the NYCF, and then with Albert Ayler. Toward the end of 1964 he formed his first steady group in Paris. During an engagement at the "Chat qui pêche," a jazz club which is one of free jazz's leading European strongholds (others include Copenhagen's "Montmartre" and the "Gyllene Cirkeln" in Stockholm), Don Cherry met musicians with whom he subsequently achieved a unity of conception all too rare in the rapidly changing ensembles of the free-jazz scene. Those players are: Argentinian tenor saxophonist Leandro "Gato" Barbieri, German vibraphonist and pianist Karlhanns Berger, French bassist Jean François Jenny-Clark, and Italian drummer Aldo Romano.

Karlhanns Berger, who had worked with Jenny-Clark and Romano before, says about this period: "Getting together with Don gave us all a terrific boost. For the first time in my experience there was a kind of music with absolutely no problems; there was no need to talk about style and that sort of thing. It was all done without words; since we spoke different languages, it was hardly possible to communicate verbally, let alone discuss anything . . . Everything we later played evolved collectively" (Berger 1967).

In this truly international quintet, which — with a few short breaks — stayed together until about the middle of 1966, Cherry was able for the first time to put his ideas into practice, not only as an improviser, but in a much broader way. Unfortunately, the music of this group appears on just one LP issued by a little-known French firm (Durium A77 127); it is not available in Germany, where this book was written. To get some idea of it *a posteriori,* we must fall back on two records produced by Blue Note while Cherry and one or more members of the quintet were playing in the USA. The first LP, *Complete Communion,* was made on December 24, 1965, when Don Cherry and Gato Barbieri were in New York (the group having no European engagement at the time). For the rhythm section, Cherry called in two old friends: one was bassist Henry Grimes, with whom he had played in the Rollins Quartet, and who had become one of the ablest bassists in free jazz during his work with Cecil Taylor (1961), Albert Ayler (1963) and Archie Shepp (1965); the other was drummer Ed Blackwell, who like Cherry was a former member of the Ornette Coleman Quartet.

Henry Grimes and Ed Blackwell also took part in the other Blue Note recording that Cherry made in New York in September 1966, *Symphony for Improvisers.* In addition to tenor saxophonist Pharoah Sanders (who is heard quite a lot on piccolo on this LP), three members of Cherry's "European" quintet were in the session: Gato Barbieri, Karlhanns Berger, and Jean François Jenny-Clark as second bassist.

Complete Communion and *Symphony for Improvisers* are among the most important LPs Don Cherry made, if not among the most important in free jazz of the Sixties. They have a central idea in common: monothematic pieces are dropped and several thematic complexes are integrated into a suite whose "movements," while clearly identifiable thanks to their contrasted thematic material, are linked with one another. Now, this procedure recalls the pieces by Charles Mingus which resemble suites in structure, and is certainly not new in jazz. Nevertheless, its adoption into the idiom of free jazz possessed a significance not forseeable at the time. As we remember, Coleman's *Free Jazz,* Ayler's *New York Eye and Ear Control* and Coltrane's *Ascension* had begun the practice of negating "tune-playing." *Complete Communion* presented, for the first time, an alternative which can be regarded as a negation of the negation. The stereotype monothematic framework is disposed of, but at the same time the improviser is not forced to work without the inspiration and sense of direction provided by a theme. Without intending to establish priorities or postulate any direct influence, works like Archie Shepp's *Portrait of Robert Thompson* and Cecil Taylor's *Conquistador* — both recorded about a year after *Complete Communion* and similar to it in conception — show that this kind of formal organization was fully accepted by Don Cherry's free-jazz contemporaries as an alternative both to a-thematic improvising and to monothematic pieces. What's more, that formal concept later had an effect on the peripheral areas of free jazz. This is demonstrated toward the end of the Sixties in the groups led by Miles Davis and Phil Woods, as well as in numerous ensembles playing so-called progressive rock.

Both *Complete Communion* and *Symphony for Improvisers* are governed, as we have said, by the idea of expanded form, and in that regard have a number of things in common. In both cases, Don Cherry matches the formal structure to the time limits of the LP, *i. e.,* each suite consists of two self-contained complexes, and the duration of each corresponds to the normal playing time of a record side. To denounce this procedure as subjugation to the non-musical dictates of technology would be worse than silly, actually, Cherry overcomes them in this way. By making allowances in his formal plan for the LP — as probably the most important medium in jazz — Cherry achieves an optimum utilization of the possibilities that medium presents. He also avoids those disturbing cuts and splices which — done by ignoramuses — chop up many of the longer free-jazz works at the most nonsensical places. Fears that Cherry's acceptance of a given time limit might hamper the spontaneity of the improvisations are easily overcome by listening to the music of *Communion* and *Symphony*.

Taking the LP into account as a formal factor, however important for the evolution of free jazz it may be, is of course only a relatively minor point as far as the musical totality of *Complete Communion* and *Symphony for Improvisers* is concerned. The essential element of Don Cherry's formal conception is the above-mentioned fusion of several different thematic and improvisation complexes into a unified whole. In a brief analysis of *Complete Communion,* I will try to demonstrate how this conception functions, and how it is musically realized. Most of the resultant observations can be applied to the second part of the album and to *Symphony for Improvisers.* For easier comprehension, I have made a schematic diagram of the structure of *Complete Communion,* Part I (Example 53). The horizontal lines have the following meaning:

(1) Division into thematic and improvised sections; the themes and the fragments derived from them are numbered;

(2) the instruments playing;

(3) the tonal centre or mode on which the section is based;

(4) tempo in approximate metronome markings (per minute);

(5) time axis (in minutes).

Naturally, this type of diagram can only give a rough idea and needs further comment. The compositional framework of the piece consists of four themes *(Complete, And Now, Golden Heart* and *Remembrance),* the first of which returns at the end as a recapitulation. The specific characteristics of Don Cherry's composing style will be discussed in more detail later. Here we need say that Cherry's themes very often have a heterogeneous structure, that is, they consist of several parts whose motives, tonal points of reference, rhythm and sometimes tempo diverge[5]. As a rule, one part forms something like a thematic centre in which the rhythm and the tonal framework consolidate to become the basis of the improvisations that follow. One important feature of the thematic material is that each of the structurally divergent thematic sections, when taken out of

---

5) In this respect, Cherry's themes are perhaps the most successful descendants of Coleman's *Congeniality* model (*cf.* p. 57 f.).

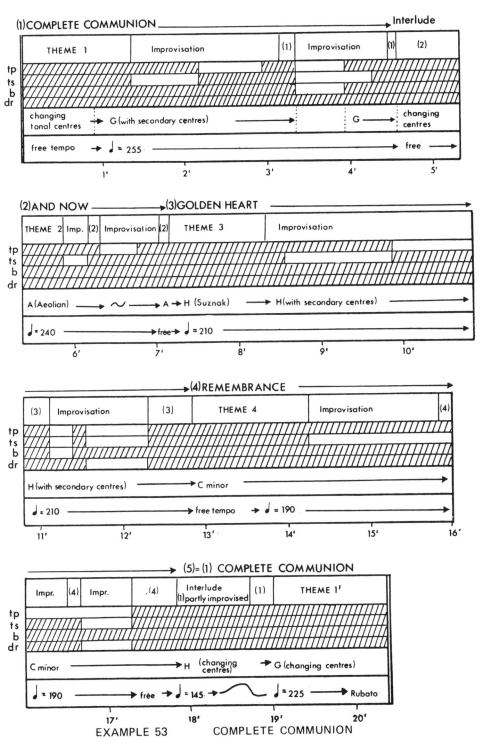

EXAMPLE 53   COMPLETE COMMUNION

143

context, is a musical entity and not simply a fragment. From this circumstance, Cherry draws a consequence that is of decisive importance not only for the form of the piece: he takes segments of the themes and gives them independence as short "interludes" inserted, as A. B. Spellman says (Blue Note 84247), at the "strategic points" of the piece. As the diagram in Example 53 shows, this usually happens where a new soloist takes over, or before a new thematic complex begins.

It is obvious that the interludes extracted from the thematic material are a means of formal articulation. But they have another purpose too, one that goes beyond organizational considerations. "We improvised from the flavor of the tunes" (from Spellman, *loc. cit.*); what Don Cherry says about *Symphony for Improvisers* applies just as well to *Complete Communion.* He means — and the music confirms it — that what the players primarily improvise on are not tonal centres, modes or even chord patterns, but the themes themselves and their motivic substance. Seen from this angle, the real meaning of the thematic interludes becomes plain: they serve not only to delineate the form, but even more to strengthen the motivic connections which govern the improvisations. Those connections are present in varying degree in the solos and collective improvisations of the four musicians. They are strongest in Cherry's playing; alternating between blurred runs with "sound" character and melodic improvising, he returns again and again to melodic models derived from the themes.

Gato Barbieri, whose playing on this LP sounds like a cross between Coltrane's broadly-spun melody and Coleman's intricate motivic work[6], does not keep as close to the motivic material. But he, too, comes back to anchor phrases originating in the thematic framework. It is left to Ed Blackwell to give what is probably the most effective demonstration of this kind of thematic improvisation. As we know, drum solos in jazz (whatever the stylistic area) very often deteriorate into a show of virtuosity without recognizable thought or direction, and have little or nothing to do with the music. This is not the case with Blackwell. Building on the rhythmic patterns of the tunes, he develops his solos into variations on those patterns by playing round them, breaking them up, putting them back together, superimposing others, etc. (In this respect Blackwell's free-jazz drum solos are a good deal less "free" than the long-winded solo excursions of Buddy Rich, for example. This is one of the ironies that arise in jazz when the concept of freedom is used without defining it.)

Closely tied up with the significance of motivic improvisation in Cherry's suites is the matter of tonality. The reader may have observed that until now I have referred very cautiously to "tonal points of reference." The system of tonal relationships on which *Communion* and *Symphony* are based is, in fact, more than a tonal centre (as in Coleman or Taylor), less than a functional harmonic skeleton (as in traditional jazz), and something

---

6) In fairness to Barbieri we must add that he overcame his eclecticism with time. *The Third World* (Flying Dutchman 117), an album he recorded in 1969, shows that he continues to play along lines mapped out by Coltrane, but that like Pharoah Sanders he has found his way to a musical idiom that is very much his own.

different from a modal scale as used by Coltrane or Davis. Cherry also works with scales in a certain way. The scales he uses, however, are not pre-formed but are more or less casually derived from the melodic line of his themes. That is, the tonal basis is not represented by a scale which the tune follows and on which the improvisations are built; instead, the melody is itself the basis. This may sound a bit sophistic, but it is of decisive importance in that Cherry's modality very rarely coincides with the modes common in jazz, and the melodies of his tunes seldom comprise a full seven-tone scale but are often simply a scale fragment.

I would like to illustrate both these points with concrete examples from *Complete Communion.*

1. The first theme of the suite, *Complete Communion,* leads in a series of shifts (not modulations!) from A via the "reference tones" G - F - E - F sharp - G - E - A finally back to G, on which tone the central motive of the theme is based (central in that it functions as the improvisation's anchor phrase). This motive — like the whole suite, incidentally — has an indefinable minor mood which is established in the foregoing phrases, and consists of only three notes: e - f sharp - g. The "goal tone" g acts as a kind of central tone, but the general tonal frame of reference for succeeding improvisations is neither the note g (as tonal centre), nor the key of G minor, nor any mode constructed on g, but rather the brief succession of pitches e - f sharp - g, a scale fragment.

2. The third tune of the suite, *Golden Heart,* is based on a scale whose interval structure is not identical to any of the common Euro-American modes, but which does coincide with modal scales found in Arabic and Turkish music (Example 54). The scale reads f sharp - g - a sharp - b - c sharp - d - e - (f) - f sharp, with b as principal tone and f sharp as final tone. It corresponds in principle to the harmonic minor (b minor) of Occidental music, but with the important difference that a sharp has no leading-tone function. What

EXAMPLE 54   GOLDEN HEART

gives this scale its specific flavour is the augmented second g - a sharp, and the diminished fifth which takes the place of the perfect fifth, depending on the melodic context (f instead of f sharp). Both of these features are just as uncommon in modal jazz of the Sixties as they are common in Arabic music, for there we not only find numerous modes with augmented seconds, but also modes whose interval structure alters according to whether the melody rises or falls. It may be an accident that the scale of *Golden Heart* is identical to the Arabic mode Râhât Fazâ and the Turkish Suznak. In any event, it is idle to speculate as to whether Don Cherry was directly inspired by Arabic music (he was in North Africa a short time before the LP was made), or whether he intuitively grasped its tonal characteristics. What is significant is the kind of modality manifest in Cherry's compositions. This modality obviously has its roots in another cultural background than does the early modal playing of Coltrane and Davis, in which traditional Occidental modes predominate.

The forms of modality described above are of great importance for Don Cherry's whole musical conception after 1965; their significance goes far beyond *Communion* and *Symphony.* This does not mean, however, that Cherry's music is generally modal, or modal in a strict sense. There is always a certain amount of freedom in the way modality is handled, especially in the improvisations; the scales of the thematic sections linger on as modal coloration in the solos. These scales do not constitute a tonal material which must be observed at all costs, so much as they do a loose system of references, always open to alternatives.

This free modality may recall the phenomenon of "modal disorientation" discussed in connection with the music of John Coltrane. But the two principles differ in a very important respect. In Coltrane's music the modal frame of reference established by the piano is usually present throughout the piece, and is merely expanded when the improvising horns move to tones outside the scale. In Cherry's music the frame of reference is completely abandoned at times, and its place is taken by changing tonal centres which have a logical connection with the thematic structure. This is quite clear in Cherry's first solo in *Complete Communion:* on the one hand, the scale fragment of the central theme (e - f sharp - g) serves as a modal point of reference; on the other hand, scale shifts in the first thematic section inspire him to move to different tonal centres.

These observations could lead to the conclusion that Cherry's treatment of tonality is, in the final analysis, a synthesis of Coltrane's modal playing (in modified form) and Coleman's improvising on tonal centres. This conclusion is as logical as it is wrong, for the real system of references in Cherry's music is not modal scales, tonal centres or a combination of the two, but the themes themselves, and the melodic and rhythmic patterns they contain. And even in the rare case where a theme implies functional harmonic progressions (in *Complete Communion,* for example, *Remembrance* has the form of an expanded blues in minor), it too is echoed in the improvisations.

While there is much agreement between *Complete Communion* and *Symphony for Improvisers* as to conception, there is substantial difference as to how the concept of expanded form is developed. The first impression one gets in listening to *Complete Communion* is of ensemble precision achieved in an utterly unpedantic way. The transitions, for example, are relatively complicated: various musical figures are linked together; there are no schematic patterns; and yet the transitions are accomplished with astonishing ease, as though they were the most natural thing in the world. The reason is without question the rapport between Cherry and Barbieri, gained in months of playing together. Both of them know the thematic and motivic material of *Communion* so well that they can do what they want with it without having to agree on things first, and each can be sure that the other will immediately go along with his ideas. Added to this is a veritably somnambulistic empathy between Henry Grimes and Ed Blackwell, who not only produce a stable rhythmic foundation, but — more important — react quickly and accurately to changes in direction taken by the horns.

This precision of ensemble — together with a concise disposition of thematic material and relatively short solos — gives *Complete Communion* a transparent structure, in which the individual formal complexes stand out sharply. *Symphony for Improvisers,* on the other hand, is more open in form, despite an almost identical construction. Transitions between the thematic sections are frequently fluid, as are the boundaries between composed material and improvisations. A great deal more time is spent on improvisations, as opposed to the themes, which become more and more fragmentary.

Not the least of the things responsible for this change of emphasis is the presence of tenor saxophonist Pharoah Sanders on *Symphony for Improvisers.* Accustomed as a result of his work with Coltrane to handling large-scale musical structures, in which only the musicians' powers of improvisation set the boundaries, Sanders is relatively indifferent to Cherry's compactly formed music, and the resultant emphasis on details. Part of that indifference may, of course, arise from the fact that he is not as familiar with Cherry's thematic material as are Gato Barbieri and Karlhanns Berger. Thus Sanders often ignores the formal caesuras placed by Cherry; and he hardly allows the motivic content of thematic interludes to influence his improvisations. In this way, he overlays the formal framework of the suite with a second layer whose contours are primarily shaped by his own stream of consciousness. Although the listener occasionally gets the impression that music is being made on separate tracks, the two layers naturally cannot remain independent of one another. The influence is mutual; on the one hand, Pharoah Sanders cannot wholly escape or ignore Cherry's "strategic points," and he certainly does not deliberately try to; on the other hand, the propellant vitality of Sanders's improvisations inspires Cherry, Barbieri and Berger to treat the stipulated thematic passages of the piece less respectfully than is the case in *Complete Communion.*

The musical qualities of the two albums, by the way, are very aptly characterized by their titles: in one instance the musical totality is marked by the "complete communion" (*i. e.,* the full accord) of the players, while in the other the predominant element is improvisation.

During and after the latter half of the Sixties, Don Cherry's music follows the direction taken by *Complete Communion* and *Symphony for Improvisers,* at least in conception. To recapitulate, the most important features are: integration of several thematic and

147

improvisation complexes into a suite form[7]; thematically controlled improvisation; a specific kind of modality which only rarely coincides with the scales commonly used in jazz.

While these outward formative principles are retained, there is a gradual change in the musical substance. In other words, while the forms and the methods of filling them stay relatively constant, the content itself changes. The reason for this is Don Cherry's growing awareness of musical cultures of the so-called Third World, especially those of Arabia, India and Indonesia. That awareness led to the exploration of new (old) rhythms, melodies and timbres. The outcome was that Cherry, in the ensuing years, gradually turned away from what came to be the mainstream of free jazz.

The first recorded document of this evolution is an LP Don Cherry made in Berlin in 1968: *Eternal Rhythm*. The piece was recorded in the wake of a concert during the Berlin Jazztage, for which jazz critic and entrepreneur Joachim Ernst Berendt gave Don Cherry the chance to assemble a big band in line with his own ideas. At the concert, between the orchestras of Maynard Ferguson and Count Basie, Cherry's big band ultimately demolished everything the Berlin audience was accustomed to thinking about the big band institution. Cherry accomplished this by employing his ten musicians not as sections, as players who either lead or accompany, but as the individualists they were. The result was a larger-scale *Symphony for Improvisers*[8].

The musicians Cherry (with Berendt's help) brought together in the studio to record *Eternal Rhythm* on November 11 and 12, 1968, were among the best available on the European free-jazz scene at that time: trombonists Albert Mangelsdorff and Eje Thelin, saxophonist Bernt Rosengren, pianist Joachim Kühn, Arild Anderson on bass and Jacques Thollot on drums. Included in the group were two musicians from New York, the guitarist Sonny Sharrock, and Karlhanns Berger, who on this occasion played various metallophones.

A necessary point in understanding *Eternal Rhythm* is that despite its *ad hoc* assembly, put together for Berlin, the piece is by no means all a product of spontaneous ideas organized and laid down in a few rehearsals, but rather an extract of Cherry's previous work with his Swedish-Turkish groups in Stockholm[9].

---

7) In *Where is Brooklyn* (Blue Note 84 3119), which Cherry made with Pharoah Sanders one month after *Symphony*, monothematic pieces are used; this, however, was and remained an exception.

8) It should be mentioned in passing that the concert (of which I have a tape) was stronger as a whole than the record made after it. Part of the reason is surely that some of the players in the concert do not appear on the record (tenor saxophonists Barney Wilen and Pharoah Sanders, and Turkish trumpeter Muffy Fallay, with whom Cherry regularly worked in Stockholm); another cause could be the difference in atmosphere between a live performance and studio work, plus the fact that at the concert the musicians had more time available than in the studio.

9) In Sweden — where Cherry has lived since about 1964 and is active as a teacher — he usually played in 1968 with Muffy Fallay (trumpet), Bernt Rosengren and Tommy Koverhult (woodwinds), Torbjörn Hultkrantz (bass), Leif Wennerström (drums) and several Turkish percussionists.

The group conception of *Eternal Rhythm,* as in *Communion* and *Symphony,* consists of a composed or agreed-upon system of references, within which the musicians have a maximum amount of individual freedom. Within this framework, Don Cherry acts as catalyst: "Don is a natural conductor of music through playing" (Berger 1968). He is supported in that role chiefly by Bernt Rosengren, who is familiar with the thematic material of *Eternal Rhythm* from his work in Don Cherry's Stockholm group. (Thus Rosengren has the same job that Gato Barbieri had in the New York recordings; moreover, the two have much in common with regard to style.)

In *Eternal Rhythm,* as in *Communion* and *Symphony,* themes are played at the "strategic points" of the piece, which create structural differentiation and formal articulation. In this instance, however, they hardly figure as motivic material in the improvisations. There are two probable reasons for the absence of motivic connections between themes and improvisations, a surprising phenomenon in Cherry's music. First, the ensemble is a group of players for whom — with the exception of Rosengren — Cherry's material is relatively new. Moreover, their improvising habits are not always the same as Cherry's. Second (and this is probably the more decisive point), *Eternal Rhythm* seems to be designed from the outset for evolving sounds and rhythms, rather than for developing motivic and melodic interconnections. Part of this shift of emphasis is the fact that the solos are relatively few and short; collective improvisations predominate. When solo instruments do emerge, they are almost always surrounded by a dense web of sounds which (partly diffuse and partly rhythmically accentuated) provide a constantly changing background. Occasionally, as in the piano solo by Joachim Kühn, the background is gradually heightened in dynamics, intensity and density until it becomes the foreground and submerges the solo.

A new element in Cherry's music underscores the dominance of tone colour and rhythm which makes it appearance here: the rhythms and sounds of the Third World. The most obvious indication of its influence is the many instruments, especially the instruments doubled by the musicians in addition to their main horn. Cherry, for instance, plays a whole assortment of differently tuned flutes and recorders of Far Eastern origin. Rosengren plays a normal "Occidental" oboe, but he uses it more like an Indian Sânâi. The chief contribution to the Oriental coloration of the *Eternal Rhythm* orchestra is made by the percussion section, whose arsenal includes gongs, chimes and Balinese gamelan instruments, the gender and saron. The latter are metal idiophones resembling the xylophone in form, and owe their specific sound to the tuned bamboo resonators fixed below the metal bars.

Now, the presence of a certain kind of instruments must not necessarily change the music's character. Swing played on a gender, or cool jazz on a flute from Bengal, is theoretically within the realm of possibility. What counts is not the instrumentation, but how it is used.

On this point, the introduction to *Eternal Rhythm* gives us an idea of what is in store. It is a solo played by Don Cherry on two bamboo flutes tuned roughly a major third apart. The melodic shape of this solo (an excerpt is given in Example 55) is largely dependent on the limited possibilities in playing two flutes at once. The primary aspects of this passage are its asymmetrical rhythm and the tone colour. The sound of slightly out-of-tune parallel thirds is additionally coloured by differential tones arising from the two parts. These differential tones create a third part which, although diffuse in pitch, is sometimes distinctly audible, especially in sustained tones[10].

EXAMPLE 55   BABY BREATH

If Don Cherry's double-flute solos stand alone as self-contained, independent musical units (in this case quasi as prologue and epilogue), the saron and gender act first as a sound continuum, and second as a rhythmic continuum *(Eternal Rhythm!)*. On the rare occasions when the gender and saron stand out more prominently, the result — in combination with the other instruments — is an unusual strata formation of sounds and rhythms. Example 56 is a short excerpt from such a heterogeneous, "multi-strata" structure, with the sounds of the gamelan instruments written as indeterminate pitches[11]. An ostinato pattern, played in unison by piano, bass and tenor, is overlaid by very dynamic accents in the two trombones; these have primarily a rhythmic function and destroy all harmonic associations by the acute interval, the minor second behaving like a "mini-cluster." The third stratum is represented by the saron and gender. Without any rhythmic differentiation to speak of, and unclear in pitch, this is the opposite pole in timbre to the trombone accents on one side, and the ostinato pattern on the other. At the same time, the fact that this timbre stratum is metrically completely independent of the others (the ratio is only approximately 6 : 7) causes a pronounced rhythmic tension between the strata.

---

10) Similar playing techniques are used in Arabia, especially on the oboe instruments (arghûl, zummâra). Double flutes are widespread in the Balkans (kaval, dvojuice); there too, differential tones are used consciously as a formative means.

11) It was impossible to determine the exact pitches.

EXAMPLE 56   TURKISH PRAYER

On the whole, *Eternal Rhythm* — in line with the trend of the times — is more open in its rhythmic conception than *Communion* and *Symphony*, where there were long stretches with a steady, accentuated 4/4 metre. *Eternal Rhythm* gets the benefit of all the knowledge of rhythm gleaned in free jazz over the years: free accentuation in the manner of Cecil Taylor, rubato, superimposition of various rhythmic planes, etc. In addition, irregular metres like those in Examples 57a and 57b — a direct consequence of orientation toward

(a)   (b)
EXAMPLE 57   ETERNAL RHYTHM

Third World music — play an important role. The first rhythmic pattern, which incidentally is identical to Bartók's "à la Bulgarese" rhythm, is played by Jacques Thollot, behind a very sustained rubato melody by Cherry; the second pattern derives from the melody rhythm of a theme *(Endless Beginnings)*.

Here the objection could be raised that after the intricate irregular metres played by the Don Ellis big band, nine and ten-beat patterns like these are nothing sensational. As obvious as that sort of comparison seems, if we listen closely we will discover that the conceptions of Cherry and Ellis differ in one very important respect. For Ellis, irregular metres are ends in themselves, a fetish which, discussed in detail in the sleeve notes of each and every record, puts a veneer of avantgardism over what is, in reality, merely a hip dressed up, musty big-band conception. For Cherry, however, these same metres are always just one creative means among many, one that temporarily ties down energies released by abandoning the beat, and that is never employed for its own sake. Furthermore, these metres emerge so inconspicuously from Cherry's thematic material — occasionally folk-like in its unpretentiousness — that one becomes aware of their asymmetrical structure only if one counts along.

Don Cherry's *Eternal Rhythm,* with its own particular kind of emphasis on near and far Eastern musical elements, by no means stands alone in the history of free jazz. It must be viewed together with similar ventures undertaken by musicians like John Coltrane, Pharoah Sanders, Archie Shepp, Sunny Murray, Sun Ra etc., as the consequence of a growing affinity with the musical cultures of Africa and Asia. Within this stylistic metamorphosis, *Eternal Rhythm* has the status of an individual variant, but it definitely belongs there. On no account should it be placed in the same category as the "Jazz meets the World" recordings made about the same time in Germany, which signalled (sometimes in a very self-conscious way) that the Third World was en vogue, just as bossa nova or Baroque jazz before it, and rock jazz later.

For Don Cherry, as opposed to most of the European musicians riding the "Oriental wave," occupation with African and Asian music signified more than just a short-lived fad. *Eternal Rhythm* should be considered as one long stride in a march which gradually increased the distance between Cherry and the "rules of the game" of the free jazz mainstream.

Two factors played an important role in making Cherry's music increasingly individualistic. For one thing, he reduces his groups to three players, and sometimes two. This means that he is in the musical limelight most of the time, and that the interactions between him and the players become more direct and intensive. Second, Cherry himself began to play even more instruments, going far beyond the non-European instrumentation he used in *Eternal Rhythm.* In the process, his trumpet playing, the actual connecting link with the free jazz of the past, gradually faded into the background. Among the instruments Cherry played in the late Sixties are the already mentioned bamboo flutes, the Turkish Zurnâ (a kind of shawm), large earthen flutes that sound rather like a European ocarina, various kinds of xylophones, and — looking slightly out of place in such exotic company — the piano. Added to this array is his voice, which now and then comes to be the predominant "instrument." Again, the objection could be raised — this time with more reason — that none of this is really extraordinary, for musicians like Pharoah Sanders, Sunny Murray, Alan Silva and many others, now use a battery of instruments that would be a credit to any ethnological museum. Once more, however, it is not the *what* but the *how* that sets Cherry apart from his colleagues in the mainstream of free jazz. There the manifold "Third World" instruments are usually employed chiefly as sound additives which contribute to the coloration of the music without actually influencing its form. In Cherry's music, on the contrary, the same instruments have an intrinsic value which is not limited to determining only the sound. A principal cause of this structural function is that Cherry no longer makes a distinction between primary and secondary instruments. Cornet, flutes, xylophones, piano and voice are all equal alternatives for him. True, they do give a variety of tone colour, but beyond that their use leads to melodic and rhythmic differentiation and thus has a direct effect on the substance of his music.

The most important documentation of Don Cherry's music around 1970 are two records he made with Ed Blackwell in August 1969 in Paris: *Mu* — Parts I and II.

Stripped of all frills and governed solely by the creative will and musical experience of Cherry as "agent," and the sensitivity of Blackwell as "reagent," these duo recordings afford a unique view of the quintessence of Cherry's music. It is important to stress that *Mu* is not the LP evidence of a unique event, an artificial situation staged in the studio, as duo recordings are often inclined to be. In every respect, it is symptomatic of Cherry's work at the time, as live performances have since demonstrated.

That the stylistic features of Cherry's music are not affected by his partner of the moment is confirmed in a telling way by a concert Cherry and Dutch percussionist Han Bennink played in the summer of 1971 in Carpentras in Southern France. Han Bennink's sweeping energy, as compared to Ed Blackwell's balanced and rhythmically highly complex playing in *Mu,* brought with it an undeniable change in relationships, because Bennink's erratic vitality forced Cherry to react more often than he did to the more adaptable Blackwell; but this difference did not have any effect on Cherry's creative ideas.

The individuality of those creative ideas can be observed first and foremost in Cherry's thematic material. His themes in *Mu* and the Carpentras concert[12] have a significance that goes beyond their earlier function of formal disposition and motivic definition (e. g. in *Communion, Improvisers* and *Rhythm*). The most obvious result of this new development is the duration of thematic material as compared to that of free improvisation. A Don Cherry "theme" can last up to ten minutes, only to lead into another theme without a trace of "solo improvisation" in between. Even so, it cannot be said that Cherry neglects improvisation in favour of composition. What he does is to place improvisation on a level other than that which listeners who have grown up in the mainstream of free jazz are used to. Thus in Cherry's case both "theme" and "improvisation" require a new definition.

In traditional jazz, the primary purpose of the theme or tune is to provide a harmonic and metrical framework as a basis for improvisation. In free jazz, which does not observe fixed patterns of bars or functional harmony, this purpose no longer exists. Themes establish tonal centres (Coleman) or modal levels (Taylor, Cherry), furnish motivic material (Taylor, Cherry), and otherwise act as emotional points of reference (Shepp, Coleman) or elements of contrast (Ayler). Whatever purpose they serve, themes and solo or collective improvisations are usually clearly distinguishable from one another; they are separate and distinct parts of the musical totality. The themes are the constants, the improvisations the variables. A partial fusion of the two — as sometimes happens in Cecil Taylor — is always the exception rather than the rule.

---

12) This concert, which was never issued on LP, was taped by the author. Here I must depart from the guideline I have otherwise observed in this book: to discuss only recordings that are generally available (*cf.* p. 15). The Carpentras recording illustrates several essential points of Don Cherry's present work which in the older *Mu* are not yet fully developed.

In Don Cherry's music, the thematic section itself now becomes an object of improvisation in two ways. For one thing, Cherry's compositions are no longer musical units planned from the outset for inclusion in a piece or suite, thereby defining it as a "work" distinct from any other work. Instead, they function as separate and independent members of a thematic "catalogue," a list of alternatives to be chosen from during a concert or recording; that is, they are used when and where it occurs to Cherry to use them. Spontaneously deciding to pick a theme from that catalogue at a given time and in a given musical context, is itself an act of improvisation. Cherry improvises not *on* his themes, but *with* them. Occasionally this gives the thematic material a great amount of autonomy vis-à-vis conventional improvisation, in that Cherry plays tunes for their own sake without taking them in any way as a basis for improvisatory elaboration.

Opposed to this ready availability of thematic material is a high degree of variability in the compositions themselves. Cherry's themes very often consist of short, rhythmically and melodically clear-cut patterns. These he repeats several times in ostinato fashion, while gradually getting away from mere literal repetition of the model and evolving variants of it. These consist, as a rule, of a very subtle metamorphosis of the melody rhythm, shifts of accent, and sometimes of metrical alteration. The original melodic shape of the theme, however, is not entirely abandoned. During this process of variation, Cherry arrives now and then at variants which he stabilizes by repetition; the outcome is a new ostinato and a new thematic model.

To sum up, this means that, on the one hand, thematic material is no longer relatively neutral. It has another purpose than merely acting as a trigger for improvisations; the theme itself is an object of variation. On the other hand, patterns evolved while the model is, so to speak, in the works, can become new themes, their contours related to the original model but not identical to it.

This specifically Cherryesque kind of *spontaneous composition* (significantly, that is the title of one of his *Mu I* pieces) is enhanced by two further improvisatory principles. In both cases, Cherry alternates between a constant or nearly constant melodic model as antecedent phrase and an improvised consequent phrase, in what is a quasi call-and-response pattern. In one case, the response is a varied continuation of the call, and both are generally based on a common motive. In the other, call and response are diametrically opposed, the *cantabile* simplicity of the call evoking a response of sound-energy playing à la Shepp. Thus one principle is continuity, the other is contrast. In Example 58, the three procedures we have discussed are shown schematically, but the use of a diagram is not meant to suggest that there is anything formalistic about Cherry's music. For one thing, the procedures in question are largely row-forms similar to those found in many folk-music genres, and grow more from a "playful" encounter with the material than from a process of reflection and conscious construction. For another, an important cause of the thoroughly unacademic nature of Cherry's music is the thematic material itself.

a)	theme 1	variants	theme 2	variants
	A A ... A	A1 A2 A3 A4	A4 A4 ... A4 = B	B1 B2 B3
	ostinato	improvisation	ostinato	improvisation

b) A - B1 - A - B2 - A - B3 - A - ...

c) A - B - A - C - A - D - A - ...

EXAMPLE 58

If one has to resort to a catchword, one could call Don Cherry's themes "songlike," as many commentators have in fact done. But this says very little about their specific qualities. As it happens, there are several very different types of compositions in his repertoire, and while they all have a certain songlike nature, they do show considerable differences in structure and function.

One of the most prominent features allowing a classification of Cherry's themes is the cultural background in which they are rooted, or the extent to which the elements and flavour of various musical cultures are reflected in them. At the risk of over-simplifying, I will try to describe the most important of these theme types, with an example of each.

   1. "Arabic-Turkish" themes (Example 59): these are primarily ornamental melodies in semitone and whole-tone steps; they frequently end in falling sequences and are, as a rule, in complex metres. The predominant tonal foundation is the Turkish Suznak mode or transpositions of it *(Brilliant Action, Sun of the East).* Cherry had worked with themes like this for some time, and we may assume that his affinity with the music of the Near East was further strengthened at the start of the Seventies by steadily working with the Turkish drummer Okay Temiz.

EXAMPLE 59   SUN OF THE EAST

155

2. "South African" themes: some of Cherry's compositions (or are they adoptions?) show distinct parallels to patterns present in the urbanized folk music of the South African Negroes (Examples 60a and 60b). Their distinguishing marks are: triadic melody, parallel thirds, the simplest functional harmonic progressions (as in Example 60a) or a kind of two-degree modality (as in Example 60b), as well as strongly syncopated rhythms in uneven metres[13].

EXAMPLE 60a

EXAMPLE 60b

3. "Indian" themes: the result of Don Cherry's investigations into the music of India can be heard first and foremost in his vocal solos. There are two chief influences, both of which act more as sources of inspiration than as immediate models. One is the Dhrupad, the sustained vocal style of the Delhi region; clear echoes of its specific manner of articulation and embellishment can be heard in Cherry's songs. The other is South Indian theatre music, to whose dancing songs Cherry's thematic material shows clear structural analogies (Example 61).

EXAMPLE 61

4. "Rhythm-and-Blues" themes: these are principally piano pieces with strongly accentuated bass progressions and simple blues-like harmony and melody, the stylistic features of the blues and the stereotyped phraseology of soul music being alienated by

---

13) During a conversation at the 4th International Music Forum in Carinthia (Austria) in 1972, Don Cherry told me that he got the first of the two themes (Example 60a) from South African pianist Dollar Brand.

a complex rhythmic structure. A good example is *The Mysticism of My Sound* in *Mu II*, in which Cherry alternates between four and five-beat metres.

5. "Hymns": although most of Cherry's pieces are probably vocally conceived, there are some whose vocal qualities are especially prominent. These are usually sustained melodies with a wide range and a certain amount of pathos; they are in many ways reminiscent of Coltrane's "rubato ballads" (Example 62).

EXAMPLE 62

6. "Endless melodies": theoretically, almost all of Cherry's thematic types can become "endless melodies" (*i. e.,* melodies repeated countless times without giving rise to improvisations), the South African patterns as well as the "Indian" songs and the "hymns." In the present case, however, I mean those compositions in which the principle of repetition is built in. These themes usually manage without any harmonic development whatever (there is often a drone as a foundation); they have hardly any rhythmic differentiation, and their melodic lay-out is cyclic. One of Cherry's most clearly-drawn "endless melodies" is reproduced in the upper stave of Example 63. When there is a second horn, the melody can be overlaid with a contrasting pattern in smaller note values.

EXAMPLE 63

Although it creates an internal rhythmic animation, such a pattern emphasizes rather than cancels the principal melody's rotating motion.

A similarly conceived model, played by Cherry on piano, is given in Example 64. In this example two rotating patterns are superimposed. They are identical, but are played in tempos that are completely independent of one another. The upper part is thus the lower part compressed.

EXAMPLE 64

Don Cherry's "endless melodies" have a special significance for his music in general, in that they create a new attitude toward time. For what happens are not developmental processes, in which time is filled and articulated by a variety of changing occurrences; the laws of dynamic impetus do not apply; there is a meditative lack of motion, a situation of repose in which movement is reduced to cycles of the smallest possible dimensions. The role of time consists only of its passing.

Obviously, what the listener hears goes counter to the Western conception of both "classical" music and jazz, which are guaged to a processive flow of musical occurrences or, to put it more plainly, to the fact that something happens. For this reason it is important to identify the cultural background of Don Cherry's "endless melodies." That background is found neither in Afro-American nor European music, but in the music of the Orient. My principal grounds for making what is admittedly a hypothetical statement are not so much the musical structure of the melodies, as the emotional effect they have on the listener. Compared to Afro-American music, the motoric qualities of these melodies are infinitesimal. They create a feeling of repose rather than motion experienced in a psycho-physical way. Their paradigm is not the dance but the lotus seat[14]. Moreover, the point of these "endless melodies" is not to

---

14)   And Don Cherry does in fact play sitting cross-legged most of the time.

convey musical occurrences that will surprise the listener, arouse his intellectual interest or demand rational cognition. The point is to communicate an emotional equilibrium, something that occurs in Indian vocal music, in the sacrificial songs of Turkish Mevlevi dervishes, and in the monotonous hymns of Tibetan monks, as a necessary condition of meditation and contemplation.

7. "Riff" themes: the rhythmic counterpart to the meditative "endless melodies," this type of theme is also marked by repetition; but it has clear metrical proportions, that is, the beginning and end of the repeated segments can be identified as such. This type frequently coincides with Cherry's "Turkish" themes (see above) in melody and rhythm. Its main point of contact with the riffs of traditional jazz is that, like them, it serves to create psychic tension. It sometimes acts as an unchanging connecting link in freely improvised energy-sound solos, as in Example 58c (*cf.* p. 155).

The riff theme in Example 65 is a kind of standard pattern in Cherry's repertoire, and has been heard regularly in his live performances since 1970. This theme, incidentally, has a predecessor in a thematic fragment from *Symphony for Improvisers*. This is not an isolated case: it is interesting to note that there are many things in Cherry's thematic material of the Seventies that were already shaped some years before, and now turn up again in modified form, among them the "endless melody" in Example 64, which is identical to a pattern from *Eternal Rhythm* in Example 56.

EXAMPLE 65

The type classification I have made here loses validity, the more varied the phenomena are which it seeks to embrace. The seven types of Cherry themes discussed above make up only part of a reservoir that escapes any definitive classification because of its diversity. So the seven types are merely meant to illustrate the broad spectrum of Cherry's expressive means. His thematic writing is "multi-dimensional" as a matter of principle, that is, it cannot be reduced to the "slow-fast" polarity that is usually the only denominator in jazz and that circumscribes at the same time the emotional expression of the theme in question.

The variability of Cherry's thematic material is matched by the variety of his instrumentation and by the forms of improvisatory creation it brings about.

Although it cannot really be said that singing has a quantitative dominance in Cherry's music, the vocal element does seem to be central in a qualitative way. Instrumental passages very often prove to be continuations of vocal passages, as for example in *Teo Teo (Mu II)*, where a sung rhythmic pattern is worked out by the flute, or in the riff theme of Example 65, in whose development Cherry alternates between vocal and trumpet passages.

The main function of Don Cherry's piano playing is to accompany vocal pieces. In this, his playing is reminiscent of Alice Coltrane's work behind her husband's rubato ballads, with tremolos in the bass and wide arpeggios or glissandos in the upper register. On the other hand, the piano — and the xylophone, incidentally — has a rhythmic function for Cherry. He is fond of evolving and varying on it those asymmetrical patterns that have a strong tendency to rhythmic disorientation. A characteristic example of this is a passage from *Terrestrial Beings (Mu I)*, in which a ten-beat pattern with a 4+3+3+4+2+4 accentuation (in eighths) is repeated several times in slightly different variants (Example 66).

EXAMPLE 66   TERRESTRIAL BEINGS

If Don Cherry's piano playing is a synthesis of different influences and musical trends[15], the folk ties of his music emerge in his flute playing very directly and, as it were, unfiltered. In keeping with the structure of his Oriental flutes, Cherry's improvisation is definitely modal and the melodies are relatively simple. The special charm of his flute improvisations (which begin as far back as *Eternal Rhythm,* Example 55) lies primarily in their uneven metres, with extra rhythmic tension added when Cherry and his drummer play on different metrical levels. Example 67 is an excerpt from *Omejelo (Mu I)*. Here Cherry repeats a seven-beat pattern on the flute, to which Ed Blackwell contrasts a syncopated six-beat rhythm. The resultant crossing and constant shift of accents create a rhythmic conflict similar to that found in African drum and xylophone music.

How much Don Cherry's "style" is tied up with the instrument he is playing becomes clear when he turns to the trumpet after long flute or vocal passages. With just a few notes, a connection to the past is re-established, and the listener would swear he is hearing free jazz as of old. But the initial impression is misleading, for even though Cherry's trumpet playing, more so then any other element of his music, calls up associations with what almost seems to be a forgotten idiom, the change in his musical self-awareness has left its mark. True, there are still those high-register, blurred runs blending into atonal sounds. This feature of Cherry's playing — otherwise mostly motivic — has always come

---

15) Cherry names Thelonious Monk and Dollar Brand as his most important "piano teachers" (personal communication at the 4th Music Forum, Carinthia).

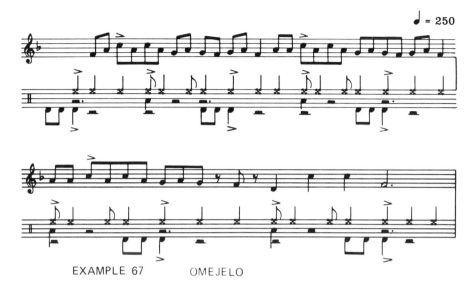

EXAMPLE 67   OMEJELO

the closest to what is generally expected of free-jazz improvisation, and continues to maintain his connection with the mainstream of free jazz. But the passages of his trumpet solos that aim at melodic evolution, quite clearly reflect his experience with the music of the Orient. The excerpt from *Total Vibration (Mu I)* given in Example 68 is far from being an exception; on the contrary, it is almost symptomatic. It shows a simple *cantabile*

EXAMPLE 68   TOTAL VIBRATION

melody (Suznak mode), with individual phrases mostly composed of stepwise motion and separated from one another by large intervals. The falling sequence in the second section of the excerpt resembles the riff theme quoted above (*cf.* Example 65), and the end of the passage has the same asymmetrical disposition prevalent in Cherry's flute pieces.

The method of dissection I have pursued in approaching Don Cherry's music around 1970 may give the impression that it is a puzzling conglomerate of disjointed exoticisms, traditionalisms and avantgardisms which no power on earth could blend into an independent, personal musical language. But appearances are deceptive. There is a factor that links all of Cherry's music together: it is not a stylistic concept of homogeneity of means, but a consistent inconsistency. The essence of Cherry's music lies in its contradictions. It is at once humorous and melancholy, full of pathos and full of fun, energy-laden and meditative, songlike and chaotic, complicated and simple, with complexity often giving an impression of simplicity, too.

Certain aspects of Cherry's music have a high degree of familiarity, but this is balanced by the unpredictability with which those familiar aspects are combined. It is not the freedom *from* something but the freedom *to do* something that determines the direction; that is, not the avoidance of tonality, consonance, metre and everything else likely to awaken associations with the past, but the unlimited possibilities of choice. And in precisely the degree to which the contradiction of creative principles is itself raised to a principle, Cherry's music evades stylistic classification.

It is often said that Don Cherry plays folklore. I for one never know whether "folklore" is meant to be a category, and whether it is a term of praise or blame. But this is not important, since if Don Cherry plays folklore, what kind of folklore is it? What folk musician from what region comes close to making music like Cherry's? His exoticism — as Alain Gerber (1971) poetically put it — is "not that of the Orient and not that of Africa; it is the exoticism of Somewhere, the Here and Somewhere; and this means it is the exoticism of dreams."

When asked what he would call his music, Don Cherry said (in 1965): "I am an improviser. All I want is that people can say about me, 'This is Don Cherry improvising, that's him, and he improvises . . . '"16)

From this statement we could perhaps derive a name for what he plays: Doncherrymusic.

---

16) *Jazz Magazine* 119 (June 1965), p. 28, retranslated from the French text.

Chapter 9

THE CHICAGOANS

There is hardly any other group of individuals in free jazz that is so tightly enclosed by a classification as those Chicago musicians who banded together in the mid-Sixties under the heading of The Association for the Advancement of Creative Musicians (AACM) and who later, in several formations — the most outstanding of which was the Art Ensemble of Chicago — spread throughout the world the tidings of a new kind of Chicago jazz.

The specific nature of Chicago free jazz can only be partly explained by the geographical location of the city, where the music arose relatively unaffected by what was musically happening in New York. If location had been all that mattered, then surely distinct styles of free jazz would have arisen in Boston, Detroit and Philadelphia too, and not just in Chicago. (The term "New York School," which German jazz publicists are prone to use, is a fiction suggesting stylistic uniformity where there is, in fact, extreme heterogeneity. And the term loses all meaning when it is extended to include a number of European musicians who have only one thing in common with the New York innovators, namely, that they too play free jazz.)

The origins of the group characteristics peculiar to Chicago free jazz, therefore, are not so much geographical as they are social. In New York, constantly increasing competition led jazzmen to "do their own thing," that is, to strive for uniqueness and individuality. The "October Revolution in Jazz," which had integration as its aim, could not do much to change that, and the failure of the Jazz Composers' Guild is symptomatic, if regrettable. Chicago was different. There was a unifying bond from the outset, in that the musicians were members of a larger organization and renounced all claims to individual fame. This ultimately had an effect on the stylistic evolution of their music. When we speak of Chicago free jazz, then, we not only have to describe a certain group of musicians and a certain kind of music, but also an interdependence of social and musical factors to which that music owes its individual status within the stylistic conglomerate of free jazz.

The initiator of the Chicago free jazz movement is composer, pianist and clarinettist Richard Abrams. In the early Sixties he founded the "Experimental Band" from which the AACM later grew. From what we are told by musicians who played in this second free-jazz big band (the first was Sun Ra's "Arkestra," likewise founded in Chicago), the Experimental Band was obviously more than just an orchestra in which individuals came together for the purpose of playing music. A group identification was present from the start, which cannot be explained in financial terms, for that side of the enterprise was anything but attractive. That group feeling is expressed by saxophonist Joseph Jarman, who joined the Experimental Band in 1961: "Until I had the first meeting with Richard Abrams, I was 'like all the rest' of the 'hip' ghetto niggers; I was cool, I took dope, I smoked pot, etc. I did not *care* for the life that I had been given. In having the chance to work in the Experimental Band with Richard and the other musicians there, I found the first something with meaning/reason for doing. That band and the people there was the *most* important thing that ever happened to me" (from Figi, Delmark 410).

The growing "we" feeling in the Experimental Band and the recognition that institution-alizing the group would give it more outward impact led in 1965 to the foundation of the AACM. About the motives and aims of the Association, Joseph Jarman said in 1967: "The Association for the Advancement of Creative Musicians, a non-profit organization chartered by the State of Illinois, was formed . . . when a group of Musicians and Com-posers in the Chicago area saw an emergent *need* to expose and showcase original Music which, under the existing establishment (promoters, agents, etc.) was not receiving its just due. A prime direction of our Association has been to provide an atmosphere con-ducive to serious Music and the performance of new, unrecorded compositions. The Music presented by the various groups in our Association is jazz oriented" (Jarman, Delmark 417).

Jarman goes on to give concrete goals of the AACM. These include, among other things, sponsoring a free training programme for young musicians, furnishing job opportunities for them, and financially assisting charitable institutions. Side by side with these practical goals are aims of a more idealistic nature: "To set an example of high moral standards for Musicians, and to uplift the public image of Creative Musicians . . . To uphold the tradition of elevated, cultured Musicians handed down from the past" *(loc. cit.)*.

What is revolutionary about this programme is not only what it sets out to do, but even more the fact that it was created by jazz musicians, that is, by a group which had always thought of itself as a fringe group of society (society thought so too). For jazzmen, any degree of organization beyond what was absolutely essential for playing in an orchestra or a combo, was normally a concession to a bourgeois style of behaviour, and that they did their best to avoid by non-conformity[1]. The ideas behind the AACM programme, then, are the very antithesis of the traditional definition of the role of the jazz musician in society. By taking the organization of his appearances in hand, he defends himself against exploitation by agents and promoters; he accepts responsibility toward the members of his own group (the training of young musicians) and toward society (supporting charitable

---

1) As a number of investigations into the social psychology of jazz have shown, this non-conformity can be explained in part as a reaction to the stereotype bourgeois image of the jazz musician as an anti-social creature and as a musical entertainer who is not to be taken seriously. It also resulted in part from the musicians' awareness that the public they play to in bars and clubs is only in the rarest instances capable of judging their music in terms of criteria appropriate to it. *Cf. inter alia* Becker (1951 and 1953), Cameron (1954), Merrian/Mack (1960).

institutions); and he does not withdraw as it were to lick the wounds of misunderstanding, but attempts instead to make society aware of his own value.

Although the economic situation of the Chicago free-jazz musicians during the years following the foundation of the AACM was hardly more advantageous than that of the New Yorkers (Litweiler 1967)[2], the Association was quite active. Regular concerts by the Experimental Band at the Abraham Lincoln Center, informal jam sessions by some of its groups at the University of Chicago, and theatrical performances and discussions kept the members busy, so there was no unproductive idleness that might have endangered the AACM's existence.

From the Experimental Band, as the musical core of the AACM, a number of "bands within the band" emerged during the latter half of the Sixties. Proceeding from a common musical basis but employing different means, these smaller groups consolidated the knowledge gained in the experimental workshop of the big band into the specific "Chicago style of free jazz." As far as I know, none of the performances of the original Experimental Band exists on records, but the music of the smaller ensembles (some of whose players worked in more than one group) is comprehensively documented. The broad musical spectrum of these groups, whose playing — as Joseph Jarman says — was "jazz oriented," but which also acquired many elements once regarded as alien to jazz, was determined to a good extent by the players' different musical backgrounds, and also by their extra-musical interests. Before we turn to the music of these groups, then, here are some biographical data on their most prominent members[3].

Richard Abrams, born in Chicago in 1929, was the first president of the AACM. At 17, he began studying piano at a private conservatory (Litweiler 1967). During the late Forties he played in local blues and bebop groups as a pianist and worked on the side as an arranger and composer. In 1955, he founded a group called MJT+3 with tenor saxophonist Nicky Hill, bassist Bob Cranshaw and drummer Walter Perkins. According to Litweiler, it was one of the best groups in Chicago at the time. When the group broke up in 1959, Abrams devoted himself mainly to studying composition. With the foundation of the Experimental Band in 1961, Abrams became the initiator of the Chicago free jazz movement. Abrams's piano playing, as he himself says, is greatly influenced by Art Tatum (!) (from Litweiler 1967). There are unmistakable reminiscences of Cecil Taylor too, but Abrams's playing is more flowing and less rhythmically contrasted than Taylor's. As a clarinettist, Abrams dispenses with traditional virtuosity of every kind; he uses the instrument primarily in collective improvisations for playing long sustained, static tones, and hardly at all in solo improvisations. Under Richard Abrams's direction, the album *Levels and Degrees of Light* was recorded in 1968.

---

2) In order to earn a living, many of the AACM musicians played dance music and rhythm-and-blues on the side.

3) The full list of musicians who took part in concerts and recordings is too long to give here. See the details in the discography (Appendix).

Joseph Jarman, born in 1937 in Pine Bluff, Arkansas, has lived in Chicago since 1938. He began his musical career as a saxophonist in a military band. After 1958, he played in various Chicago jazz groups, principally blues and rock-and-roll bands. The profound effect that meeting Richard Abrams and joining the Experimental Band had on his psychical development is expressed in his own words on p. 164. During the Sixties, Jarman developed into one of the most important composers in the AACM. In addition, his interest in literature and the theatre had a lasting influence on the group's work. Many of the performances directed by Jarman were actually multi-media shows incorporating elements of contemporary musical theatre. Experience gained in the commedia dell'arte troupe he founded with Roscoe Mitchell still determines, to a great extent, his music today (more about that later). Like most of the AACM musicians, Joseph Jarman plays a number of instruments: alto, tenor and soprano saxophone, oboe, clarinet, and several more whose function in the music of the AACM will be discussed later. On his main horn, the alto, Jarman is an utterly individual stylist. His particular strength lies in lyrical, restrained passages, but he is also capable of very intensive energy-sound playing. His blues background is noticeably revealed at the end of his piece *Noncognitive Aspects of the City.* Two LPs have been issued under Jarman's name: *Song For* (1967) and *As If it Were the Seasons* (1968).

Roscoe Mitchell, born in Chicago in 1940, began playing the clarinet at 13, added the alto a short time later, and then — in the AACM — a whole arsenal of other woodwind instruments. During the Fifties, following the trend of the times, he played hard bop until he was inspired to leave that well-worn path through acquaintance with the music of Ornette Coleman (Endress 1970). Like Joseph Jarman, Roscoe Mitchell began his actual musical apprenticeship in the Experimental Band. Mitchell's playing is more aggressive than Jarman's, and his tone is harder. He is prone to fragmentary flourishes and unpredictable leaps in his angular phrases. Of outstanding stylistic significance is his use of tone colour. This is shown quite clearly in his unaccompanied solo piece *Tkhke* (on *Congliptious*), in which he blows, among other things, two alternate tones an octave apart, with continuous changes of tone colour. The albums *Sound* (1966) and *Congliptious* (1968) were made under Roscoe Mitchell's direction.

Lester Bowie, born in 1941 in Frederick, Maryland, grew up in St. Louis. At 5 he began taking trumpet lessons from his father, and he was just 14 when he founded his first band. Before Bowie went to Chicago and joined the AACM (he later became its second president) he had already had direct playing experience of the whole spectrum of Afro-American music. He toured the southern states with rhythm-and-blues bands (Gene Chandler, Joe Tex and others) and even temporarily worked in the tent shows of a wandering carnival troupe (Endress 1970, Wilmer 1971). During his studies at Lincoln University in St. Louis, and later at North Texas State University in Dallas, he played in several bebop and hard bop groups. Two of his partners were saxophonists James Clay and David Newman. He then went on tour again with rhythm-and-blues bands (Albert King and Oliver Sain). In Chicago, Bowie began by working as a studio musician. He became a member of the AACM in 1965. Lester Bowie's trumpet playing reveals a synthesis of traditional and advanced stylistic elements such as no other free-jazz trumpeter achieved with similar consistency. His playing has the power of the New Orleans veterans, as well as the vocalized sound of Ellington trumpeters Cootie Williams and Rex Stewart, plus the reflective subtlety of Miles Davis in his *Sketches of Spain* period. Half-open valves, growl tones, a wide vibrato and shrill cascades in the highest register, create a variety of sound that the trumpet had more or less lost in modern jazz. A good insight into Bowie's improvisation is provided by his solo piece *Jazz Death?* (on Mitchell's LP *Congliptious*), in which he gives a convincing negative answer to the question in the title. Under his own name, in 1967, Bowie recorded the LP *Numbers 1 and 2* with Jarman, Mitchell and bassist Malachi Favors. This is the first recording on which the later Art Ensemble of Chicago can be heard in its original formation.

Anthony Braxton, born in Chicago in 1945, joined the AACM in 1966 after four years of study at the Chicago School of Music (1959-63), followed by military service in Korea. According to Braxton, whose chief instrument is the alto, the earliest influence on him was the music of cool-jazz saxophonists Paul Desmond, Lee Konitz and Warne Marsh (Levin 1971). Later, stimulated by the AACM musicians, he increasingly directed himself toward the music of John Coltrane and Ornette Coleman. In addition, he made a detailed study of John Cage's and Karlheinz Stockhausen's music. The LPs *Three Compositions of New Jazz* (1968) and *Anthony Braxton* (1969) were made under his direction.

John Cage and Pirandello, Paul Desmond and John Coltrane, rhythm-and-blues and bebop, the tent show and the music school — this kaleidoscope of musical and social backgrounds is reflected, with varying intensity and clarity, in the music of the Chicago groups. The extent to which the AACM was successful in absorbing all these heterogeneous influences and in blending them into a new Chicago style is the subject of the following examination of the "Chicagoans'" music. Without meaning to imply that historic or stylistic dividing lines can be drawn, two phases of evolution can be recognized in the recorded music of the AACM (now about 15 LPs). The first phase is represented by records made from 1966 to 1968, involving various groups that emerged from the Experimental Band. These groups, led by Richard Abrams, Joseph Jarman, Roscoe Mitchell, Lester Bowie and Anthony Braxton among others, were generally not permanent, that is, they did not work steadily together, but were assembled especially for concerts, record dates, etc. The second documented phase of the AACM's activity appears on the records made by the Art Ensemble of Chicago. Founded in the summer of 1968 by Bowie, Jarman, Mitchell and bassist Malachi Favors, the Art Ensemble represents, so to speak, a concentrated charge of the most creative energies within the AACM. The group began to make itself known outside the narrower limits of the Chicago circle by a series of concerts at American universities, but is scored its real break-through when it settled in Paris in 1969. There the Théâtre des Vieux Colombier gave it a musical home, and there it made a number of records.

The first phase of Chicago free jazz can be identified as the search for an individual musical language. Many different influences are present in a relatively unfiltered condition, and "originality" at times consists of nothing more than a multitude of unrelated elements. The second phase, centred on the music of the Art Ensemble, is marked by a synthesis of the varied experience gained in Phase 1, and progresses from experimentation to the systematic working out of a multi-facetted, but now clearly oriented, musical conception.

The very first AACM recordings, Mitchell's *Sound* (1966) and Jarman's *Song For* (1967), plainly show that the music of the Chicagoans is first and foremost group music in which the main emphasis is on collective interaction, with less importance given to the solo playing. In this respect, solos are often of episodic brevity and act more as structural contrast to the collective sound than as long stretches of "self-projection" on the part of the soloists playing them.

I cannot agree with G. Endress when she states (1970) that a "retreat from soloistic virtuosity . . . which they [the musicians] do not yet possess" can be deduced from the fact that solo improvisation is minimized. On the contrary, there is much to indicate that in this music soloistic virtuosity of the traditional kind is deliberately pushed into the background because it goes against the grain of the music's conception. The solo is not abolished in the process. Far from it. It is even occasionally emphasized by solo improvisation in the literal sense, that is, without any accompanying background whatever. But at the same time, the role of the solo in the total structure of a piece is newly defined. The solo is no longer the culminating point of an individual show of creativity, but is one of many possible structural units within the sonic and formal organization. Considering the dominance of collective ensemble playing over the individual, it is obvious that what sets Chicago free jazz apart from the New York and European varieties is chiefly the Chicagoans' group conception. It must be noted here, however, that the Chicago musicians' individual styles of playing also become unique as time goes on, presumably because of interactions between collective and solo playing.

One of the prominent features of Chicago free jazz is its concern with tone colour. The titles of some compositions, like Roscoe Mitchell's *Sound* and Richard Abrams's *Levels and Degrees of Light,* tell us that sounds are the central element of the music. Other pieces in which the evolution of sound structures is in the foreground are Abrams's *Bird Song* and Jarman's *Song For.* What is decisive here, however, is not the fact that the Chicagoans concentrate on exploring the principles of working with tone colour; that was happening everywhere in free jazz during these years. The point is the way in which they went about it. As the reader will recall, Archie Shepp, in classifying his saxophonist colleagues, spoke of energy-sound players (*cf.* p. 71). The combination of energy and sound is typical not only of saxophonists but also of Cecil Taylor's piano playing and the collective improvisations in Coltrane's *Ascension.* In these cases sound-playing always implies, at the same time, rhythmic or, if you will, kinetic energy. Taylor's clusters have primarily a rhythmic-energetic function and only secondarily a sound function. And in Shepp's motion-clusters too, the element of motion dominates, and not that of sound — at least in the listener's awareness.

Things are different in the music of the Chicagoans. For them, working with sound often means the evolution of sound structures for their own sake, with all rhythmic motion and rhythmic articulation abandoned. "Sound surfaces" or "layers of sound" such as those that occur in *Levels and Degrees of Light* and *Noncognitive Aspects of the City,* are primarily given differentiation by instrumental shadings and dynamic gradations, and by a diffuse internal motion. The sound is created not by what the listener hears as a fusion of very fast consecutive tones which cannot be identified singly (as in Shepp or in *Ascension*), but by the superimposition of long sustained sounds that cannot be defined as chords. Unlike the static atonal clusters of avantgarde music, these sounds, despite their harmonic vagueness, are as a rule fixed to a tonal centre in the form of a pedal point in the bass. The percussion instruments used in such passages generally serve not as a means of accentuation, but as additional sound coloration. Usually they are instruments which by nature are vague in accentuation, such as gongs, bells, rattles, etc.

Not only with regard to motion do the Chicago sound improvisations differ markedly from the usual ways of treating sound in free jazz. A further specific feature is their intensity, or rather lack of intensity. Whereas Shepp's or Taylor's sound improvisations are generally climactic points in the course of a piece, the Chicagoans' sound structures are more restrained and meditative. In their music, sound improvisation is an element of psychical tranquillity rather than of agitation.

If the kind of sound improvisation I have described were the only creative principle in the music of the AACM, or even only the predominant one, it would be difficult to call the music the Chicagoans play free jazz. (This says nothing against its quality. But considering the theme of this book it would doubtless be an argument against including it.) As it happens, however, the static, tonally-centred sound surfaces — like the strictly solo improvisations — are just one of many means of musical organization; to be sure, they are a means rarely employed in New York or European free jazz, and are thus a perfectly legitimate feature of classification. Moreover, the Chicagoans' sound surfaces are often part of larger formal complexes, which are laid out according to a relatively simple but highly effective plan: static sound surfaces produced by long sustained tones and the undifferentiated clanking and jingling of percussion lead to rhythmically accentuated collective improvisations on the energy-sound principle, from which a solo (usually melodic as opposed to energetic) later proceeds. Each of the three phases of this formal complex, then, has a predominance of only one basic musical element: sound — rhythm — melody. Transitions between the parts can be gradual (as, for example, in Jarman's *Song For*); or the parts can be sharply distinguished from one another, as in Jarman's *Song for Christopher,* where a collective energy-sound improvisation breaks off abruptly and a static sound-field is established.

There is obviously a direct connection between the importance of tone colour in the Chicagoans' musical conception and the instrumentation they use, which in quantity and variety far exceeds the multi-instrumentalism normally found in free jazz. (The full instrumentation is not given on the record sleeves until the later recordings of the AACM, in particular those of the Art Ensemble. On earlier LPs there are only the words "little instruments.") A remarkably broad palette of unconventional instrumental colours is present from the start. Here are a few, chosen at random: slide whistles, recorders, harp, Japanese koto, harmonica, kazoo, police whistles, thunder sheet, bells and gongs, plus countless other percussion instruments. In contrast to other free-jazz groups which use a similarly variegated instrumentation (cf. for example Alexander v. Schlippenbach's Globe Unity, Saba 15109), these unorthodox sound-producers and noisemakers do not have the status of an exceptional artistic means in the music of the Chicagoans; they are not used "every so often," and then more or less as an experiment. On the contrary, they are present as a characteristic of style in almost all AACM records. One could call this instrumentation a "trade-mark" of Chicago free jazz.

The function of the "little instruments" in the music of the AACM is not always the same. In passages conceived as sound surfaces they either serve to enrich and colour the horn sounds by blending with them, or — as in the case of unpitched percussion — they enliven the sounds with irregular accents. But they also have a thematic function, and are frequently employed to form unusual sound combinations, as, for example, in Roscoe Mitchell's *Little Suite,* where one thematic section is presented by recorder and double bass in unison, and another by unison clarinet, bowed bass and harmonica, all to the rhythmic accompaniment of a ratchet. In Joseph Jarman's *Song to Make the Sun Come up* there is a trio consisting of alto saxophone, koto and percussion.

From time to time, the Chicago musicians seem to take their unorthodox sound-tools as sufficient reason for pure playfulness, flitting from one instrument to another in a rather hectic way. When done to excess, sequences like this often produce fascinating, opalescent, dense sound configurations, but there is occasionally a considerable amount of confusion and lack of direction. (It must be mentioned, however, that in all probability the AACM musicians — who are fond of musical happenings — quite deliberately set out to produce chaos.)

The thematic material of the AACM, as might be expected from the different temperaments and musical backgrounds of its important composers (Abrams, Jarman and Mitchell), has great variety. It includes such disparates as conventional modal tunes like Joseph Jarman's *Little Fox Run* or *Adam's Rib,* Roscoe Mitchell's angular *Ornette* (composed à la Coleman), and the complex sound compositions of Richard Abrams, which are sketched only in outlines. Among the latter are *Levels and Degrees of Light* and *Bird Song,* in which probably only the melodic line for vocalist Penelope Taylor is really written out.

A comparison of Jarman's and Mitchell's compositions is especially instructive, for it reveals some of the things which later, in the music of the Art Ensemble, were to lead to a productive field of tension between the two composers' musical temperaments. At the core, Joseph Jarman's compositions are lyrical, reflective and restrained, as is particularly evident in his "songs" *As If it Were the Seasons, Song to Make the Sun Come up,* and

Song for Christopher. In Jarman's pieces too, there are passages of considerable density and rhythmic energy, but from the composition point of view the predominant atmosphere is one of balance and tranquillity produced by clear, flowing melodic lines and symmetrical rhythms. Roscoe Mitchell's pieces, on the other hand, have a scurrilous and rather rustic gaiety about them. A sometimes extremely awkward instrumentation (recorder and bowed bass!) is paired with a kind of melody in which the banality of ironically exaggerated vaudeville music enters into a paradoxical union with tonally very advanced ideas. In an unconventional way, Mitchell's compositions seem conventional, without really being that at all.

As in the thematic material, there is no uniform conception of formal organization in the music of the AACM. Traditional "pieces" in the "theme-improvisation-theme" formula have a certain place at the beginning (Mitchell's *Ornette*, Jarman's *Adam's Rib* and *Little Fox Run*), but are later dropped. A great deal more numerous are multi-thematic suites, or pieces in which one or more melodic models serve as the contents of a collective or "group memory" improvisation. A notable example of this is Joseph Jarman's *As If it Were the Seasons:* the music revolves around a theme which is, so to speak, kept under wraps. The theme is obviously tucked away in the memory of all the musicians concerned; it turns up in fragments now and then during the piece, but not until the end is it presented in its entirety. The gradual evolution of thematic interconnections determines the direction the music takes, but at the same time guarantees enough room for free musical development.

Spoken and sung words play a significant role in the Chicagoans' music. As we know, there is a much stronger tendency in free jazz than in earlier styles to verbally incorporate ideological aspects into the context of the music. Coltrane, for instance, prefaces *Om* with a philosophical motto in the form of a pan-denominational prayer. Others, like Shepp, ridicule the "American dream" in poetic fashion *(The Wedding)* or give voice to rage at the assassination of Malcolm X. These manifestations of an awakening consciousness, which occurred within the black American minority during the Sixties, are too important to be dismissed as a fashion and thus an aberration in what is otherwise thought of as an intact and unblemished world of jazz. One must of course beware of the opposite extreme, which would be to interpret the music of a given composer or group only as a reflection of an ideological concept. Analogies, however, can be drawn in many cases between verbal programmes and the emotional content of free-jazz improvisations (which have themselves increasingly moved closer to language in their expression). The problems this poses are much too complex to be dealt with exhaustively here, but one more aspect should be mentioned. To what extent, one is bound to ask, are the words integrated into the music, or are they simply an appendage to it? Conversely, to what extent are words and music two isolated levels (meaning versus expression) which, although mutually supplementary in theory, are held together in the final analysis in that they co-exist without fusing into a structural entity?

A comparison of the examples given above (Coltrane, Shepp) with the music of the AACM shows that in the latter the integration of language into music is plainly further advanced. This is not to say that the Chicago musicians are more able to handle the problem of coupling language and music than were Coltrane or Shepp (who were probably not aware that there was a problem). The causes lie rather in the specific frame of reference in which the music of the AACM was placed from the very start. As we have seen, the AACM performances were very often on the order of contemporary musical theatre, with music as just one element among many, even if it was the most important. The combination of stage action, spoken words and music is therefore not on the periphery of the AACM's artistic "self-identification" but squarely in the centre. It is only natural that on recordings by the Chicagoans (which must be considered in a sense as acoustical extracts of their shows) at least the verbal, communicative component is incorporated and — thanks to years of experience in coping with the problems this presents — is more smoothly integrated than is elsewhere the case.

The functions of vocal elements in the music of the Chicagoans, and the forms they take, are multifarious and occasionally overlap one another. The most important are singing, spoken poetry, symbolic word-signals, and finally, vocalism as a means of representing alienation and as pure buffoonery.

Comparatively, the most conventional vocal form in the music of the AACM is singing, although it is not unlikely that the voice is used principally in a quasi-instrumental way, with the words' message secondary. The lines sung by Penelope Taylor (who has a "classical" timbre) in Abrams's *Levels and Degrees of Light,* and by Sherri Scott (whose singing is closer to jazz) in Jarman's *Song to Make the Sun Come up,* are instrumental in conception and seem designed more for musical interaction with the instruments than to be accompanied by them in a traditional way. The dialectical relationship between voice and instruments is especially clear in *Song to Make the Sun Come up,* where from time to time a bubbling agitation in the horns and percussion is superimposed on the vocalist's calmly flowing melodic line.

When spoken poetry and music are combined, the message of the words is obviously much more prominent than when a text is sung. There is real danger that the music will be reduced to a mere sound backdrop, or — as is the case in many rigged-up "jazz and poetry" experiments involving words and music not written for each other — that the two will run as it were on separate tracks. But Joseph Jarman's *Noncognitive Aspects of the City* (among other pieces) demonstrates that a very intensive interaction between words and music can indeed be attained. There are passages in this piece in which parallel spans of verbal and musical tension are created, when Joseph Jarman as reciter achieves an emotional intensification by repeating sentences and words, setting off a matching rhythmic-dynamic compression in the music. This means that there is a feedback process in which Jarman's voice and phrasing, and the collective improvisations by his companions, influence each other. Furthermore, there are passages in Jarman's *Aspects* when the speaking voice not only has something to say verbally, but clearly dominates as a rhythmic (and thus musical) element, while the players provide a diffuse, undelineated background of sounds.

Using the voice as a signal for individual emotional or social situations gains importance after 1968 in the Art Ensemble recordings, but is comparatively rare in the early records of the AACM. Without question, this vocal form also has something to do with the Chicagoans' theatre-oriented performances, in which the cries of an anguished creature, insane laughter or dull muttering are connected with dramatic situations. Transferring such vocal (but usually non-verbal) elements to the "blind" medium of the record is risky, since the meaning that arose from the dramatic context is lost and the originally "meaningful" signal appears to be purely a joke (which is not to say that there is anything bad about jokes).

Striking examples of vocal signals in a musical context are found in Lester Bowie's *Numbers 1 and 2*. Unintelligible commands are shouted to the accompaniment of a police whistle. Over a sustained, melancholic melody played by Malachi Favors and Lester Bowie, Jarman and Mitchell sing nonsense syllables in falsetto, like nervous opera singers. After a general rest, someone shouts "Ring the bell, man!" and the hectic clanking of a cowbell is heard. As these examples (which I have taken at random) show, the boundary between symbolic signals and happenings is fluid, and interpreting these signals is problematic. But one should bear in mind, in any event, that these sometimes seemingly absurd vocal actions must on no account be considered as mere stylistic additives that give an extra (and extraneous) effect to the music. The combination of music, coherent words and seemingly incoherent happenings results directly from the Chicagoans' style of performance. The AACM recordings are reductions of those performances, made necessary by the medium itself.

The reader may have noticed that so far I have referred to the music of groups led by Richard Abrams, Joseph Jarman, Roscoe Mitchell and Lester Bowie, and have omitted the contribution of the youngest leader in the AACM, Anthony Braxton. This was intentional, for saxophonist and composer Braxton does in fact occupy — musically speaking — the position of an outsider in Chicago free jazz, and this makes it seem advisable to discuss his music separately.

As is made clear by the LPs *Three Compositions of New Jazz* (1968) and *Anthony Braxton* (1969), both recorded by Braxton with trumpeter Leo Smith, violinist Leroy Jenkins and others, there is a startling conceptual difference between his music and that of the other AACM groups. As I mentioned in Braxton's biographical data (p. 167), Cage and Stockhausen were among the decisive musical influences on him. Presumably this is the clue to the distinguishing marks of his music, for like no other musician of the AACM, Braxton has adapted the creative ideas of Euro-American avantgarde music. At the same time, he has drawn away from the jazz-based stylistic elements that form the foundation of the music of the other Chicago groups — if not always, then at least in large measure. One of the important distinguishing features here lies in the rhythm, or — more precisely — in those verbally elusive qualities that result from motion and are psycho-physically felt as motion, which form one of the decisive criteria of every kind of jazz, be it swing, bebop or free jazz. Those qualities are lacking almost everywhere in Braxton's music. Their place is taken by a certain rhythmic sterility, which is also peculiar to a good percentage of advanced European improvised music. In the slow passages of Braxton's pieces, accents crumble into disconnected sound occurrences, void of all tension. Fast passages simulate the energetic rhythm of free jazz à la Cecil Taylor, but ultimately turn out to be merely acceleration, rather than rhythmic intensification.

Two factors are probably chiefly responsible for the absence of a jazz-like kinetic energy in the music of Anthony Braxton's groups: the first is the attitude toward rhythm on the part of Braxton and his violinist Leroy Jenkins; the second is a lack of rhythmic interaction within the group. As regards the first point, it is noticeable that the phrasing of both Braxton and Jenkins tends to be relatively unaccentuated and thus lacking in clear rhythmic delineation. Braxton's playing has a certain droning monotony, while Jenkins's improvisations sometimes recall the cadenzas of a romantic violin concerto that aim at beauty of tone and have little rhythmic differentiation. How remote the playing of these two musicians is from jazz becomes evident when it is compared to the playing of the third permanent member of the group, the trumpeter Leo Smith, whose improvisations — especially in combination with Richard Abrams in Braxton's piece *"N-M488-44M"*– are marked by a strong drive. As to the second point, the musical interactions within the group are concentrated primarily on developing structural differentiation; only rarely, however, do these interactions produce an even detectable common rhythmic basis (I do not mean a beat). And this does appear, after all, to be indispensable to the creation of propellant chains of impulses and thus to a new kind of collective drive, as the music of Taylor, Shepp and Ayler shows — and the music of Jarman, Mitchell and Bowie too.

Anthony Braxton has protested with some vehemence against having his music compared with that of his AACM colleagues, and against value judgements being drawn from such a comparison (Levin 1971). On the latter point he is absolutely in the right, especially if he wishes to have his music understood as something fundamentally different from free jazz in general and from the Chicago variety in particular. This granted, the absence of jazz rhythm (which I have already noted) should not be thought of as a shortcoming but either as a neutral fact that invites no evaluation, or as the consequence of a musical conception in which jazz rhythm has no place. But what is that musical conception? Anthony Braxton tells us in the article by Robert Levin mentioned above: "I myself saw . . . music from a mathematical perspective and worked with mathematical systems. I wanted to arrive at a vocabulary of my own, and not take over somebody else's . . . My music is now a combination of all the things I learned in the AACM, plus the knowledge I have gained from mathematics concerning sounds, relationships, density, structures, various forms; I call it conceptional transference, a mixture of the most different elements."[4] The most obvious realization of this ambitious programme, which describes a kind of music determined by constructionist principles, is found in the titles of Braxton's pieces as they appear on the record sleeves. The complicated graphic diagrams with lines, numbers and letters, have no resemblance at all to what we are accustomed to think of as titles; they would be likely to give any conscientious discographer a headache.

---

4) Retranslated from German, Levin 1971.

The constructionism that these titles suggest, however, is hardly ever found in the music of Braxton's groups. The general formal layout of the pieces is doubtless pre-planned, and there is sometimes an organization of musical details that guarantees structural differentiation. But in the end, the predominant impression is that of spontaneous improvisation running neither together nor counter, but simply side by side, improvisations that in general are neither slack nor taut, with an aimlessness that does not in the least make one suspect a system of mathematical relationships as a groundwork.

I hope that this excursion to the outskirts of Chicago free jazz — and that is where I consider Anthony Braxton's musical position to be — will not be taken as a malicious criticism of a man whose music I do not care for. The purpose of the excursion was rather to point out a trend that has gained more ground in free jazz than at any other time in jazz history: a movement in all directions, toward all aspects of world music. This could become possible only when the formal, tonal and rhythmic canons of traditional jazz were overthrown, and it has led not only to incorporating musical elements of the Third World, but equally to adapting the materials and creative ideas of the European avant-garde. Anthony Braxton's music, and all the consequences it involves, seems to me to be symptomatic of the latter part of that trend. That Cecil Taylor, Archie Shepp and Don Cherry could, without detriment to their own music, absorb Bartók and Stravinsky, African drum rhythms, and Arabic and Indian melodic models respectively, doubtless had something to do with their ability at synthesizing, but it had even more to do with the characteristics of the material they brought in from "outside." The qualities and creative principles of the newest European music, however, are possibly too unmalleable to be integrated into the substance of jazz, without leading at the same time to a metamorphosis in which jazz itself is lost.*)

The most important alternative in Chicago free jazz to Anthony Braxton's musical conception has been, since 1968, the music of the Art Ensemble of Chicago, a formation consisting of Lester Bowie, Joseph Jarman, Roscoe Mitchell and Malachi Favors. On a very distinct jazz foundation, the experience gained in the various AACM groups is expanded and consolidated into an unmistakeable musical language in this quartet. In the evolution of Chicago free jazz, the music of the Art Ensemble represents the time of maturity.

---

*) The example of Anthony Braxton's music shows to which extent the time-lag between the writing of a book and its final publication may relativate the analyses given in it. Although there is hardly anything to add to the remarks made about Braxton's recordings of the Sixties we have to state that his music underwent some remarkable changes during the beginning of the Seventies: While working with groups outside the AACM, namely with Chick Corea's "Circle" and later with Dave Holland and Sam Rivers, the music of Anthony Braxton got a rhythmical drive and melodical inventiveness, that made him one of the most exciting improvisers of the time. (See for example: "Circle — Paris-Concert," ECM 1018/19, and Dave Holland — Conference of the Birds, ECM 1027).

While the Art Ensemble was in France, it made a number of records (1969/70) which provide a mass of material for discussing its music. The main albums are *A Jackson in Your House, Reese and the Smooth Ones, Message to Our Folks, People in Sorrow,* plus the music to a film by Moshe Mizrah, *Les Stances à Sophie,* in which Lester Bowie's wife, vocalist Fontella Bass, also takes part. With the Chicago blues musicians Julio Finn and Chicago Beau (both of whom had worked with Archie Shepp in Paris), the Art Ensemble recorded the ironic-critical work *Certain Blacks Do What They Wanna.* The group also appeared at the "Free-Jazz-Meeting" organized by J. E. Berendt in Baden-Baden in December 1969, which led, among other things, to recording a big-band composition by Lester Bowie called *Gettin' to Know Y'all.*

Although I intend to discuss the music of the Art Ensemble of Chicago mainly as a group style and not as a concentration of personal styles, a few prefatory remarks are necessary about the musical traits of each of the four members, Bowie, Jarman, Mitchell and Favors.

In the biographical notes on Lester Bowie I mentioned his ability to blend the most varied "historical" trumpet playing techniques into a style that is autonomous and very advanced, despite its "historizing" aspects. While Bowie's versatility and technical potential are apparent enough on the records of the Art Ensemble, there are two expressive features in the foreground which are in some ways reminiscent of Don Cherry: the first is a sense of humour which finds an outlet in a deliberately "crumpled" manner of articulation and in a certain tendency to hoary musical jokes; the second is a pronounced lyric streak, which is shown to particularly good effect in Bowie's minor-mood balladesque improvisations in *A Brain for the Seine (Message to Our Folks)* and *People in Sorrow.*

Pinning down the style characteristics of Joseph Jarman and Roscoe Mitchell involves some difficulty for two reasons. First, their saxophone playing, compared to earlier AACM records, becomes increasingly similar in tone and phrasing; this is possibly due to the mutual influence and adjustment that comes from close musical contact. Second, they both have such a broad range of technical and expressive means that their individual contribution to the music of the Art Ensemble can hardly be reduced to a few salient features. (And this does not take into account their multi-instrumentalism, which sometimes pushes their alto playing into a subordinate role.) The spectrum extends from the rough timbre and rhythmic aggressiveness of a rhythm-and-blues player (as in *Rock Out* and *Bye Bye Baby*), to swinging and melodically complex improvisations à la Eric Dolphy (as in Parker's *Dexterity*), and to frugal sound improvisations interspersed with long rests (as in *A Brain for the Seine*). Both musicians' "style" lies in their versatility — like Don Cherry's style in the late Sixties — and their eclecticism is made legitimate by their competence in doing justice to the musical context of the moment.

The rhythmic motor of the Art Ensemble, in the absence of a drummer, is bassist Malachi Favors, who can do absolutely everything. Favors has the driving swing of a

Henry Grimes, the quasi "singing" pizzicato of a Charles Haden, the advanced bowing techniques of a David Izenzon, plus a lot more. He alone often provides the rhythmic groundwork for three improvising horns and occasionally arrives at a manner of playing reminiscent of African drum techniques (cf., among others, *People in Sorrow*): very fast, short-tone patterns that make any percussion superfluous.

The conceptual bases of the Art Ensemble's music, as evident in the first four recordings mentioned above, are identical in many respects to those of the earlier AACM groups. Since I do not want to repeat here what I have already written, I will limit myself to describing the changes that occurred after 1968 in the music of the Art Ensemble. Those changes are in general neither sudden nor fundamental, but more gradual.

One of the important stylistic factors in the music of the AACM from the very beginning was an exploration of tone colour, which led to the use of an unusual quantity of diverse instruments and also had a direct effect on creative principles (development of static sound-fields, etc.). The Art Ensemble expands the tone-colour aspect of its music by bringing in a multitude of new instruments. Gudrun Endress (1970) reports that when the group went to Europe it took more than 500 musical instruments along. A first impression of what that array included can be gained by summarizing the instruments listed on the records made by the Art Ensemble in France:

Lester Bowie: trumpet, flügelhorn, cowhorn, bass drum;

Roscoe Mitchell: soprano, alto and bass saxophone, clarinet, flute, cymbals, gongs, conga drums, steel drum, logs, bells, siren, whistles;

Joseph Jarman: soprano, alto and tenor saxophone, clarinet, oboe, bassoon, flutes, marimba, vibraphone, guitar, conga drums, bells, gongs, whistles, sirens, etc.;

Malachi Favors: double bass, fender bass, banjo, zither, log drum and other percussion instruments.

On some recordings there are also piano and accordion.

Considering the quantity of equipment and the availability of a wide range of sounds and colours, there is an astounding economy in their use. One of the decisive achievements of the Art Ensemble lies precisely in turning away from every kind of musical muscle-flexing. What creates the impression of intensity and enhancement is not decibels, but density and drive. Moreover, the music gains greatly in transparency by dispensing with a drummer. Actually, what is dispensed with is jazz percussion of the traditional kind, for each of the musicians plays several percussion instruments. However, by spreading the instruments over the quartet, by a division of labour into bass drum, cymbals, melodic percussion (marimba and vibraphone), and other percussion instruments, percussion is employed selectively, and to a considerable degree as a means of structural differentiation, and is not constantly present as a matter of course.

Isolating the various elements of conventional jazz percussion goes hand in hand with a partial rejection of customary ways of playing other instruments. The piano for example, whose role in the Art Ensemble puts it paradoxically into the "little instrument" category, is generally used to provide just a sound background *(People in Sorrow)*. The accordion does not play melodies — its traditional function — but produces long sustained, static tones. The strings of the zither are not plucked but are struck with a stick, which either produces sharply accentuated clusters of indeterminate pitch or (as in *People in Sorrow*) a short-lived rhythmic continuum. It is important to note that these and other examples of sound alienation (which can of course be heard in the earlier AACM recordings too) very rarely appear for their own sake in the Art Ensemble. That is, the denatured sound is not to be comprehended as an isolated occurrence sufficient unto itself; in general, it stands in a dialectical relationship to the music around it. In a piece by Anthony Braxton, for instance, the squeaks and squawks of four rubbed, inflated balloons are the whole musical "substance" for a length of time. In the Art Ensemble, on the other hand, the denatured percussive or static instrumental sound usually complements some other musical element. Art Ensemble themes drawn from traditional jazz, like Parker's *Dexterity (Message to Our Folks)* or the soul piece *Theme de Yoyo (Stances à Sophie)*, are deliberately disrupted by the interpolation of denatured sounds and noises. Similar things happen during some "lyrical" solos by Lester Bowie, whose beauty of melody and tone is contrasted to the rattle and click of "little instruments." This confrontation of various levels of expression and style, in which the expressive power of one level is relativized by the other, is an important part of the basic conception of the Art Ensemble's music, even though the passages in question may not be pre-planned in detail, but result from spontaneous interactions between the musicians.

The ways and means of musical organization prove to be just as numerous in the Art Ensemble as in the earlier records of the AACM. But a gradually changing attitude to time can be noticed which appears similarly in the music of Don Cherry (*cf.* p. 158). Pieces like *People in Sorrow, A Brain for the Seine* and *Song for Charles* reveal spacious and "quiet" processes of evolution that demand a good deal of patience and adaptation from listeners accustomed to the more active music of Coltrane, Taylor and Shepp.

Two important creative means employed in these long processes of development are pedal points and rests. They have very different functions to fulfil. While the pedal points bind the musical progress to a central point for a period of time and thus give a sense of repose, the primary purpose of rests is to heighten tension. The recognition on the part of the Art Ensemble that absolute silence has a tension-producing effect is also manifest in some of the unaccompanied solo improvisations by the four musicians, whose phrases are occasionally punctuated by long pauses — sometimes painfully long for the listener.

Compared to the music of the AACM up to 1968, there is a considerable expansion in the Art Ensemble's thematic material. The group shows a partiality to traditional elements from all conceivable musical and cultural areas. A brief list will serve to illustrate this: *Reese and the Smooth Ones* begins with a "tootling" waltz, which conjures up an atmosphere similar to that of the fair scene in Stravinsky's *Petrouchka*. The structure and melody of another theme in the same piece evoke associations with Charles Mingus's melancholy *What Love* (*cf.* p. 37). *A Jackson in Your House,* likewise built as a suite, begins with a pompous overture whose Baroque grace is considerably impaired by percussive interjections and laughter. Later comes a Dixieland piece with slapped bass and a clarinet whose syncopated phrasing is insistently corny. Finally, there is an episode in imitation of the swing style.

On the same LP *(Jackson)* is the march *Get in Line* that goes at an unmilitary headlong pace until it ends in the total pandemonium of a collective cymbal-crashing session; and a waltz *(The Waltz)* whose Viennese charm is rather adversely affected by the hacking accentuations of the accompanying bass.

The two Art Ensemble pieces in the style of contemporary rock, *Theme de Yoyo (Stances à Sophie)* and *Rock Out (Message to Our Folks)* are each treated in different ways. While the former (whose film music function presumably protects it from too much denaturing at the hands of the Chicagoans) is only "broken up" by the interpolation of free collectively improvised breaks, *Rock Out* proves to be a parodistic lark: its ingenuous bass pattern is drowned out by noise at the end.

The examples I have given denote just one aspect of the Art Ensemble's creative work, and remembering the group's suites and their broadly proportioned processes of evolution, that aspect may not even be the most significant. Still, precisely those examples give some clues to the musical self-identification of the Art Ensemble. In somewhat the same way as Archie Shepp, the group introduces into its music influences from a number of stylistic areas of jazz and other musical cultures. Only in the rarest instances does that "historical" material appear unfiltered. It is shaped to match the specific group stylistic features of the Art Ensemble; the time-honoured clichés of traditional music remain recognizable by allusion and occasionally by ironic overstatement, but they are never brought directly into play. Many of these pieces are funny (to use a word that is taboo in jazz criticism) and are doubtless meant to be exactly that way. Others obviously are tied up with the socio-critical message of the Art Ensemble *(Message to Our Folks)*, which takes a much more direct and aggressive line than was the case in the AACM. Ideology is no longer disguised as poetry, but appears as a sermon *(Old Time Religion)*; metaphorical trappings are stripped away and replaced by open agitation *(Certain Blacks Do What They Wanna! — Join Them!)*. Getting this message across in a medium as non-political as music means necessarily going back to models whose meaning the listener can decipher. But reversion does not unavoidably have to end in triviality; this is demonstrated quite conclusively by the "traditional" themes of the Art Ensemble. To measure them exclusively by an aesthetic yardstick, however, would be just as senseless as to interpret the sound improvisations of the group as protest.

Chapter 10

SUN RA

"With the current lack of new ideas in jazz, charlatans have a chance too," wrote an anonymous German jazz critic in 1970[1]. The cause of his indignation and the object of his wrath was Sun Ra.

What is a charlatan? According to the Oxford Universal Dictionary: "a mountebank, an empiric who pretends to wonderful knowledge or secrets, an impostor, a quack." In terms of free jazz this would be a man who buys a saxophone today, walks out on the stage with it tomorrow, simulates "freedom" by blowing away like mad with a lot of haphazard fingerwork (not having the faintest idea about the keys), and then swears to us that the whole sorry demonstration is great art.

I do not think our anonymous critic had this kind of charlatan in mind, for anybody who has followed Sun Ra's musical development over the last 16 years knows that he has complete command of the manual side of his music. From what, then, does the charge of charlatanry arise?

In Sun Ra's biography and in his unusual philosophical conception (as has been recorded in a large number of interviews), there are many things that are bound to puzzle a sober-sided central European. Neither the place nor the date of his birth is known. Sun Ra him-self — whose real name, according to various sources, is either Sonny Blondt or Blount — has given to understand that he was born "under the sign of Gemini in the month of May," in "arrival zone USA" (from Fiofori 1970). We have further managed to learn that he grew up in Gary, Indiana, lived for a few years in Washington, where he began to study music, and that he went to Chicago in the Forties. After that, his biography takes on clearer contours[2].

In Chicago, he worked for several years under the name Le Sony'r Ra as a pianist and arranger in various bands that accompanied the shows in Club DeLisa, a variety theatre. Among them were the orchestras of Jesse Miller and Fletcher Henderson. Occasional jobs brought him together with Stuff Smith and Coleman Hawkins, and in November 1948 he took part with tenor saxophonist Yusef Lateef in a recording date for Aristocrat, led

---

1) "Der Spiegel," 24th year (1970), No. 47, p. 228.

2) For biographical data I refer to Figi (Delmark 411), Noames (1955), McRae (1966), Carles (1968, 1972) and Fiofori (1970, 1971).

by bassist Gene Wright *(Eugene Wright and his Dukes of Swing)*. In 1953 Sun Ra formed his first group with tenor saxophonist John Gilmore (who is still playing with him today), bassist Richard Evans and drummer Robert Barry. The quartet soon expanded into a big band, and in 1956 the first LP under Sun Ra's name was made: *Jazz by Sun Ra,* Transition TRLP 10, reissued in 1967 by Delmark under the title *Sun Song.* The "Arkestra," as Sun Ra has called his band since then (with changing attributives), attracted during these years — like Richard Abrams's Experimental Band was later to do — a number of talented musicians from Chicago and the vicinity. They lived together in a kind of musicians' commune, constantly rehearsing and experimenting, and many of Sun Ra's compositions originated during these rehearsals directly from the interactions between himself and his musicians.

Toward the end of 1961, the Arkestra went to Montreal for an engagement, about the success and length of which there is some confusion in the literature[3]. What is certain is that afterward Sun Ra did not return to Chicago but settled in New York, where most of his musicians followed him in the succeeding weeks and months. In 1964, the Arkestra took part in the "October Revolution in Jazz" staged by Bill Dixon. Sun Ra joined the Jazz Composers' Guild, which emerged from that first modest free-jazz festival, but soon left it, partly for ideological reasons. Later he said about Archie Shepp and Cecil Taylor: "They were doing their thing, but they were not talking about Space or Intergalactic things ... They were talking about Avant Garde and the New Thing" (from Fiofori 1970).

The reproachful undertone in these words and the mention of space and galaxy bring us to the side of Sun Ra that continues to provoke the greatest mistrust and the most violent reactions in the ranks of jazz publicists today. Sun Ra, who according to his own declarations thinks of himself more as a scientist than as a musician (Noames 1965), and for whom free jazz has never had the same political implications as it had for Shepp and Taylor, claims that he is playing the "music of the universe" and outlines various stages of development, analogous to the changing designations of the Arkestra[4]. In 1970, he said in an interview with Tam Fiofori, a Nigerian jazz critic and poet living in New York: "I'm not playing Space Music as the ultimate reach anymore. That is, not in the interplanetary sense alone. I'm playing intergalactic music, which is beyond the other idea of space music, because it is of the natural infinity of the eternal universe ... Music is a universal language. The intergalactic music in its present phase of presentation will be correlative to the key synopsis of the past and to the uncharted multi-potential planes outside the bounds of the limited earth-eternity future. The intergalactic music is in hieroglyphic sound: an abstract analysis and synthesis of man's relationship to the universe, visible and invisible first man and second man."

---

3) J. B. Figi (Delmark 411) says that the engagement was cancelled. Sun Ra says it lasted five days (from Kaiser 1968), and Barry McRae (1965) talks about four months.

4) Sun Ra's orchestra has had the following names: Myth-Science Arkestra, Solar Arkestra, Astro-Infinity Arkestra, and Intergalactic-Research Arkestra.

It is not my intention here to ruminate over the cryptic meaning of these words, which say absolutely nothing about Sun Ra's music. But we must ask ourselves whether the irrationalism audible in them justifies the accusation of charlatanry which I mentioned at the beginning of this chapter, or whether these utopian speculations may perhaps be the extreme form of a phenomenon that puts a stronger stamp on musician-critic communication in the jazz of the Sixties than ever before. In the past, jazz musicians, in response to interviewers' questions, usually said nice things about their colleagues, described funny or tragic events that had occurred early in their careers, spoke about the jazzmen who had been their ideals, or complained about the shoddy conditions of nightclub work[5]. In conversations with free-jazz musicians, however, a theme comes more frequently into the picture that points beyond the tangible facts of music-making and its social and economic aspects. The repeated emphasis by John Coltrane, Albert Ayler, Pharoah Sanders, Don Cherry and others on the spiritual aspects of their music, the use of a terminology in which transcendence, spiritual vibration and the magic word "Om" are among the basic concepts — all this doubtless differs from the utopias of Sun Ra. But the difference is of degree and not of principle.

When the creative ideas of free jazz, developed for the most part in small groups, are transferred to a big band, the problems that arise are both musical and economic in nature, and the latter unfortunately very often decide whether an orchestra stays together or breaks up.

One of the musical problems is due to the fact that a larger group requires a larger measure of musical organization and pre-planning than a small group, in which spontaneous inter-actions between the musicians work out more smoothly. The "classical" big band, with its sections and settings, is opposed to individual development. Organized discipline leaves little room for spontaneous processes of evolution. And "modernizing" the ensemble sound by written-out clusters (as happened in the Jazz Composers' Orchestra) does not eliminate the problem. The individual musician is just as much forced into the not very creative role of a re-interpreter, as he is playing the same riff throughout a dozen choruses in the Count Basie band. The problem of the big band in free jazz, then, lies first and foremost in employing the sound potential of a large apparatus structurally, without having to revert to the normative organization of the "classical" big band, that is, without having to reduce the individual creativity of a majority of the players to merely reading notes.

The economic problems of a free-jazz orchestra do not fundamentally differ from those of big bands in traditional jazz, but they do differ in proportion. At a time when the US State Department has repeatedly sent the orchestras of Duke Ellington and Benny Goodman on world tours to make propaganda for an American culture of yesterday; at a time when the nostalgia of a frustrated bourgeoisie is helping the reconstructed "original"

---

5) *Cf.* in particular Shapiro/Hentoff (1955)

orchestra of the late Glenn Miller to new fame and a full till; at a time like this, nothing much is going to change the reduced economic viability of a big band that attempts to play free jazz. That Sun Ra's orchestra is the only one to date in free jazz whose musical development shows continuity, that it has survived despite a minimum of jobs, may have to do with the circumstance that financial success, or lack of it, has a very low place in the scale of values that is part of Sun Ra's philosophy[6], and that both the human and the musical bond between himself and his musicians is tighter than is usually the case in a big band.

Attempts to play "big band free jazz" have remained limited as a rule to sporadic concerts or scattered recordings. The Jazz Composers' Orchestra led by trumpeter Mike Mantler and pianist Carla Bley, and firmly anchored in a registered association, has been comparatively the most stable. But even this formation, in which all the more outstanding free-jazz musicians of the New York circle have taken part over the years, meets relatively rarely. In 1968, a double album was privately issued. The compositions are by Mike Mantler. Cecil Taylor, Don Cherry, Roswell Rudd, Pharoah Sanders and Gato Barbieri (among others) are heard as soloists. The album showed with some success that advanced European composing techniques can be transferred to free jazz. But the standard division of roles into soloists and accompanists was not even remotely overcome, nor are the compositions and improvisations integrated into an organic whole.

The activities of the Globe Unity Orchestra, a group of predominantly German musicians under the direction of pianist Alexander von Schlippenbach, have likewise been restricted so far to a single LP (1966) and a few concerts. The quality of the concerts, moreover, has occasionally suffered from the relatively small amount of rehearsal time the musicians have had available.

The London Jazz Composers Orchestra, created in 1970 by the English composer and bassist Barry Guy, has fared similarly. Guy's *Ode for Jazz Orchestra* is one of the most convincing free-jazz compositions anywhere, but Guy has not yet been able to find a record company willing to risk a production.

During the past sixteen years, Sun Ra has made nearly 30 LPs with his orchestra, more than any other free-jazz musician with the exception of Coltrane. Only a fraction of this immense production has ever been available to the public at large, however, since the majority of the records, issued by Sun Ra himself on his Saturn label, can only be obtained from a mail-order service that most of the time does not seem to work[7]. At the

---

6) The realization that even the black bourgeoisie was hostile to his music, while the people of under-privileged districts like Harlem received it with enthusiasm, did not lead Sun Ra to adapt to "paying audiences," but instead led him to play in the streets of Harlem (*cf.* the interview with Sun Ra by Rolf-Ulrich Kaiser (1968).

7) The Chicago address given on some Saturn productions does not exist.

risk of leaving out one or another detail in the development of Sun Ra's music, I will refer in my comments to the recordings of the Arkestra that have been issued in Europe. The material on those eight LPs (cf. the discography) can be regarded as fairly representative.

"He [Sun Ra] was playing free jazz before there was even the term 'free jazz' — since the first half of the Fifties" (Berendt 1970, p. 62).

One often runs across comments like this in writings about jazz. It may be that critics, having more or less ignored Sun Ra's music for years, later tended to over-compensate. There is absolutely no foundation for styling him a prophet of free jazz. As is evident in the albums *Sun Song* and *Sound of Joy* (recorded 1956/57), Sun Ra's orchestra played what can be called at best a relatively unconventional variety of hard bop with Ellington influences that add a certain element of timelessness. The album *The Futuristic Sounds of Sun Ra,* recorded in 1961 in New York, also promises more in its title than it actually delivers. When placed alongside Coleman's collective improvisation *Free Jazz,* which was made at about the same time (1960), and Cecil Taylor's *Into the Hot* (recorded in 1961), Sun Ra's "futuristic sounds" appear pretty conservative. These remarks are not meant to detract in the slightest from Sun Ra's significance for the further development of free jazz. But it is important to establish a precise chronology.

Although the Chicago recordings of the Arkestra can hardly be said to have anticipated free jazz, there are some important indications in them of stylistic features that were to be part of Sun Ra's music during the decade that followed. Taken together, these records are swinging big-band jazz between jump and hard bop. Their arrangements and harmony occasionally recall the music of the Shorty Rogers big band on the West Coast. (The 12-bar blues *Two Tones,* for example, begins with some of the favourite changes in West Coast jazz: Bb Bb^7/Am^7 D^7/Gm^7/Fm^7 Bb^7/Eb^7 etc.)

Most of Sun Ra's pieces of that time have a structure based predominantly on functional harmony (many also follow the blues pattern). But there are a few exceptions which could be called modal, for example *El is a Sound of Joy* and *Fall of the Log.* In the latter, there is an eight-bar alternation between D flat major and F major. Modality, however, is obviously mainly a compositional device; there is nothing to show that it was intended to be a point of departure for a new concept of improvisation, as it was later for Davis and Coltrane.

In Sun Ra's thematic material of the Fifties, one section of one piece stands out: the introduction to his composition *Saturn* (Example 69). Over a simple ostinato pattern in the piano, there is an unusually angular 7-bar melody with a range of more than two octaves, whose tonal relationships are heavily veiled and at some points completely cancelled. But this escape from tonality is short-lived. The introduction, which sounds quite unusual for 1957, is followed by a very conventional theme, and this is followed in turn by equally conventional solos by John Gilmore, Dave Young, Art Hoyle and Pat Patrick. Nevertheless, *Saturn* was one of the pieces that remained longest in the Arkestra repertoire, an indication of the exceptional position it held at the time among Sun Ra's compositions.

EXAMPLE 69   SATURN

If, generally speaking, neither the harmonic-melodic nor the rhythmic components of Sun Ra's music during the Fifties tell us much about its later development, the element of sound does suggest a new departure. The sound of the orchestra is strikingly "low register." Two baritone saxophones (in *Sound of Joy*), trombone and tenor saxophone create a definite preponderance of lower registers, also characteristic of Sun Ra's recordings during the Sixties. Furthermore, there is besides the normal jazz percussion a copious use of timpani, rare in jazz groups up to that time. Their main purpose is to give colour to the rhythmic foundation. But the timpani are also used soloistically; in *El Viktor* and *Street Named Hell,* for example, there are out-and-out chase choruses with percussion and timpani taking turns as solo instruments. Of particular importance here is the variability of sound that timpanist Jim Herndorn (who is otherwise not very swinging) achieves with the pedals.

Apart from solos, which are mostly independent of the tune being played (in the jump-oriented *Reflections in Blue* there is a timpani solo, too), the job of the timpani is usually to create an emotional atmosphere that musically reinforces the predilection for the mysterious expressed in Sun Ra's titles: *Call for All Demons, Planet Earth, Sun Song,* etc. Orchestral chimes (used less often) likewise mainly serve to express programmatic titles in sound. In this connection, it must be said that pieces like *Overtones of China* and *Sun Song,* with their exoticism and "celestial sounds," are sometimes alarmingly close to pompous, trashy film music. But this too is part of Sun Ra, as we shall see: the pomposity of a latter-day Paul Whiteman, combined with the blues power of a Chicago jump band.

The same paradox of stylistic levels evident in the contrast of swing-bop-jump pieces like *Two Tones, Lullaby for Realville* and *Reflections in Blue* on one side, and what can be called tone paintings like *Sun Song* or *Overtones of China* on the other, is heard in Sun Ra's piano playing. It becomes clear that as a pianist he does not keep to a single stylistic conception, but matches the emotional tone of each one of his pieces and thus necessarily arrives at very different techniques and means of expression. His playing in *Lullaby for Realville* and *Reflections in Blue* is blues-like in mood. *Call for All Demons* and *El is a Sound of Joy* show influences of Monk. And in *Paradise* and *Sun Song* he falls into the bombastic gestures of a Rachmaninoff piano concerto.

Important for the later development of Sun Ra as a soloist is his use of the electric piano and Hammond organ. While he employs the latter like timpani and chimes, chiefly as a means of creating an atmosphere of mystery (in *Sun Song* the organ sounds painfully cinematic), he finds in the electric piano an inspiring alternative to the normal piano sound. An important hint of Sun Ra's playing techniques during the next years is found in *El is a Sound of Joy.* He begins by alternating between the normal and electric piano, and then goes on to play both instruments at once, the piano with his left hand, the electric piano with his right. What may seem at this stage to be an instrumental gag later leads, in connection with the increasing electrification of his keyboard instruments, to one of the most salient features of Sun Ra's approach to instrumental technique.

At the beginning of the Sixties, with the orchestra's move to New York, a gradual change of style takes place in Sun Ra's music. The transition from hard bop to free jazz is preserved in the above-mentioned album *The Futuristic Sounds of Sun Ra,* recorded in 1961. Although, as I have mentioned, the playing on this LP is not "free" in the same sense and with the same consistency as Ornette Coleman's, for instance, the record does show a few substantial changes compared to the Chicago recordings *Sun Song* and *Sound of Joy,* which are four and five years older respectively.

The improvising continues to be predominantly tonal, but there is now a pronounced trend to modal playing (*e. g.,* in *Bassism* and *Where is Tomorrow*). 12-bar blues patterns, as in *Wounds and Something Else* and *What's that,* now exist solely as a metric framework and have been divested — as in Coleman's *Tears Inside* (p. 47 f.) — of their functional harmonic content. That is, the structure of the blues is retained as an "empty formula"; the four and twelve-bar caesuras are observed in phrasing and in change of soloist. But apart from that, the harmonies on which the blues are usually based are often ignored and replaced by modal levels or tonal centres. Collective improvisation takes on more weight (*What's that* and *The Beginning*), and so do improvised "dialogues" between two horns *(Where is Tomorrow).* The stylistic proximity to Mingus cannot be overlooked.

In Sun Ra's own playing, hard bop elements fade further into the background. His phrasing becomes more discontinuous and the harmony more dissonant. Solo introductions are very often reminiscent of Thelonious Monk.

The Arkestra takes what is probably its biggest step forward with regard to sound. Although the group involved in *Futuristic Sounds* is relatively small (an octet), there is a striking variety of instrumental colours and unusual sound combinations. Much of what later came to have a style function for the AACM in Chicago is anticipated here — more or less incidentally. One decisive point in this connection is that the Arkestra soloists become increasingly multi-instrumental. Saxophonist John Gilmore plays bass clarinet, trombonist Bernard McKinney plays euphonium, and Sun Ra, who refers to himself in the English(!) listings as "Pianist," "komponiste" and "leiter," plays percussion in *The Beginning.*

The Beginning, by the way, proves to be the most advanced piece on *Futuristic Sounds.* It is a-thematic; what carries it along is principally an interest in timbric and rhythmic exploration. Here the group's instrumentation resembles that of an Afro-Cuban band: bongos, ratchet, claves, rattles, cowbell, etc. Over the heterogeneous sounds and rhythms of the percussion instruments, the bass clarinet, flute and trombone engage in collective improvisation whose elegiac character presents a strong contrast to the very lively rhythmic groundwork. The whole thing happens within a freely manipulated modal framework, without any periodic subdivision or limitations imposed by bar patterns.

The incipient break with traditional norms in *Beginning* is an exception in the music of Sun Ra at the start of the Sixties, but renunciation of functional harmony, formal schemes and a continuous beat becomes the rule by 1965 at the latest. It is very difficult to subject the albums recorded for ESP that year, *The Heliocentric Worlds of Sun Ra* (Vol. 1 and 2) to objective musical analysis. When one hears them today (seven years later), they suggest comparison with things that originated at the same time, or just before or after, in the adjacent stylistic areas of free jazz. One is reminded of the monumental collective improvisation in Coltrane's *Ascension* (recorded the same year); of the playing with unorthodox tone colours and the courageous use of silence in the music of the Chicago AACM; of the "collective composing" in Cecil Taylor's groups. But beyond all musical and technical parallels — and having nothing to do with the extent to which tradition is overcome — there is a component in Sun Ra's music, during his *Heliocentric Worlds* period, that distinguishes it from every other kind of free jazz. That component is a form of interweaving compositional and improvisatory creative principles with programmed affects, *i. e.,* emotional qualities.

Regarding *Heliocentric Worlds,* one can hardly talk about composition in the customary sense anymore. Not one of the ten pieces in the two albums has fixed thematic material; there are no written-out horn arrangements; there is not even a tiny unison melodic line. Abstaining in this way from everything that can be pre-fabricated in the form of notes does not lead to disorganization. On the contrary, the music on these two LPs has extraordinary clarity of structure and a broad range of emotional levels. This circumstance can presumably be traced to three different factors:

(1)   programmatic establishment of musical processes on various levels of expression,

(2)   a specific kind of communication between Sun Ra and his musicians, and

(3)   the high standard of those musicians.

Concerning the first factor, there are clear indications in *Heliocentric Worlds* that Sun Ra's real "thematic material" is found in the titles of his pieces, that the "themes" are thus formulated verbally and not musically.

As we learn from numerous jazz magazine interviews with Sun Ra and his musicians, Sun Ra has always been concerned with translating an idea into music, illustrating an emotional state, or sketching a picture. The titles of his pieces function in that process as captions or mottos. During the Fifties, as I have already mentioned, translation of a verbal programme was more or less accomplished in the composition (*i. e.,* the arrangements, instrumentation, etc.), while improvisation by the soloists — who were still playing hard bop — was for the most part untouched by the programmatic aspects of the thematic material. Now (1965) the transformation of figurative or emotional ideas no longer occurs by writing out a composition. Instead, the motto expressed in the title of a piece directly intervenes in the process of improvisatory creation.

(One can call this programme music, with a good conscience, but one should not overlook the fact that in highly emotional music like jazz the expression of something, be it happiness, sadness, anger, sex, loneliness, peace or whatever, has always been one of the usually unmentioned triggers of musical creation. Renouncing emotion does not necessarily result in bad music, but it often does result in dull jazz.)

So that the theoretical considerations I have advanced so far do not remain as mysterious and cryptic as Sun Ra's own explanations of his music generally are, I will illustrate by three examples the translation of programmatic ideas into musical form.

1. *Outer Nothingness:* The "emptiness" of space is translated into a musical context by coupling two expressive ideas: a strong emphasis on the low instrumental register, and tonal and rhythmic indeterminacy. Timpani, bongos and bass marimba (the latter played by Sun Ra) provide a rhythmic background that is lively but very diffuse in accentuations; against it, trombone, bass trombone, bass clarinet and baritone saxophone play long sustained, dissonant fortissimo sounds in their lowest registers. The entrances do not all occur at once; the sounds overlap each other, creating an impression of turgid, narrow clusters. The combination of bass register, atonality, rhythmic diffuseness and aggressive dynamics sets off that "magical" and "threatening" atmosphere which is present as an emotional basis in the ensemble passages of *Outer Nothingness.* The collective improvisations in this piece, then, are as it were verbally pre-programmed, and the motto is also realized in some of the solos. Example 70 is an excerpt from a bass clarinet solo by John Gilmore in which "nothingness" is suggested in a very significant way: melodic evolution is dispensed with; there are fragmentary phrases in half-steps, irregular single accents, and a great deal of "space," *i. e.* rests. (Since the solo is in a free tempo and is played against a rhythmically unorganized, diffuse backdrop of drums, cymbals and bass marimba, the notation of rhythmic values in the transcription had to be simplified. The solo ends with overblown multi-phonics in the highest register, which proved to be impossible to notate.)

38 sec.

EXAMPLE 70   OUTER NOTHINGNESS

2. *Dancing in the Sun:* The title is translated into music by means of rhythm. In this piece, the only one in *Heliocentric Worlds* that has a continuous beat, the improvisations swing in a traditional manner.

3. *Nebulae:* This piece is a solo improvisation by Sun Ra on celesta, an instrument whose timbre is relatively thin and yet diffuse. The sound itself is enough to awaken associations with something "nebulous" and indeterminate, and the instrument is therefore frequently used by Sun Ra in ensemble passages to create a quasi "spheric" sound background. The non-transparency of the celesta timbre is augmented in *Nebulae* by the way Sun Ra improvises: atonal lines in free tempo criss-cross, becoming interwoven into a dense melodic web, while irregularly interjected dissonant chords or clusters contribute to rhythmic insecurity.

The relationships between verbal theme and musical structure in *Heliocentric Worlds* are not all as easy to pin down as in the three examples I have given. The longer compositions in particular — *Sun Myth, House of Beauty* and *Cosmic Chaos* (in Vol. II) — contain a profusion of forms and a diversity of emotional levels which can hardly be reduced to a single programmatic theme. The tendency to translate ideas or emotional states into music is nevertheless noticeable almost throughout. And that translation of thoughts or feelings proves to be what really governs the progress of Sun Ra's music. "My rule is that every note written or played must be a living note. In order to achieve this, I use notes like words in a sentence, making each series of sounds a separate thought" (from McRae 1966).

189

One consequence of this conception is that motivic improvising and motivic-thematic links between formal sections will be found almost nowhere in *Heliocentric Worlds.* Melodic-rhythmic motives and their subsequent development by variation are obviously much too abstract to convey extra-musical content, and to achieve the "tone-painting" effect at which Sun Ra is aiming. The means he employs in their place consist chiefly of combinations of rhythms, tone colours and dynamic values, and the emotional contrast engendered by structural non-transparency on the one hand and clarity on the other; that is, the opposite poles of "cosmos" and "chaos," which Sun Ra frequently develops, are reflected in his music by relatively veiled or straightforward tonal and rhythmic relationships.

Eliminating composed or written-out musical processes in *Heliocentric Worlds* means that intensive communication is required between Sun Ra and his players. The larger outlines of formal organization are probably agreed upon in advance, but the music of the Arkestra also shows such precise organization of material right down to the details that head arrangements alone can scarcely achieve. The inner clarity of even the most complex musical processes, the sure-fire combinations of instrumental colours and the telling expressive effect they achieve, all are a result of the way Sun Ra works with his orchestra. We know that during the time when *Heliocentric Worlds* originated, the Arkestra made hardly any public appearances except for regular Monday night dates at New York's "Slugs Club." Sun Ra's participation in events like Bill Dixon's "October Revolution in Jazz" or the "New Black Music" concert organized by LeRoi Jones were isolated occurrences that made little change in the orchestra's permanent state of under-employment. Sun Ra made up for the lack of chances to play in public — indispensable if a big band is to have any musical homogeneity at all — by concentrated rehearsals. (In this respect he found himself in a situation similar to that of Cecil Taylor who, as the reader will recall, had to depend on simulating at home the conditions of a working musician (*cf.* p. 68).

The Arkestra rehearsals take place either in Sun Ra's apartment or in a nearby studio and usually proceed in a way that differs from that of a so-called rehearsal band, in which musicians employed in studio orchestras or smaller groups get together once or twice a week to play big band jazz. The purpose of the Arkestra rehearsals, held almost daily, is not to perfect the playing of complicated arrangements or to master difficult rhythms and metres. More time is spent rehearsing reactions than anything else: that is, the spontaneous translation of a framework (whose outlines are set) into a musical message. As alto saxophonist Marion Brown says: Sun Ra plays the piano but his real instrument is the orchestra (from Fiofori 1971, p. 50). This shows how close Sun Ra's conception is to Duke Ellington's. Both know their players' style characteristics and musical capabilities from years of contact with them, and both do not write *for* their orchestras but compose *with* them. In the same way as a pianist's nerve-fibres become set in certain reaction patterns after years of playing, specific reaction patterns became set over the years in the Ellington and Sun Ra orchestras, which often made verbal communication and — in Sun Ra's case — notated compositions superfluous. The process of musical interaction between Sun Ra and his musicians required only very subtle signals (which the listener is hardly able to identify) to set off certain collective reactions and to establish a certain emotional state. In *Heliocentric Worlds* the secret of structural clarity, in the midst of unpredictability, is not the rule of an imaginary "cosmic" force (as Sun Ra sometimes likes to suggest in his commentaries) but, above all, a uniformity of concept and execution that he achieves by unremitting work with his musicians.

Although the translation of figurative ideas into music continued to play a major role in Sun Ra's musical self-perception in the years after *Heliocentric Worlds* (an LP made in 1968 is significantly entitled *Pictures of Infinity*), the ties binding music to a given verbal idea did become looser toward the end of the Sixties. We may surmise that growing involvement with a theatre-oriented mode of performance caused figurative and symbolic aspects to increasingly shift from the music to the decoration, stage action, singing, etc., while the music itself began to follow its own laws of creation.

In the summer of 1967, Sun Ra gave a mixed-media show in New York's Central Park with about one hundred players, singers and dancers, plus a large crew of light and sound technicians. This break with the traditional jazz concert — a move that had already been made by the Chicago AACM — irritated New York jazz critics, and it perplexed European listeners when the orchestra came to Europe for the first time in the autumn of 1970 on the initiative of Joachim E. Berendt, after overcoming a multitude of organizatorial difficulties. The light-show, the musicians' bizarre costumes and fantastic headdresses, the girl dancers, the fire-eater, the songs extolling the "joys of space travel," the march through the audience (à la "Living Theater"), and Sun Ra's pretended star-gazing with a telescope through the solid roof of the Berlin Kongresshalle — all this clashed violently with the expectations of a public who could not (or would not) understand that Sun Ra's performance ideas run on very different lines than those customary in the conventional routine of the jazz concert. Furious "boos" from the audience and attacks from "jazz critics" who wrote with a superior smile about "mystical vapours" (K. Albrecht Hinze), "secret agent of the flying saucer government" (Kurt Honolka) and "half-baked visions of space music" (Wolfgang Burde), proved how easy it is to lower the threshold of tolerance, in otherwise relatively liberal people, when a performance does not measure up to their definition of seriousness. The boos and acid comments also revealed an ignorance of the cultural background in which this kind of "musical theatre" is rooted, a background that has as little to do with the stupid flashiness of Broadway shows as it does with the intellectually calculated surrealism of Mauricio Kagel's "instrumental theatre."

As cultural and psychological points of reference in the show by the Intergalactic Research Arkestra (as Sun Ra called his group around 1970), its "futuristic" aspects are, in the last analysis, irrelevant. The roots of this show lie rather in the origins of Afro-American music: in the rites of the voodoo cult, a blend of magic, music and dance; and in the vaudeville shows of itinerant troupes of actors and musicians, where there was room for gaudily tinselled costumes and the stunts of supple acrobats, as well as for the emotional depths of blues sung by a Ma Rainey or a Bessie Smith.

These relationships between Sun Ra and the traditions of Afro-American music must be taken into consideration before the listener — annoyed by the motley paraphernalia of a pseudo-scientific, intergalactic view of the world — becomes exasperated at the way the whole thing is presented and cuts himself entirely off from Sun Ra's music.

Excerpts from three of the "concerts" played by Sun Ra and his 22-man orchestra in France, England and West Germany in the autumn of 1970 are available on records. The Arkestra's performances at the "Tage für Neue Musik" in Donaueschingen and the "Jazztage" in Berlin were issued by MPS on a single rigorously cut LP, with only fragments of most of the pieces. Two more albums were made from an appearance sponsored by the Maeght Foundation in Saint-Paul-de-Vence in southern France. On these latter LPs, issued by Shandar, the large-scale processes of evolution in Sun Ra's music fare better than on the MPS record. Even so, one must always be aware that — quite apart from the editing problems involved in selecting "representative" passages from a performance lasting several hours — the music on these records is only part of a larger entity.

The music of the Arkestra recorded in Berlin, Donaueschingen and Saint-Paul-de-Vence differs in a number of ways from the music of the *Heliocentric Worlds* phase, five years earlier. Gone is the homogeneity of style which exists in *Heliocentric Worlds,* despite the diversity of structure, thanks to the uniform advanced stage of creative development. The 1970 recordings show an extreme heterogeneity of means and styles, entirely in keeping with the variety of a mixed-media show. This is the same phenomenon we have already encountered in the music of Shepp, Cherry and the Art Ensemble, namely the linkage of jazz tradition and exoticism with the advanced playing techniques of free jazz. In Sun Ra's music, as in the others', there is now a co-existence of atonality and modality, free tempo and beat, simple melodic formulas and a-melodic sounds, the connecting link between these diverse elements of creation and expression being rhythm.

As the reader will remember, percussion had a special purpose in even the earliest Sun Ra recordings. The timpani solos and timpani-percussion duets in pieces like *El Viktor* and *Street Named Hell,* and the long percussion-only passages in *Sun Myth, Cosmic Chaos* and *The Cosmos (Heliocentric Worlds),* show that percussion has always been more than merely a necessary layer in the total structure of Sun Ra's music. In the recordings the Arkestra made in Europe, the percussion section is augmented by countless Latin American and African instruments; consequently, the rhythm gains steadily in intensity and density (there are times when the whole orchestra plays drums). But something else happens too: the rhythm, as the predominant factor, begins to lead a life of its own; there are lengthy stretches when the lead is no longer taken by the horns; instead, the dynamic and formal processes of development (disposition and intensification) are initiated and guided by the percussion[8].

---

8) *Cf.* among others *Egyptian March* (MPS) and *Spontaneous Simplicity* (Shandar II)

The basic approach to rhythm in the 1970 recordings differs from that of *Heliocentric Worlds* in that the effort is not to create a diffuse, irregularly articulated rhythm-sound mixture, a rhythmic disorientation to deepen the "mystification" of musical processes, but rather to evolve a rhythmic groundwork which is adequate to dance, as one of the components of Sun Ra's performances. This is accomplished by an adaptation of African drum playing, chiefly by superimposing different patterns to form a complex polyrhythmic fabric, which means that the drum passages demand a large measure of discipline.

The renunciation of rhythmic freedom is matched by a new attitude toward melody and tonality. Especially — but not only — in the thematic material, there is a turn toward simple and usually modal melodic lines, encountered only rarely in the music of the Arkestra after *Futuristic Sounds*. Of surprisingly uncomplicated structure are *Friendly Galaxy No. 2* and *Spontaneous Simplicity* (Shandar II). Both tunes are modal, and the harmony and setting of the latter recall the homophonic, parallel-motion arrangements written by Booker Little in the early Sixties for his recordings with Eric Dolphy or Max Roach. Clearly analogous to the Africanisms in the percussion is the thematic material of *Shadow World* (Shandar I), in which superimposition of several patterns in the horns and organ creates a dense melodic-rhythmic web similar to the melodic structure of African xylophone music (which is, however, more precisely coordinated).

Despite all their conventional features, the Sun Ra instrumental compositions I have mentioned fit into the avantgarde character of his music (thanks partly to the specific way these tunes are interpreted by his players). On the other hand, his poems and songs (sung by June Tyson and John Gilmore), when detached from the show and placed in relation to the musical totality, form an element that can hardly be integrated. Sun Ra's poetry is simple and really very old-fashioned. It has none of the aggressiveness and irony present in the texts by Archie Shepp and Joseph Jarman, and behaves either mystically, evocatively, or romantically, or else is content with the simplicity of nursery rhymes : "If you're not a reality, whose myth are you? If you're not a myth, whose reality are you?" .

The effects of going back to traditional models and of an orientation on Third World musical elements are limited in the music of the Arkestra — as I have said — primarily to the thematic material and the rhythm. (In this connection it must be emphasized that while the rhythm is marked by Africanisms for long stretches, it is by no means exclusively so.) There are scattered improvisations by Sun Ra which are as simple as the thematic material, such as his solo in *Spontaneous Simplicity* when he plays "Caribbean" phrases like those Harry Belafonte sings. But that sort of stylistic adjustment to the nature of the theme remains an exception. In Archie Shepp, a blues theme will be followed, as a rule, by an improvisation in the same vein. In Don Cherry, a tune from North Africa provides the material for the improvisations too. But in Sun Ra the musical development usually leads away from the theme. The notated composition is an episode in the musical action, just as the fire-eater stunt is an episode in the stage action. A theme is introduced, serves for a short while to focus the centrifugal energies of the orchestra, but seldom has consequences for the further course of the action. "Pieces" of a traditional kind, with a beginning and an end, occur only very rarely. (*Spontaneous Simplicity*, which follows the theme-improvisation-theme pattern, is one such exception.) On the records discussed here "pieces" are usually the work of the sound engineer, who intervenes in a continuously evolving process of musical creation.

One should not take the generally low level of coherence between composition and improvisation, and the absence of large self-contained formal complexes, as evidence that the music of the Arkestra is formless. Seen as a whole there is, to be sure, something episodical about it and occasionally something sketchy, rather like what one hears in Don Cherry's live performances. But the open form in Sun Ra (and in Cherry) shows a very distinct inner order, with two extremes of structural differentiation coming into play. The first is continuous evolution or cumulation, for example, from an unaccompanied horn solo to collective energy-sound playing in which the elements blend into undifferentiated and very loud motion clusters, out of which another solo improvisation emerges. The other extreme consists of discontinuous sequences of contrasting formal blocks, with abrupt changes of instrumentation, kinetic density, intensity and rhythmic basis. Between these opposite poles of musical organization, continuity and discontinuity, the Arkestra reaches a "plateau," from which no further development seems possible. These plateaus are as a rule homogeneous and — for all their internal motion — static structures. A typical example is the drumming collective; this actually leads nowhere, but is a ritual that is its own reason for being. Another example is the passage in which the main point is vertical tension rather than horizontal development; this is achieved by superimposing layers of tone colour. The latter is illustrated very well by *Friendly Galaxy No. 2:* the focus of the musical action is a (bowed) cello solo by Alan Silva, which is quite restrained, has little rhythmic accentuation, and is chiefly concerned with nuances of sound (harmonics, glissandos, etc.). The rhythmic groundwork is laid by uniform 6/8 rhythms played by percussion and organ, with two trumpets monotonously accentuating the "6-1." The whole thing is tied together by five or six flutes playing long sustained pianissimo clusters, which later dissolve into diffuse falling glissandos. This passage gets its specific effect not from something *changing,* but from something being; what is decisive here is not development but a state or condition.

The models of structural differentiation sketched out here are doubtless somewhat too schematic to establish a wide-range formal organization. The alternation of solo and collective improvisation; the continuous growth of clusters; the spread of static sound and rhythm plateaus; the interpolation of simple themes — there is, in all this, a risk of becoming stereotyped, and the vitality of the orchestra, which continues to be an unceasing source of fascination, cannot always make up for it. As it happens, the musical processes of evolution in Sun Ra's 1970 concerts are easier to survey than in *Heliocentric Worlds,* and they are also comparatively easy to predict. But we must keep two things in mind. First, the basic emotional mood of these concerts is utterly different from that of *Heliocentric Worlds.* This music is less mystical and more aggressive, more immediate in effect and occasionally happier too, which surely comes not only from the singable tunes and danceable rhythms, but also from the fact that the former predominance of the lowest registers is replaced by a distinct emphasis on the discant register in the orchestral sound. It is plain that this change in the affective qualities of the music brings about a change in form. Second, and perhaps the more important point, we must realize that this kind of formal organization agrees in principle with the order of "numbers" in a show. Although the music of the Arkestra cannot be called functional in the strict sense (the music does not accompany the show, the show accompanies the music), reciprocal influences between stage action and musical form cannot be excluded.

One of the emancipatory effects of free jazz throughout its evolution, is that each and every member of a group is theoretically equal to all the others — if we leave aside the characteristics and capabilities of the instruments, which continue to imply a certain division of roles. Coleman's *Free Jazz,* Ayler's *Eye and Ear Control* and Coltrane's *Ascension* have become the classic examples of "musical democratization" in the jazz ensemble, in which the "star" is recognized by his name and not by the length of his solo improvisations. As in every other big band in the history of jazz, there have always been individual musicians in Sun Ra's Arkestra who occupied prominent positions as soloists within the musical collective. What players like Johnny Hodges, Harry Carney and Cootie Williams were for Duke Ellington, and Lester Young, Harry Edison and Buck Clayton for Count Basie, saxophonists John Gilmore, Marshall Allen and Pat Patrick are for Sun Ra[9]. In *Heliocentric Worlds,* conceived predominantly as collective ensemble playing, the distinction between soloists and accompanists is mostly absent. In the 1970 Arkestra concerts, however, the "stars" have regained the upper hand, with first place in the hierarchy of soloist self-projection falling to Sun Ra himself. No longer, as in *Heliocentric Worlds,* does he stay in the background pulling the strings as initiator and guide. Now he stands forth as a soloist, and his improvisations dominate over all the others, both in the amount of time they take and in their dynamic level[10]. The instrumentation that Sun Ra has available is so extensive that one might say it forms an orchestra within the orchestra: piano, organ, clavinet, spacemaster, roc-si-chord, electra and Moog synthesizer. Except for the piano, which in Sun Ra's music leads a much diminished existence from now on, all these keyboard instruments are electro-acoustical sound producers. The synthesizer is distinguished from the other instruments insofar as it permits musical processes and sound mixtures to be programmed. In addition, its keyboard is sensitive to pressure; dynamic gradations can be achieved by varying the pressure of the touch, and the pitch of the tones can be manipulated by moving the keys slightly in a horizontal direction.

---

9) The only "big" big band in free jazz today where the division into "stars" and "non-stars," soloists and sidemen, seems to be completely abandoned is — as far as I know — the Globe Unity Orchestra, which meets sporadically under the leadership of Alexander von Schlippenbach.

10) The latter feature had a negative effect in live performances. At a concentrated volume of about 130 decibels the inner structures of his improvisations could hardly be heard. Therefore the listener can only get at these Sun Ra solos, paradoxically enough, via records, thanks to the controlling hand of the sound engineer.

For Sun Ra these instruments signify a big advance, if not the ultimate realization of his personal ideas concerning sound. "It is a point where some people need the electronic form of music for the harmonization of their energies, and others need nature-forms of vibrations suitable to their psyche-needs . . . The keyboard instruments I used formerly were just preparatory instruments in order to be able to play with speed electronically, with the right kind of pressure and touch . . . I was just getting prepared for these instruments, and they are coming out now more and more" (from Fiofori 1970).

"Electronic speed" is in fact now one of the most prominent features of Sun Ra's playing, and it represents a certain danger. The relatively narrow dimensions of the keyboards and the light action make it possible to play much faster on these instruments than on the piano, which because of its mechanical properties reacts sluggishly in comparison. Sun Ra makes abundant use of the chance to play motion clusters at an extreme speed, sometimes so abundant that his improvisations become predictable to a high degree. One example of this is his solo in *Journey Through Outer Darkness* (Shandar II), in which there are long passages of motion clusters in all registers, at a constant dynamic level and density. A maximum of sound impulses per time unit very soon becomes a minimum of information. In fairness, it must be pointed out that the "speed intoxication" of Sun Ra is not the rule. There are far more improvisations with a balance between pure energy and invention, between undifferentiated motion clusters and variable, transparent sound structures (*cf.* among others *Black Forest Myth* and *Out in Space,* both on MPS).

As we may recall, during the Fifties Sun Ra began using piano and electric piano simultaneously, either playing both at once or by alternating between them in quick succession in a sort of call-and-response pattern. He now considerably expands this practice. "Rotating" in the middle of his instruments, which are placed in a circle around him, he sometimes gets astonishingly abrupt transitions between contrasting tone colours and dynamic levels, which could never be realized on a single instrument. Sometimes, however, the visual effect of passages like these takes precedence over the musical results.

By far the most instructive example of Sun Ra's improvising is *Cosmic Explorer* on Shandar I, a solo lasting about twenty minutes with only sporadic percussion accompaniment and leading to the controlled chaos of a collective improvisation involving the whole orchestra. Although *Cosmic Explorer* is listed as a Moog solo on the record sleeve, at times other instruments seem to be used too, certainly the clavinet and possibly an organ, but the Moog synthesizer is definitely in the centre of the musical action. How this instrument functions is too complicated to be explained in detail here. Therefore, I will make just a few remarks about its musically relevant properties.

As I have mentioned, musical processes can be programmed, that is, rhythmic patterns, melodic formulas, repetition and continuous alteration of given patterns, etc., can be stored and recalled any time the player wishes in the course of a piece. As far as I can judge from an aural impression, Sun Ra makes hardly any use of programming; he plays the instrument manually in the same way as an organ. It may be that he feels improvisation and programming are mutually exclusive. But even when programming is omitted, the synthesizer's capabilities make it superior in many ways to standard electronic organs.

Probably the most important Moog attribute for Sun Ra's improvising is the possibility of continuous variation of all sound parameters. The simplest example for this procedure are sine tones (like those produced by any frequency generator) being made to "slide"; but also whole sound complexes can be gradually altered in pitch on the synthesizer. A not less significant property is "dynamic tone colour variation": proceeding from a single sine oscillation, other oscillations can gradually be superimposed on it, creating a constantly expanding complex sound which can be reduced again to the single sine oscillation. Furthermore, by filtering so-called white noise (a stochastic sound mixture in which all frequency ranges are nearly equally represented), single noise bands differing in breadth and register (coloured noise) can be obtained, i. e. very compact clusters which can be gradually varied in height and breadth. Of special value for the horizontal (time) structure of sounds and noises are pulsation patterns established with the aid of amplitude modulation.

In view of all this potential, the question arises as to how Sun Ra deals with it. Is he dominated by it, or does he manage to make music that is more than just an accumulation of interesting and imposing effects? *Cosmic Explorer* gives a clear answer: Sun Ra neither tries to do everything at once, to match maximum potential by maximum action, nor does he fall into the austerity of certain Western electronic compositions. Construction, playfulness and ecstasy strike a balance in Sun Ra.

In the formal structure of the piece, Sun Ra follows the principle of tension-relaxation. A brief exposition serves to introduce the material: atonal scraps of melody, sliding noise bands that condense into shrill single tones, and static sounds in various registers. Following are a number of more or less extensive structural units which are differentiated as to tone colour, kinetic density and the changing predominance of certain musical parameters — pitch, tone colour, rhythm. That means that the primary emphasis of each section is placed on varying the particular colour, the density, or the pitch. Among Sun Ra's multifarious creative principles, formation and deformation of complex sounds have a leading place: sliding noise bands contract into shrill single tones. Long sustained, static sounds of various registers, colours and densities are overlaid by "howling" glissandos and interrupted by short impulse-like clusters. Bass tremolos like motor noises expand and end in undifferentiated sound textures, in which a clear "shining" tone unexpectedly appears.

Melodic improvisation very often emerges from sound improvising: for example, at the beginning of the piece when sliding pitches gradually crystallize into distinct scale degrees and thus into clearly definable melodic lines. These are given increased significance by a sudden change of register, and take on sharpness of contour by the addition of harmonic overtones. Here Sun Ra's melody is predominantly atonal, and its rhythmic structure occasionally recalls Cecil Taylor's style of improvisation.

In contrast to rhythmically diffuse passages whose sole point is evolution of tone colour, there are others in which the rhythm — taking the form of sharply accentuated clusters — is placed squarely in the centre of the musical action, with sliding bands of coloured noise acting as a sound backdrop. Less frequent, but then more telling in effect, are sections that can be called "planned chaos." These are the culminating points of gradual intensification processes: melodies, rhythms, clusters and glissandos are concentrated into undifferentiated sound-heaps of deafening volume.

The relationship of these Sun Ra Moog improvisations to what we have become accustomed to classify as free jazz is ambivalent. On the one hand, there are passages that presumably could not be played by anyone but a jazz musician. The decisive criterion — as always — is the rhythmic substance, which despite freedom from tempo and absence of recognizable accentuation patterns still has that psycho-physically sensible kinetic energy that corresponds, however remotely, to the phenomenon of swing. On the other hand, in passages concerned with tone colour variation, there is nothing at all to tell us that this is jazz. One reason for this — apart from the rhythmic aspect — is that the second characteristic of jazz, tone production, is replaced by synthetic sounds. The solo unfolds as it were between the poles of avantgarde music and free jazz, between Mauricio Kagel's *Improvisation ajoutée* and Cecil Taylor's *Unit Structures*. Sun Ra's achievement is that he turns tension between those poles to such good advantage that a new quality results.

Of the musical sum total of the Arkestra, the Moog improvisations prove to be the furthest removed from all the now established creative principles of free jazz. This is particularly evident with regard to tonality. In solo horn improvisations, insofar as they are not limited to energy-sound playing, tonal centres can usually be recognized. In collective improvisation, the many independent parts have tonal bearings when taken separately, while together they create a sort of polytonality. Sun Ra's Moog solo, however, is consistently atonal.

The stylistic heterogeneity of Sun Ra's music, evident in the musical distance between Moog improvisations and contemplative songs like *The Star Gazers*; his reversion to forms and creative principles of the past, and his anticipation of an imaginary music of the future (both of which, in the final analysis, always only create another form of the present); the irrational ritual of his show and the musical discipline of his players, who look anything but disciplined — all this fits just as badly into the formula of a linear evolution of jazz as does the music of Don Cherry and the Art Ensemble of Chicago. In all three (Sun Ra, Cherry and Art Ensemble) the development of a qualitatively new musical language is no longer achieved primarily by overthrowing the conventions of the moment. Instead of a progressive negation of established creative principles (one of the things that had always guaranteed the continuity of stylistic change in jazz), there is a renunciation of the compulsion for formal, rhythmic and tonal emancipation that is immanent in free jazz.

An expansion in all directions began around 1960 with Charles Mingus and his synthesis of Tijuana, Ellington, gospel music and Jelly Roll Morton. It led Archie Shepp to blues and to *Magic of Juju,* and allowed Don Cherry to discover North Africa and India for himself. And it finally guided both the Art Ensemble and Sun Ra to an almost unsurveyable diversity of techniques and means of expression. This receptivity to all aspects of world music reduces to an absurdity the insistence on a system of aesthetic criteria according to which progressiveness of material and creative originality are automatically marked down on the credit side of the ledger, while regression and eclecticism are noted in the debit column.

The psychological and ideological reasons for absorbing creative principles that are chronologically and geographically far apart — and some of them are indeed very remote from jazz — and for reaching back to traditional forms of Afro-American music may differ greatly from individual to individual. The politically accentuated reminiscences in the music of the Art Ensemble, Don Cherry's efforts toward "musical world peace," and Sun Ra's mysticism dressed in the costumes of a utopian minstrel show, all represent levels of consciousness that can by no means be reduced to the equation "free jazz = Black Power." Nevertheless, there is in the style changes manifest in the music of Sun Ra, Don Cherry and the Art Ensemble, a tendency that is probably tied up with the change of consciousness that took place in the Sixties among the American black population. The significance of the non-American world in the emancipation of the American Negro has not only political but cultural implications as well. The third acculturation in jazz is a counter-acculturation. Sun Ra, despite his verbal excursions into the galaxy, is one of its most important exponents.

DISCOGRAPHICAL NOTES

Records are listed here in the order in which they are mentioned in the book. The following particulars are given:

1. Performer or bandleader (if not the same as the name in the title of the chapter);
2. Title of the record, the year made, label and number*);
3. Titles of the pieces (extracts) and names of players (extracts).

For more complete data, readers are advised to consult Erik Raben, *A Discography of Free Jazz* (Copenhagen 1969) and the *Bielefelder Katalog der Jazzschallplatten*, 12th year, 1970/71 edition.

Chapter 1: John Coltrane and Modal Playing

Miles Davis
Milestones (1958), Columbia CL 1193
   Milestones, Straight No Chaser (with Coltrane, Adderly)

Miles Davis
Kind of Blue (1959), CBS 62066
   So What, Freddie Freeloader, All Blues, Flamenco Sketches (with Coltrane, Adderly, Evans)

Miles Davis and Gil Evans
Sketches of Spain (1959/60), Columbia CL 1480
   Concierto de Aranjuez, Solea, Saeta (big band)

John Coltrane
Giant Steps (1959), Atlantic 1311
   Giant Steps, Count Down, Spiral, Naima

My Favorite Things (1960), Atlantic 128006
   Favorite Things, Summertime, But Not For Me (with Tyner, Jones)

John Coltrane and Don Cherry
The Avant-Garde (1960), Atlantic 1451
   Cherryco, The Blessing (with Haden, Blackwell)

John Coltrane
Olé Coltrane (1961), Atlantic 1373
   Olé, Dahomey Dance, Aisha (with Hubbard, Dolphy, Tyner)

Impressions (1961/62/63), Impulse AS - 42
   India, Up Against the Wall (with Dolphy, Tyner, Jones)

Live at Birdland (1963), Impulse AS - 50
   Afro-Blue, Alabama, The Promise (quartet)

---

*) As a rule, the record numbers are those of the issues available in Europe.

200

A Love Supreme (1964), Impulse AS-66
  A Love Supreme (quartet)

Charles Mingus Presents Charles Mingus (1960), America AM 6082
  Folk Forms No. 1, Original Faubus Fables, What Love, All the Things You Could Be . . . (with Dolphy, Curson, Richmond)

Tijuana Moods (1957), RCA LPM 2533
  Ysabell's Table Dance, Los Mariachis

The Clown (1957), Atlantic 1260
  Reincarnation of a Lovebird

Duke's Choice (1957), Polydor Special 545 111
  New York Sketchbook

Tonight at Noon (1957/1961), Atlantic 1416
  Passions of a Woman Loved

The Black Saint and the Sinner Lady (1963), Impulse AS-35

Pre Bird (1960), Mercury MG 20627
  Prayer for Passive Resistance (big band with Curson, Knepper, Dolphy, Richmond)

Chapter 3: Ornette Coleman

Something Else (1958), Contemporary S 7551
  When Will the Blues Leave, Chippie, Jayne (with Cherry, Norris, Higgins)

Ornette Coleman
Tomorrow is the Question (1959), Contemporary S 7569
  Tears Inside, Mind and Time, Compassion, Rejoicing, Lorraine (with Cherry, Heath, Mitchell, Manne)

The Shape of Jazz to Come (1959), Atlantic 1317
  Lonely Woman, Congeniality, Chronology (with Cherry, Haden, Higgins)

Change of the Century (1959), Atlantic 1327
  Forerunner, Una Muy Bonita, The Face of the Bass (with Cherry, Haden, Higgins)

Ornette! (1961), Atlantic 1378
  (with Cherry, LaFaro, Blackwell)

Ornette on Tenor (1961), Atlantic 1394
  (with Cherry, Garrison, Blackwell)

Free Jazz (1960), Atlantic 1364
  (with Cherry, Hubbard, Dolphy, LaFaro, Haden, Blackwell, Higgins)

An Evening with Ornette Coleman (1965), Polydor 623.246/247
  Sadness, Falling Stars, Silence; Forms and Sounds for Wind Quintet (with Izenzon, Moffett, Virtuoso Ensemble, London)

At the "Golden Circle" Stockholm, Vol. I and II (1965), Blue Note 84224/5
Dee Dee, Snowflakes and Sunshine, The Riddle (with Izenzon, Moffett)

The Empty Foxhole (1966), Blue Note 84246
Good Old Days, Sound Gravitation (with Haden, Denardo Coleman)

New York is Now (1968), Blue Note 84287
Garden of Souls, Round Trip (with Redman, Haden, Blackwell)

Friends and Neighbors (1969 or 1970), Flying Dutchman 123
Long Time No See, Forgotten Songs (with Redman, Haden, Blackwell)

Chapter 4: Cecil Taylor

Looking Ahead (1958), Contemporary 3562
Luyah! The Glorious Step, Of What (with Griffith, Neidlinger, Charles)

The Hard Driving Jazz (1958), United Artists UAS 5014
Shifting Down, Just Friends (with Dorham, Coltrane, Israels, Haynes)

The World of Cecil Taylor (1960), Candid 8006
Air, Lazy Afternoon (with Shepp, Neidlinger, Charles)

Into the Hot (1961), Impulse A-9
Bulbs, Mixed, Pots (with Curson, Lyons, Shepp, Rudd, Grimes, Murray)

Conquistador (1966), Blue Note 84260
(with Dixon, Lyons, Grimes, Silva, Cyrille)

Unit Structures (1966), Blue Note 84237
(with Stevens, Lyons, McIntyre, Grimes, Silva, Cyrille)

Chapter 5: John Coltrane 1965 - 1967

Ascension (1965), Impulse· AS-95
(with Hubbard, D. Johnson, Brown, Tchicai, Shepp, Sanders, Tyner, Garrison, A. Davis, Jones)

Kulu Se Mama (1965), Impulse AS-9106
(with Sanders, Tyner, Garrison, Garrett, Jones)

Om (1965), Impulse AS-9140
(with Sanders, Tyner, Garrison, Garrett, Jones)

Meditations (1966), Impulse AS-9110
(with Sanders, Tyner, Garrison, Jones, Ali)

Cosmic Music (1966), Impulse AS-9148
Manifestation, Reverend King (with Sanders, Alice Coltrane, Garrison, Ali)

Live at Village Vanguard Again (1966), Impulse AS-9124
Naima, My Favorite Things (with Sanders, A. Coltrane, Ali)

Expression (1967), Impulse AS-9120
Ogunde, To Be, Offering (with Sanders, A. Coltrane, Ali)

Chapter 6: Archie Shepp

Peace (1962), Savoy MG 12178
Trio, Peace, Quartet, Somewhere (with Dixon, Workman)

New York Contemporary Five (1963), Fontana 881013 ZY
Sound Barrier, Crepuscule with Nellie, Consequences, Rufus (with Cherry, Tchicai)

Rufus (1963), Fontana 881014 ZY
Rufus, For Helved, Funeral (with Tchicai)

New York Contemporary Five (1964), Savoy/CBS 52422
Where Poppies Bloom, Like a Blessed Lamb (with Curson, Tchicai, Murray)

Four For Trane (1964), Impulse AS-71
Mr. Syms, Cousin Mary, Naima, Rufus (with Tchicai, Rudd, Shorter, Moffett)

Fire Music (1965), Impulse AS-86
Hambone, Los Olvidados, The Girl from Ipanema, Malcolm Malcolm (with Curson, Brown, Izenzon)

On This Night (1965), Impulse AS-97
On this Night, The Original Mr. Sonny Boy Williamson, In a Sentimental Mood (with Hutcherson, Izenzon, Blackwell, Spencer)

Live in San Francisco (1966), Impulse AS-9118
Wherever June Bugs Go, The Lady Sings the Blues, In a Sentimental Mood (with Rudd, Harris, Garrett, Worrell)

Mama Too Tight (1966), Impulse AS-9134
A Portrait of Robert Thompson, Basheer (with Rudd, Moncur III, Haden, Harris)

The Magic of Ju Ju (1967), Impulse AS-9154
Shazam, Sorry 'Bout That, The Magic of Ju Ju (with Zwerin, Banks, Blackwell, D. Charles)

The Way Ahead (1968), Impulse AS-9170
Damn if I Know, Fiesta, Sophisticated Lady (with Moncur III, Jimmy Owens, Ron Carter, Beaver Harris)

Chapter 7: Albert Ayler

The First Recordings (1962), Sonet SNTF 604
I'll Remember April, Tune Up

Free Jazz or My Name is Albert Ayler (1963), America AM 6100
Bye Bye Blackbird, Billie's Bounce, Summertime, C. T.

Spirits (1964), Transatlantic 130
Spirits, Holy Holy, Witches and Devils (with Howard, Grimes, Murray)

Spiritual Unity (1964), ESP 1002
Ghosts, The Wizzard, Spirits (with Peacock, Murray)

Ghosts (1964), Fontana 925 888 ZY
Ghosts, Holy Spirits, Children, Mothers (with Cherry, Peacock, Murray)

New York Eye and Ear Control (1964), ESP 1061
Don's Dawn, Ay, Itt (with Cherry, Tchicai, Rudd, Peacock, Murray)

Spirits Rejoice (1965), ESP 1020
  Spirits Rejoice, Holy Family, Angels, Prophets (with Don Ayler, Tyler, Peacock, Grimes, Murray)

In Greenwich Village (1966/67), Impulse AS-9155
  For John Coltrane, Change Has Come, Truth is Marching In (with Don Ayler, Friedman, Sampson, Silva, Grimes, Harris)

Love Cry (1967), Impulse AS-9165
  Ghosts, Bells, Dancing Flowers (with Don Ayler, Cobbs, Silva, Graves)

New Grass (1968), Impulse AS-9175
  New Generation, Free At Last

Music is the Healing Force (1969), Impulse AS-9191
  Masonic Inborn, Island Harvest

Chapter 8: Don Cherry

(*cf.* also the notes to Chapters 3, 6, and 7)

Sonny Rollins
Our Man in Jazz (1962), RCA 2612
  Oleo, Dearly Beloved, Doxy (with Cherry, Higgins)

Don Cherry
Complete Communion (1965), Blue Note 84226
  (with Barbieri, Grimes, Blackwell)

Symphony for Improvisers (1966), Blue Note 84247
  (with Barbieri, Sanders, Berger, Grimes, Jenny-Clark, Blackwell)

Where is Brooklyn (1966), Blue Note 84311
  (with Sanders, Grimes, Blackwell)

The Eternal Rhythm (1968), MPS 15204
  (with Mangelsdorff, Thelin, Rosengren, Sharrock, Berger, Kühn, Anderson, Thollot)

Mu — First Part (1969), Byg Actuel 1 (529.301)
  Brilliant Action, Total Vibration, Sun of the East, Terrestrial Beings (with Blackwell)

Mu — Second Part (1969), Byg Actuel 31 (529.331)
  The Mysticism of My Sound, Smiling Faces Going Places (with Blackwell)

Chapter 9: The Chicagoans

Summary of musicians appearing on recordings by the AACM, with principal instruments:
Trumpet: Lester Bowie, William Brimfield, John Jackson, Leo Smith
Trombone: Lester Lashley
Woodwinds: Fred Anderson, Joel Brandon, Anthony Braxton, Maurice McIntyre, Joseph Jarman, Roscoe Mitchell, John Stubblefield
Piano: Richard Abrams, Christopher Gaddy
Violin: Leroy Jenkins
Vibraphone: Gordon Emmanuel
Double Bass: Charles Clark, Malachi Favors, Leonard Jones
Percussion: Thurman Barker, Robert Crowder, Alvin Fielder, Steve McCall
Vocals: Sherri Scott, Penelope Taylor, Fontella Bass

Richard Abrams
Levels and Degrees of Light (1968), Delmark 413
  My Thoughts Are My Future, The Bird Song (with Braxton, Jenkins, Clark, Barker)

Joseph Jarman
Song For (1967), Delmark 410
  Little Fox Run, Non-Cognitive Aspects of the City, Adam's Rib, Song For (with Brimfield, Anderson, Gaddy)

Joseph Jarman
As If It Were The Seasons (1968), Delmark 417
  As if it Were the Seasons, Song to Make the Sun Come Up, Song for Christopher (with Abrams, Clark, Barker, Lashley, Scott)

Roscoe Mitchell
Sound (1966), Delmark 408
  Ornette, The Little Suite, Sound (with Bowie, Lashley, Favors, McIntyre, Fielder)

Roscoe Mitchell
Congliptious (1968), Nessa n - 2
  Tutankhamen, Tkhke, Jazz Death? (with Bowie, Favors, Crowder)

Lester Bowie
Numbers 1 and 2 (1967), Nessa n - 1
  (with Mitchell, Jarman, Favors)

Anthony Braxton
Three Compositions of New Jazz (1968), Delmark 415
  (with Jenkins, Smith, Abrams)

Anthony Braxton
B-X^{O} NOI 47^{A} (1969), Byg Actuel 15 (529.315)
  The Light on the Dalta, Simple Like (with Smith, Jenkins)

Art Ensemble of Chicago (Bowie, Jarman, Mitchell, Favors)
A Jackson in Your House (1969), Byg Actuel 2 (529.302)
  A Jackson in Your House, Get in Line, The Waltz, Ericka, Song for Charles

Message to Our Folks (1969), Byg Actuel 28 (529.328)
  Old Time Religion, Dexterity, Rock Out, A Brain for the Seine

Reese and the Smooth Ones (1969), Byg Actuel 29 (529.329)

Certain Blacks (1969), America AM 6098
  One for Jarman, Bye Bye Baby (with Chicago Beau, Julio Finn)

Gettin' to Know Y'All (1969), MPS 15269
  (with the Baden-Baden Free Jazz Orchestra)

Les Stances à Sophie (1970), Pathé Marconi 2 C 062-11365
  Theme de Yoyo, Theme de Celine, Theme Amour Universel (with Fontella Bass)

Chapter 10: Sun Ra

Sun Song (1965), Delmark 411
  Call for All Demons, Fall of the Log, Lullaby for Realville, Sun Song, Street Named Hell

Sound of Joy (1966), Delmark 414
El is a Sound of Joy, Overtones of China, Two Tones, Saturn, El Viktor, Reflections in Blue, Planet Earth, Paradise

The Futuristic Sounds of Sun Ra (1961), Savoy MG 12138
Bassim, Where is Tomorrow, What's That, The Beginning

The Heliocentric Worlds of Sun Ra, Vol. I (1965), ESP 1014
Outer Nothingness, Dancing in the Sun, Nebulae

The Heliocentric Worlds of Sun Ra, Vol. II (1965), ESP 1017
Sun Myth, A House of Beauty, Cosmic Chaos

Live at the Donaueschingen and Berlin Festivals (1970), MPS CRM 748
Black Forest Myth, Out in Space, Myth Versus Reality

Nuits de la Fondation Maeght, Vol. I (1970), Shandar SR 10.001
Shadow World, Cosmic Explorer, The Star Gazers

Nuits de la Fondation Maeght, Vol. II (1970), Shandar SR 10.003
Friendly Galaxy, Spontaneous Simplicity, Journey Through Outer Darkness

LITERATURE

A. Books and Magazine Articles

Balliett, Whitney, *The Sound of Surprise,* Harmondsworth 1963; 1st impression, New York 1959 [Balliett 1963]

Balliett, Whitney, *Such Sweet Thunder,* London 1968 [Balliett 1968]

Bartolozzi, Bruno, *New Sounds for Woodwinds,* London 1967 [Bartolozzi 1967]

Becker, Howard S., "The Professional Dance Musician and his Audience," in *Amer. Journ. Sociol. 57* (Sept. 1951), 136-144 [Becker 1951]

Becker, Howard S., "Some Contingencies of the Professional Dance Musician's Career," in *Human Organization 12* (1953), 22-26 [Becker 1953]

Behne, Klaus Ernst, "Der Einfluß des Tempos auf die Beurteilung von Musik," dissertation, Hamburg 1971 [Behne 1971]

Berendt, Joachim Ernst, *Variationen über Jazz,* Munich 1956 [Berendt 1956]

Berendt, Joachim Ernst, *Das Jazzbuch. Von New Orleans bis Free Jazz,* Frankfurt/M. 1968 [Berendt 1968]

Berendt, Joachim Ernst, "Sun Ra — zweimal die Sonne," in programme notes for the Berliner Jazztage 1970, Berlin 1970, 33 and 62 [Berendt 1970]

Berger, Karlhanns, "Zwischen Cave und Five Spot," in *Jazz Podium,* March 1967, 78 [Berger 1967]

Berger, Karlhanns, "Das Don-Cherry-'Märchen,'" in programme notes for the Berliner Jazztage 1968, 12 [Berger 1968]

Borris, Siegfried, "Gegensätzliche Authentizität in der Interpretation," in *Vergleichende Interpretationskunde. Veröffentlichungen des Instituts für Neue Musik und Musikerziehung Darmstadt,* Vol. 4, Berlin 1962, 7 ff. [Borris 1962]

Cameron, Bruce, "Sociological Notes on the Jam Session," in *Social Forces 33* (1954), 177-182 [Cameron 1954]

Carles, Phillippe, "Archie méconnu," in *Jazz Magazine 119* (June 1965), 18-21 [Carles 1965]

Carles, Phillippe, "L'opéra cosmique de Sun Ra," in *Jazz Magazine 159* (Oct. 1968), 26-30, 44-46 [Carles 1968]

Carles, Phillippe, "L'impossible liberté. Entretien avec Sun Ra, John Gilmore, Marshall Allen et Pat Patrick," in *Jazz Magazine 196* (Jan. 1972), 10-13 [Carles 1972]

Carles, Phillippe and Jean-Louis Comolli, *Free Jazz / Black Power,* Paris 1971 [Carles/Comolli 1971]

Carr, Ian, "Freedom and Fish Soup," in *Melody Maker,* May 22, 1971, 41 [Carr 1971]

Coltrane, John and Don DeMichael, "Coltrane on Coltrane," in *Down Beat,* Sept. 29, 1960, 26-27 [Coltrane 1960]

Dauer, Alfons M., *Jazz — Die magische Musik,* Bremen 1961 [Dauer 1961]

DeMichael, Don, "John Coltrane and Eric Dolphy Answer the Critics," in *Down Beat,* April 12, 1962, 20-23 [DeMichael 1962]

Dibelius, Ulrich, *Moderne Musik 1945-1965,* Munich 1966 [Dibelius 1966]

Endress, Gudrun, "AACM. Die dritte Generation des Free Jazz," in *Jazz Podium,* March 1970, 96-99 [Endress 1970]

Feather, Leonard, *Encyclopedia of Jazz in the Sixties,* New York 1966 [Feather 1966]

Fiofori, Tam, "Sun Ra's Space Odyssea," in *Down Beat,* May 14, 1970, 14-17 [Fiofori 1970]

Fiofori, Tam, "Sun Ra et l'extension intergalactique," in *Jazz Magazine 185* (1971), 21-24, 50-51 [Fiofori 1971]

Gerber, Alain (A. Ger.), "Ornette Coleman — At the 'Golden Circle'" (review), in *Jazz Magazine 129* (April 1966), 48-49 [Gerber 1966]

Gerber, Alain, "Notes sur la Nouvelle Chose," in *Jazz Magazine 133* (Aug. 1966), 42-45 [Gerber 1966a]

Heckman, Don, "Inside Ornette Coleman," Part 1, in *Down Beat,* Sept. 9, 1965, 13-15; Part 2, in *Down Beat,* Dec. 16, 1965, 20-21 [Heckman 1965]

Heineman, Alan, "Archie Shepp — Three for a Quarter, One for a Dime" (review), in *Down Beat,* Sept. 18, 1969, 25-26 [Heineman 1969]

Hentoff, Nat, *The Jazz Life,* New York 1961 [Hentoff 1961]

Hentoff, Nat, "The Persistent Challenge of Cecil Taylor," in *Down Beat,* Feb. 25, 1965, 17-18, 40 [Hentoff 1965]

Carl Gregor, Duke of Mecklenburg, "Die New Yorker Schule des Free Jazz," in *Jazz Podium,* August 1969, 260-263 [Mecklenburg 1969]

Hopkins, Pandora, "The Purposes of Transcription," in *Ethnomusicology 10,* 1966, 310-317 [Hopkins 1966]

Jones, LeRoi, "Don Cherry — Making It the Hard Way," in *Down Beat,* Nov. 21, 1963, 16-18, 34 [Jones 1963]

Jones, LeRoi, "Voice From the Avant Garde — Archie Shepp," in *Down Beat,* Jan. 14, 1965, 18-20, 36 [Jones 1965]

Jones, LeRoi, *Black Music,* London 1969 [Jones 1969]

Jost, Ekkehard, "Eine experimentalpsychologische Untersuchung zu Hörgewohnheiten von Jazzmusikern," in *Jazzforschung 1,* Vienna 1970, 173-180 [Jost 1970]

Jost, Ekkehard, "Zur jüngsten Entwicklung des Jazz," in *Die Musik der sechziger Jahre; Veröffentl. des Instituts für Neue Musik und Musikerziehung Darmstadt* (ed. R. Stephan), Vol. 12, Mainz 1972, 100-116 [Jost 1972]

Jost, Ekkehard, "Zur Musik Ornette Colemans," in *Jazzforschung 2,* Vienna 1970, 105-124 [Jost 1970a]

Kagel, Mauricio, "Ton-Cluster, Anschläge, Übergänge," in *Die Reihe 5,* Vienna 1959, 23-37 [Kagel 1959]

Kaiser, Rolf-Ulrich, "Sun Ra — Scharlatan oder Weltverbesserer," in *Jazz Podium,* June 1968, 183-184 [Kaiser 1968]

Keil, Charles and Angeliki, "Musical Meaning: A Preliminary Report," in *Ethnomusicology 10,* 1966, 153-173 [Keil 1966]

Kleinen, Günter, "Experimentelle Studien zum musikalischen Ausdruck," dissertation, Hamburg 1968 [Kleinen 1968]

Kofsky, Frank, *Black Nationalism and the Revolution in Music,* New York 1970 [Kofsky 1970]

Levin, Robert, "Anthony Braxton und die dritte Garde des Free Jazz," in *Jazz Podium,* April 1971, 130-133 [Levin 1971]

Litweiler, John, "Chicago's Richard Abrams — A Man With an Idea," in *Down Beat,* Oct. 5, 1967, 23 ff. [Litweiler 1967]

List, George, "The Musical Significance of Transcription," in *Ethnomusicology 7,* 1963, 193 ff. [List 1963]

McRae, Barry, "Sun Ra," in *Jazz Journal,* Aug. 1966, 15-16 [McRae 1966]

Merriam, Alan P. and Raymond W. Mack, "The Jazz Community," in *Social Forces 38,* 1960, 211-222 [Merriam/Mack 1960]

Miller, Manfred, "Cecil Taylor — Schlüsselfigur der Jazz Avantgarde," in *Neue Musikzeitung 19,* 1 (Feb./March 1970), 10 [Miller 1970]

Morgenstern, Dan and Martin Williams, "The October Revolution — Two Views of the Avant Garde in Action," in *Down Beat,* Nov. 19, 1964, 15, 34 [Morgenstern/Williams 1964]

Morgenstern, Dan, "Point of Contact — A Discussion," in *Down Beat Music '66* (11th Yearbook), Chicago 1966, 19-31, 110-111 [Morgenstern 1966]

Nelson, Oliver, *Patterns for Saxophone,* Hollywood 1966 [Nelson 1966]

Noames, Jean-Louis, "Visite au Dieu Soleil" (interview), in *Jazz Magazine 125* (Dec. 1965), 23-25 [Noames 1965]

Noames, Jean-Louis, "Le système Taylor" (interview), in *Jazz Magazine 125* (Dec. 1965), 34-36 [Noames 1965a]

Peebles, Melvin van, "Tête à tête avec Ornette Coleman," in *Jazz Magazine 125* (Dec. 1965), 26-28 [Peebles 1965]

Pekar, Harvey, "The Critical Cult of Personality," in *Down Beat,* Jan. 13, 1966, 18-19, 39 [Pekar 1966]

Quinn, Bill, "Four Modernists" (review), in *Down Beat,* June 13, 1968, 28-29 [Quinn 1968]

Rauhe, Hermann, "Der Jazz als Objekt interdisziplinärer Forschung," in *Jazzforschung 1,* Vienna 1970, 23-61 [Rauhe 1970]

Reinecke, Hans-Peter, "Über den Zusammenhang zwischen Stereotypen und Klangbeispielen verschiedener musikalischer Epochen," in *Bericht über den internationalen musikwissensch. Kongreß Leipzig 1966,* Leipzig 1970, 499-507 [Reinecke 1970]

Schuller, Gunther, "Sonny Rollins and Thematic Improvising," in *Jazz Panorama* (ed. M. Williams), New York 1962, 239-257 [Schuller 1962]

Schuller, Gunther, *Early Jazz,* New York 1968 [Schuller 1968]

Shapiro, Nat and Nat Hentoff, *Hear Me Talkin' to Ya — The Story of Jazz by the Men Who Made it,* New York 1955 [Shapiro/Hentoff 1955]

Shepp, Archie, "A View From the Inside," in *Down Beat Music '66* (11th Yearbook), Chicago 1966, 39-44 [Shepp 1966].

Siders, Harvey, "The New Wave in Jazz" (review), in *Down Beat Music '66* (11th Yearbook), Chicago 1966, 16 [Siders 1966]

Slawe, Jan, *Einführung in die Jazzmusik,* Basel 1948 [Slawe 1948]

Spellman, A. B., *Four Lives in the Bebop Business,* London 1967 [Spellman 1967]

Stephan, Rudolf, "Das Neue der Neuen Musik," in *Das musikalisch Neue und die Neue Musik* (ed. H.-P. Reinecke), Berlin 1969, 47-64 [Stephan 1969]

Stockmann, Doris, "Das Problem der Transkription in der musikethnologischen Forschung," in *Deutsches Jahrbuch für Volkskunde 12,* 1966, 207 ff. [Stockmann 1966]

Tirro, Frank, "The Silent Theme Tradition," in *Musical Quarterly 53,* (July 1967), 313 ff. [Tirro 1967]

Williams, Martin, "John Coltrane — Man in the Middle," in *Down Beat,* Dec. 14, 1967, 15-17 [Williams 1967]

Williams, Martin, *The Jazz Tradition,* New York 1970 [Williams 1970]

Williams, Richard, "Stollman and ESP — A Label Without Myopia," in *Melody Maker,* June 5, 1971, 32 [Williams 1971]

Wilmer, Valerie, "Lester Bowie — Extending the Tradition," in *Down Beat,* April 29, 1971, 13 [Wilmer 1971]

Wilmer, Valerie, "The Art of Insecurity" (interview with Ornette Coleman), in *Melody Maker,* Nov. 6, 1971, 12 [Wilmer 1971a]

Wilson, John S., *The Transition Years — 1940-1960,* New York 1966 [Wilson 1966]

B. Sleeve Notes

Coleman, Ornette, *Change of the Century* [Atlantic 1327]

Figi, J. B., *Joseph Jarman — Song For* [Delmark 410]

Figi, J. B., *Sun Ra and his Arkestra — Sun Song* [Delmark 411]

Fox, Charles, *New York Contemporary Five — Consequences* [Fontana 881 013]

Hentoff, Nat, *Charles Mingus Presents Charles Mingus* [America 6082]

Hentoff, Nat, *Mingus — Oh Yeah!* [Atlantic 1377]

Hentoff, Nat, *John Coltrane — OM* [Impulse 9120]

Kofsky, Frank, *Albert Ayler — Love Cry* [Impulse 9165]

Schonfield, Victor, *Ornette Coleman — An Evening with Ornette Coleman* [Polydor International 623 246/247]

Shepp, Archie, *Mama Too Tight* [Impulse 9134]

Spellman, A. B., *John Coltrane — Ascension* [Impulse 95]

Spellman, A. B., *Don Cherry — Symphony for Improvisers* [Blue Note 84274]

Williams, Martin, *Free Jazz — A Collective Improvisation by the Ornette Coleman Double Quartet* [Atlantic 1364]

Taylor, Cecil, *Unit Structures* [Blue Note 84237]

INDEX

212

213

Other titles of interest

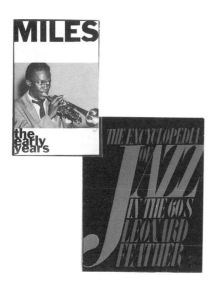

FORCES IN MOTION
The Music and Thoughts
of Anthony Braxton
Graham Lock
412 pp., 16 photos, numerous illus.
80342-9 $15.95

THE FREEDOM PRINCIPLE
Jazz After 1958
John Litweiler
324 pp., 11 photos
80377-1 $13.95

IMPROVISATION
Its Nature and Practice in Music
Derek Bailey
172 pp., 12 photos
80528-6 $13.95

JAZZ MASTERS IN
TRANSITION 1957–1969
Martin Williams
288 pp., 10 photos
80175-2 $13.95

JOHN COLTRANE
Bill Cole
278 pp., 25 photos
80530-8 $13.95

IN THE MOMENT
Jazz in the 1980s
Francis Davis
272 pp.
80708-4 $13.95

MILES DAVIS
The Early Years
Bill Cole
256 pp.   80554-5 $13.95

ASCENSION
John Coltrane and his Quest
Eric Nisenson
298 pp.
80644-4 $13.95

BIRD: The Legend
of Charlie Parker
Edited by Robert Reisner
256 pp., 50 photos
80069-1 $13.95

BLACK TALK
Ben Sidran
228 pp., 16 photos
80184-1 $10.95

CHASIN' THE TRANE
The Music and Mystique
of John Coltrane
J. C. Thomas
256 pp., 16 pp. of photos
80043-8 $12.95

DEXTER GORDON
A Musical Biography
Stan Britt
192 pp., 32 photos
80361-5 $12.95

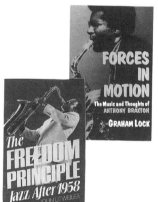